Thomas Hutchinson and the Origins of the American Revolution

The American Social Experience

SERIES

James Kirby Martin
GENERAL EDITOR

Paula S. Fass, Steven H. Mintz, Carl Prince,
James W. Reed & Peter N. Stearns
EDITORS

Thomas Hutchinson and the Origins of the American Revolution

ANDREW STEPHEN WALMSLEY

NEW YORK UNIVERSITY PRESS
New York and London

NEW YORK UNIVERSITY PRESS
New York and London

Copyright © 1999 by New York University

Library of Congress Cataloging-in-Publication Data
Walmsley, Andrew S.
Thomas Hutchinson and the origins of the American
Revolution / Andrew Stephen Walmsley.
p.   cm. — (The American social experience series ; 38)
Includes bibliographical references and index.
ISBN 0-8147-9341-X (acid-free paper)
1. Hutchinson, Thomas, 1711–1780. 2. Governors—
Massachusetts—Biography. 3. United States—History—
Revolution, 1775–1783—Causes. 4. Massachusetts—History—
Colonial period, ca. 1600–1775. 5. United States—Politics and
government—To 1775.   I. Title. II. Series.
F67.H982 W35 1999
973.3'14'092—ddc21   [B]   98-25531
                                  CIP

New York University Press books are printed on acid-free paper,
and their binding materials are chosen for strength and durability.

Manufactured in the United States of America

10 9 8 7 6 5 4 3 2 1

For my son, Alexander Ross Walmsley,
my mother, Una Alicia Walmsley, and
my wife, Shantal Marie LaViolette.

Contents

Preface and Acknowledgments

Rarely in American history has a political figure been so pilloried and despised by his contemporaries as Thomas Hutchinson. Despite his long years of successful public service in pre-Revolutionary Massachusetts, there are no monuments to commemorate his life in politics; no statues, no squares, parks, or buildings bear his name. Soon after his exile, Boston's radicals hastily renamed Hutchinson Street and Hutchinson Field. Following radical threats of reprisal his neighbors at Milton even retracted their offer to reimburse him for the price of a church pew he had acquired decades earlier. His political opponents spared no effort to eradicate from the historical record any positive reference to Hutchinson's life and career. They ensured that he would be remembered, but only, and exclusively, as an execrable traitor both to Massachusetts and to the cause of liberty.

Regardless of these efforts to demonize him, Hutchinson has proved an enduring, if enigmatic, political figure. Indeed, he remains fascinating owing to the very thoroughness with which his contemporaries besmirched his career and character. Students of the American past continue to wonder why it was so important to Boston's patriots to place him on such an unprecedented pedestal of treachery. The question, what had he done to ensure such thorough infamy and historical denunciation, remains a vital concern.

Thomas Hutchinson enjoyed a continuous and active role in the public affairs of the Bay Colony from 1737 until 1774. During this long tenure he was a central and often pivotal figure in all the major controversies of his tumultuous times. As his career flourished and progressed he attracted ever more vehement criticism and opprobrium from his enemies. Vilified, stigmatized, and ridiculed, he eventually became the pre-eminent bête noire or scapegoat of America's most vigorous radical activists. By 1774 he was arguably the most unpopular man in North America. His name had become synonymous in the popular imagination with detested loyalism, hated toryism, and treason.

In 1974 Bernard Bailyn introduced a biography of Hutchinson which recognized his profound historical importance as a leading player in the pre-Revolutionary drama. Significant as this achievement remains, Bailyn's analysis of Hutchinson's career concentrated too much on the perceived ideological shortcomings of the individual. In Bailyn's opinion Hutchinson was an isolated and remote figure who was incapable of comprehending the passion for liberty that drove America's revolutionaries. He appeared anachronistic, out-of-touch, and detached from the main currents of his time; he was haughty, disdainful, secretive, and emotionally removed from the issues of his day. Consequently, Bailyn's central explanation for Hutchinson's unfortunate "ordeal" of persecution and exile was tautological; he failed because he was himself and thus fated, tragically to fall.[1] The time has now come for a more complete contextual examination of the life and career of this vital colonial figure.

For many years Hutchinson's presence in Massachusetts politics constituted an obstacle to the forging of an effective challenge to British authority. He occupied a perennial and entrenched position in the eye of the gathering pre-Revolutionary storm. One of the greatest challenges to confront Massachusetts' radicals throughout the years of imperial crisis was to develop an effective formula for ousting Hutchinson. Without him as their foil, Boston's radicals would have had a far more difficult time engineering the crisis that produced the Revolution. His existence provided the radicals with a constant target for their attacks; his exalted status represented a constant, troubling reminder of the governing class they wished to eliminate.

This, above all, explains why it became so necessary for the radicals of Massachusetts to present him as the epitome of political evil. In demolishing Hutchinson the radicals legitimized themselves. During the embryonic, formative years of the Revolution, before Americans could bring themselves to challenge the King directly, he served as the indispensable symbol of the detested *ancien régime*.[2]

No other colony had an individual of Hutchinson's stature and acumen who challenged radical arguments so directly. No other colony possessed anyone so willing to oppose the radical position with such vigor and dogged determination. In return his antagonists came to detest him personally and politically. His removal from office and influence became the *sine qua non* of the opposition faction. Had Hutchinson not existed, Samuel Adams, James Otis, Jr., Thomas Cushing, Samuel Cooper, and John Hancock would have had to invent someone like him.

In a certain sense this is exactly what they did by successfully characterizing him as a duplicitous, selfish, and narrow-minded traitor. When we remove the whig historiographical patina of blame and recrimination, however, it becomes clear that Hutchinson's experience holds significance far beyond his designated, perennial role of archenemy of the Revolution.

Hutchinson recognized that Boston's leading radicals coveted his political power and that these men were willing to break all the traditional rules of engagement to succeed in the struggle for ascendancy. Most significantly he understood that a drama of self-interest between competing elites for control of political power, patronage, and the domination of economic resources had occurred in Massachusetts and not merely an ideological morality play between the forces of good and evil. The hyperbolic libertarian rhetoric of James Otis, Jr., Samuel Adams and other whigs did not fool Hutchinson. Behind all the boiler-plate theorizing of Boston's hysterical opposition pamphleteers he perceived clearly that a crucial battle for unadorned political power had erupted.[3]

This reality, far more than any other factor, explains why Boston's radicals came to identify him as their single most important political opponent. Hutchinson understood that without power, ideals and principles counted for little. More than any other imperial administrator in North America, he fought the radicals for the exercise of power in Massachusetts.

Therefore, if the radicals were to succeed fully, they had to defeat him politically and destroy his reputation forever. Only by doing so could the whig mandate to govern be legitimized. From the radical perspective, Hutchinsonian preservationism needed to be presented to the world as obnoxious and morally flawed if the ideological seed of early American nationalism was to flourish. Other less prominent or dedicated loyalists argued their position without necessarily risking physical danger. After the war many returned unmolested to the land of their birth. Hutchinson, however, by virtue of his enduring symbolic status as the peculiar and unique enemy, had to be thoroughly annihilated before any semblance of a whig victory could be claimed.

The price that Hutchinson eventually paid for fighting Boston's radicals was permanent exile from Massachusetts where his family had lived and prospered for five generations. In addition, he acquired the reputation of America's first great traitor and blackguard.

Hutchinson's treatment by his opponents seems too harsh, the shrillness and vehemence of his denunciation disproportionate to his actual career. His radical opponents attacked him with a singular viciousness tinged with personal hatred which betrayed an agenda more comprehensive than merely to supplant him and his circle as colonial governors. The following new look at Hutchinson's unique fate examines important insights into the complex structural and personal forces that produced and propelled the origins of the American Revolution in Massachusetts.

Throughout this book I have employed the terms "whig," "patriot," "popular party," "country party member," and "radical," interchangeably. Similarly, I have designated their opponents "tories," "loyalists," "royalists," "the prerogative party," and "court party members," quite arbitrarily. My decision to employ these terms so loosely deserves some explanation. This book is far more a biography of Hutchinson than a scholarly analysis of the evolution of party political opposition to royal authority. The precise moment in the history of Massachusetts when a radical whig became a popular party proponent and then a patriot is not a central point of inquiry in the following book. The same goes for the evolution of the loyalist position. This is not to contend that these matters are not historically significant, only that, for the purposes of this biography, these questions of nomenclature are not particularly relevant. Readers interested in the emergence of the two warring parties should consult the literature that specializes in this history.

I would particularly like to thank Professor James Kirby Martin for all the assistance rendered to me throughout the execution of this project. Professor Martin demonstrated invaluable patience, enthusiasm, rigor, and professionalism in serving as an exemplary mentor. Thanks are also due to the staff of the Massachusetts Historical Society, especially Peter Drummey, who was consistently helpful and courteous during my several research visits to that institution. The University of Houston history department solidly encouraged my scholarly efforts with substantial financial assistance as did my colleagues in the Houston Community College System.

Professors Steven Mintz and Cathy Patterson of the University of Houston deserve particular mention for their critical contributions. My thanks also go to Niko Pfund and the New York University Press for editorial help and for publication of my manuscript. Finally, my wife Shantal LaViolette wholeheartedly supported my work over a long period of time and provided much-needed encouragement when my own reserves of commitment diminished. Finally, I dedicate this book to my son, Alexander Ross Walmsley, in the hope that he will someday read it and learn a little about his nation's past.

*Thomas Hutchinson and the Origins of
the American Revolution*

Prologue: Departure

Early on Wednesday morning, June 1, 1774, Governor Thomas Hutchinson of Massachusetts embarked on the first leg of his long journey into permanent political exile. On that warm day in early summer he shook hands and exchanged leisurely farewell pleasantries with his friends and neighbors. He accepted their best wishes for the future and, with his usual restrained and gracious gentility, reassured them that he would soon return. From his comfortable country home at Milton he strolled slowly in the direction of Dorchester Neck, gradually leaving behind "the shady walks, the pleasant groves that adorn this villa."[1] While his carriage followed he deliberately lingered perhaps to enjoy once again the warm air and green pastures of the New England countryside for which he harbored such a deep attachment. Finally, he ascended into his carriage, waved a last farewell to the morning crowd, and urged his driver to accelerate toward the dock at Dorchester Point. Here a boat waited to transport him to Captain Callahan's sturdy ship the *Minerva* that would carry him across the Atlantic to England.

The aging governor departed with great reluctance. He did not relish this obligation to travel to England to defend himself. He believed that he had done everything in his power to prevent the crisis which now confronted him. Nevertheless, political turmoil gripped the colony he now left in his wake. The Massachusetts General Court had formally petitioned for

1

his removal. Ordinary Bostonians in pulpit, tavern, ropewalk, and quayside were furious, convinced that he had betrayed them. His credibility and trustworthiness as a figure of political authority had completely evaporated. He had no choice now but to physically remove himself to England and appear before his imperial superiors to explain the crisis in Boston, to endeavor to justify his own recent decisions, and to receive further instructions.

Despite the presence on the *Minerva* of his engaging son Elisha and his devoted daughter Peggy, the hours must have weighed heavily on the sixty-three-year-old Hutchinson. As he struggled with seasickness and contemplated the ceiling of his berth during the empty days of the voyage, he must have wondered many times how and why his fortunes had so reversed themselves in recent years.

Throughout a long and distinguished tenure in Massachusetts politics, Hutchinson had invariably prevailed. He had occupied every major position of power in the colonial administration of the Bay Colony and had always managed to direct his career forward and maintain an upward trajectory. During a life in politics that spanned thirty-seven years, he had succeeded far more often than he had failed. Now he faced the humiliating prospect of seeking vindication before supercilious and perhaps even openly unfriendly English officials. In the evening of his political career, as the *Minerva* pitched and rolled its way eastward, he faced his most difficult challenge, to reassure the British of his competence to govern and to secure reinstatement as governor.

He believed that he had embarked on a temporary mission to explain the apparent failure of his governorship to his British superiors who would then return him to his rightful position as chief executive. Nothing was further from the truth. In reality he had been elbowed out of Boston forever, the loser in a critically important clash of events, personalities, and ideas that characterized the early Revolution in Massachusetts. He never set foot on New England's soil again. Instead, he died in London, a lonely, disillusioned, confused, and bitter exile from his country.

If he was gone forever from Massachusetts he was certainly not to be forgotten. Even as the *Minerva* gradually disappeared over the horizon, Boston's radicals planned to consolidate and embellish the myth of Hutchinson the "damn'd arch traitor."[2] In absentia his utility to the radicals as colonial America's pre-eminent symbol of political malfeasance continued undiminished. Although unaware of it at the time, he had embarked on a permanent journey into political and historical purgatory.

Hutchinson's experiences contain fundamental lessons about the American revolutionary impulse in Massachusetts. The ensuing re-examination of his story elucidates the manifold and complex explanation of why he alone became such a particular symbol of betrayal to America's early patriots. We begin with his childhood, youth, and early political activity as the scion of one of Boston's most prominent families.

CHAPTER ONE

Boston's Fortunate Son

Thomas Hutchinson, merchant, magistrate, politician, and historian, was born in Boston, Massachusetts, on September 9, 1711. He was the son of a wealthy trader and well-respected member of the Provincial Council and represented the fifth generation of his family in British North America. No public figure of the revolutionary generation could claim a more genuine American pedigree.

After many years of conventional trading and material accumulation, the family had, by the eighteenth century, recovered from the celebrated dissidence of their troublesome progenitor Anne Hutchinson. By the second decade of the century, they had evolved to become a pillar of the Boston establishment—conventional, commercial provincials content to trade from the Long Wharf and govern from the State House as if by family birthright.

Considerable historical irony accompanies the curious development that Thomas Hutchinson, who embodied the highest expression of his family's faith in conformity, met with exactly the same fate as that of his infamous ancestor Anne, one of colonial America's most outspoken, radical, factional voices. In the seventeenth century dissent invited exile. In the eighteenth century obedience to authority courted the same result.

Those prone to a poetic view of history may conclude that perhaps these Hutchinsons were not destined to triumph. Perhaps a congenital independence of mind, some dynastic conceit, an implacable obduracy or arrogance consigned them to the losing side. In a time of growing orthodoxy, one embraced dissent; in a time of general rebelliousness the other endorsed obedience. How can this be explained beyond a cursed, perverse bloody-mindedness?

The reality, at least in the case of Thomas Hutchinson, was far more prosaic. His social background and first twenty-three years of public service reveal that he simply accumulated too many enemies to sustain his career when the imperial crisis reached a point of critical mass in the 1760s and 1770s. His long tenure in politics meant that he had crossed swords with a number of vindictive opponents who resented his power and prestige and vowed revenge against him. His upper-class status, his refined manners, and his genteel demeanor provoked hostility from provincials who were cut from rougher fabric. Broader structural economic and social developments in Boston militated against his survival as a political leader. Finally, in an age of patronage politics, his patrons failed him. Hutchinson's early life and political career illustrate the origins of these developments.

The Hutchinson dynasty originated in eastern England, in the flat, boggy farmland around Alford in Lincolnshire. William was the first Hutchinson to emigrate to America. He was accompanied by his wife Anne Marbury Hutchinson and fourteen children who arrived in Boston in 1634. William and Anne Hutchinson were followers of the Puritan divine John Cotton, whom they had emulated in crossing the Atlantic. These pious farmers emigrated primarily due to religious devotion, comprising one family among the many who contributed to the Great Migration of Puritans to the New World in the 1630s.

William and his wife Anne soon became embroiled in serious religious controversy in Boston. This stubborn, intellectually committed, and serious family almost immediately became enmeshed in Boston's Antinomian conflict with John Winthrop and the powers of the orthodox church. In 1638, after being forced out of Boston, the Hutchinsons removed themselves to the island of Aquidneck. During their forced exile they actively participated in the establishment of two new communities, Portsmouth, and Newport, Rhode Island.

Following William's death in 1642, Anne Hutchinson moved her family to an isolated spot on Long Island called Pelham Bay, which at that time fell within Dutch jurisdiction. Shortly after this move she and five of her children were murdered by Indians, who, not unreasonably, wished to eradicate all white settlers from their hunting grounds.[1]

The most distinguished survivor of the family was Edward Hutchinson. He was twenty-five years old in 1638 and intensely loyal to his mother during the time of her trial and banishment. Boston's General Court fined him during the Antinomian dispute and he probably would have been expelled too had he not been able to reconcile himself to the authorities through the more orthodox connections of his wife's family.

Despite his mother's exile, Edward remained in Boston for the rest of his life. Gradually he redeemed himself in the eyes of his peers and achieved a position of community respect. He served actively in Massachusetts public life and occupied a seat as a deputy in the General Court for seventeen years. Edward Hutchinson thus established the tradition of family public service that was to continue unbroken until his infamous descendant's exile in 1774.[2]

Edward also enjoyed a military career and acted as chief commander of horse in the colony during the calamitous and bloody King Philip's War. In the summer of 1675, while on his way to a negotiation appointment, a group of Nipmuck Indians ambushed and murdered him. Here a second of Thomas Hutchinson's ancestors fell to Indians as the English settlers slowly struggled to colonize Massachusetts.

Edward fathered twelve children, and of these his son Elisha, born in 1641, was the most politically inclined. Elisha continued his father's commitment to active participation in the public life of the colony. He served as both a judge of the Court of Common Pleas and as a member of the Provincial Council. He opposed the high-handed and unpopular government of Sir Edmund Andros. Throughout his public career he remained a strong advocate of provincial charter rights. This division between supporters of established provincial charter rights and those who favored expanded royal or executive authority eventually came to represent a significant line of distinction in Massachusetts politics. Elisha Hutchinson consistently advocated maximum colonial freedom of action during the era of salutary neglect.

When Elisha Hutchinson died in 1717 he was buried with great ceremony. The degree of commemoration illustrated unequivocal community respect. The quality of his public service was unimpeachable, and he died a popular figure. Proud of their prominent civic role, the family actively solicited visible public approval. Thomas Hutchinson, six years old in 1717, remembered with pleasure the vivid occasion and splendor of his grandfather Elisha's funeral.[3] In later years, he perceived an organic historic connection between the hardy pioneers of his family, who had met violent deaths carving out the British claim to the American wilderness, and his own right to govern.

Elisha's eldest son Thomas was born in Boston in 1674. This Thomas was the father of Thomas Hutchinson, Jr., the focus of this study. Despite the elder Thomas Hutchinson's lack of a Harvard degree—which was *de rigueur* among Boston's socioeconomic elite during this time period—he eventually went on to become a wealthy shipowner and prominent merchant. His lack of formal education did not hinder his progress into the corridors of power. Carrying on his family's already established pattern of public service, Thomas the elder served as a member of the Provincial Council for twenty-six years. This individual represented the pre-eminent formative influence on his namesake son, in politics and in life.

Colonel Thomas, as he was known, was a gentleman-politician and a man of considerable economic and political influence in Boston. He socialized with Samuel Sewall's clique; he was an executor of Increase Mather's will; he assisted in the capture of Captain Kidd; and he donated a building for the North Grammar School. Philanthropy combined with generous public service, both military and political, in exchange for deference and gratitude, was the political tradition within which Thomas Hutchinson, Sr., operated. He was to pass these values on to his own nine talented sons.

The elder Thomas Hutchinson married into the wealthy Foster family in 1703. Sarah Foster was the daughter of Colonel John Foster, another prominent trader and provincial gentleman-politician who had opposed Sir Edmund Andros during the period of the Dominion of New England. When Colonel Foster died in 1711, Thomas Hutchinson, Sr., inherited the large house on Garden Court Street as part of a bequest that gave him half of his father-in-law's estate. It was partly as a result of this inheritance that the elder Hutchinson became a very wealthy man. Notwithstanding his good fortune in marriage, however, he was a successful businessman in his own right. Later Thomas, Jr., recorded that after only seven years in business his father had "gained about three or four thousand pounds," a considerable amount of wealth for the early eighteenth century.[4]

Well connected to another prominent family and highly successful in his own business, the elder Thomas Hutchinson stressed piety, frugality, and noblesse oblige as he raised his children. "What would become of all the people in my employ if I should sell all my assets" was the question the elder Hutchinson once asked in response to the suggestion that he could make more money by selling some of his shipping interests and investing elsewhere.[5] He embodied the values of a strict yet benevolent patriarch. Some of Thomas Hutchinson's strongest childhood memories were of his father catechizing the children and instilling frugal habits by serving only plain fish dinners to his Saturday evening guests. The elder Hutchinson preferred the company of merchants and clergymen, people whom he regarded to be the custodians of New England's best traditions, those of commerce and Christianity.[6] Thomas Hutchinson, Sr., believed that gentlemen-politicians should present a modest facade to the world. They should never overtly seek office but, rather, condescend to serve as fidelity to honor dictated. They should mix with members of their own class but also be solicitous of those situated lower in the social hierarchy. Not for them was the gossip, rumor-mongering, and common camaraderie of Boston's taverns and coffee houses.

Thomas Hutchinson was thus born into an eminent and well-established founding family of Massachusetts. His ancestors had shed their blood to establish the English claim to North America. There had been dissenters in the lineage, but no one could accuse them of dishonor in the face of standing up for their principles. By the eighteenth century a tradition of assiduous wealth accumulation, public service, and a proprietary sense of belonging characterized the Hutchinson family. The younger Thomas must have felt, as soon as he was old enough, an almost dynastic sense of deserved status, security, privilege, and power as he grew up in the grandee's mansion on Garden Court Street. Young Hutchinson was well cared for, cosseted, safely tucked-in, and groomed for leadership. The thought probably never occurred to him that others resented his family's privileged position and his own advantages of birth.

Hutchinson spent his earliest years in a particularly intimate family atmosphere in the elegant home on Garden Court Street in Boston's North Square. He was the fourth child and second son of Thomas and Sarah Foster Hutchinson. His elder brother Foster died in 1721 when Thomas was ten. From that point on his family expected him to continue to direct the family business dealings and to exercise community leadership. In common with eldest sons throughout human history, he endeavored to satisfy the expectations of his father.[7]

Thomas was a bookish youngster and a withdrawn individual. As a child he preferred to remain indoors reading rather than play outdoors with other boys.[8] He absorbed royalist history, and he seemed especially moved by the tragic experiences of Charles the First. His early reading also included religious volumes sent personally by the well-known minister Cotton Mather. Throughout the elegant house busts of classical figures and British royalty reflected the political and cultural orientation of its comfortable inhabitants. All of his earliest influences suggested a prosperous environment thoroughly at ease with the status quo.

In March 1717, young Hutchinson began to attend Boston's North Grammar School, housed in a building donated by his father. As he traversed to and from school the Hutchinson family coat of arms, conspicuously on display above the lintel of the building, served as a daily reminder of his family's civic prominence. When he conjugated Latin verbs and memorized Greek vocabulary under the rigorous scrutiny of his tutors, he no doubt experienced feelings of high expectations for him on the part of his adult guardians.

His accelerated education continued when at the age of twelve he was admitted to Harvard. Although he was not a particularly dedicated student, as was the custom of the day the college placed him third in his class owing to the high social prominence of his family.

One of his main reflections on his time at Harvard recounted a story of cheating during a Latin to Greek translation exercise. The tutor in charge of the assignment discovered Hutchinson's deception and reported him to the president of the school. A fine accompanied this incident of what he referred to as "hogueing," along with a searing reprimand to the effect that from young Hutchinson, of all people, this was not expected.[9] He recalled this episode while in exile in England. The shame associated with this seemingly minor event still mattered to the exiled and discredited ex-governor from the perspective of nearly fifty-five years later. Community leaders including his tutors at Harvard as well as his family insisted that the young gentleman be held to a high standard of honesty and rectitude. Among all personal values, honesty, trustworthiness, honor, and the maintenance of an impeccable public reputation were of paramount importance to the mature Hutchinson. No doubt the memory of this youthful transgression, occurring as it did within the context of a repressive and rarified atmosphere of high moral expectation, still yielded pain for him, despite the passage of so much time. Even this small act of childhood rebellion seemed contrary to his nature.

Another incident recalled from his youth and recounted while in exile underscores his sense of shame when failing to live up to expectations. Shortly after graduating from Harvard Thomas fell into what he considered to be "gay company." Rather than apply himself to business or study, recreation with Boston's aristocratic and carefree young men temporarily triumphed over his wish to live up to the expectations dictated by his family and social status. In 1732 young Hutchinson, the governor's son Andrew Belcher, and six or eight other young blades armed a new sloop and sailed to Casco Bay in Maine for eight or ten days.[10] He did not reveal the details of what these young men did, but the recollection of the incident itself—couched as it was in vaguely disapproving terms—suggested a discomfort with leisure and a temperament ashamed of aimless recreation. Although the idea of having fun tempted him, an oppressive sense of duty burdened the young Hutchinson. He felt the pull toward seriousness much more strongly than the desire for raucous amusement.

Part of Hutchinson's personality compelled him toward material, commercial productivity. Remarkably, he set himself the task of making money while still a teenager at Harvard. "All the time he was at college he carried on a little trade," he later recalled.[11] Hutchinson maintained this distinctive habit of using the third person singular to refer to himself throughout his life. He was acutely self-conscious and appeared to watch himself so as to be perpetually on his guard against lapses from perfectly honest and upstanding behavior. While still at Harvard, he accumulated the significant sum of £500. He made this money by organizing commercial fishing ventures using his father's vessels. In his spare time he mastered the intricacies of double-entry bookkeeping. From his earliest days as a young adult he was a fastidious record keeper and accountant. He informed us that he "kept a little paper Journal and Ledger and entered in it every dinner, supper, breakfast, and every article of expense, even of a shilling; which practice soon became pleasant."[12] Throughout his days he carefully measured accounts, kept meticulous records, and organized the material elements of life much as many of his forebears had before him. He no doubt derived a sense of gratification and fulfillment from such precise behavior.

His tendency toward organization and orderliness extended beyond business concerns and spilled over into his intellectual interests. As a historian and antiquarian, Hutchinson avidly collected relevant documents and artifacts so he could write history in his spare time. John Adams, later one of his leading political enemies, recognized the unquestioned value of his historical scholarship. Adams charitably acknowledged the upper-class Bostonian's "great advantages" in writing the history of Massachusetts arising from his "birth and hereditary collections of pamphlets and manuscripts."[13] Although Hutchinson's writing style was prolix by modern standards, as a collector, compiler, collator, and curator of documents he was without peer. His three-volume *History of the Colony and Province of Massachusetts-Bay* endures today as an early classic of American historical literature. One modern historian has asserted that "of all contemporaneous histories of the American Revolution, Hutchinson's is the only one used frequently by present-day scholars almost as one of their own."[14]

After graduating from Harvard the youthful Hutchinson returned to Boston to take up employment in the family dry goods and shipping business. He dedicated himself to performing and mastering the details of a life in trade. He apparently relished the responsibility of running the family business with a steady hand. Despite his later devoutly loyalist and legalistic sentiments, as a young businessman he perhaps engaged in smuggling from Holland, which at that time was an egregious violation of British commercial law. Although not the most reliable of sources, William Palfrey, the whig merchant and sometime business partner of John Hancock, suggested that Hutchinson willingly participated in the illegal Dutch trade in a letter written to John Wilkes in 1770.[15] Whether Hutchinson smuggled or not, he certainly appeared to be a dedicated young trader. Making money was not, however, his only interest. In his spare time he studied French and Latin to catch up on what he had neglected at Harvard; he also socialized with his friends. By 1732 he was wealthy enough in his own right to be one-half owner of a ten-gun sloop, in which he and his friends followed Governor Belcher's man-of-war to Casco Bay.[16]

Before very many years of adult bachelorhood had elapsed young Hutchinson's "acquaintances began to banter with him the danger of the marriage noose."[17] Taking the hint without much prodding, the conventional and extremely eligible young man began to search for an appropriate marriage partner. The three wealthy granddaughters and heiresses of the deceased ex-Governor Peleg Sanford from Newport, Rhode Island, soon recommended themselves as potential spouses.

Initially he courted Mary Sanford, who at eighteen was the eldest of the three available sisters. This liaison soon collapsed, however, when Hutchinson turned his attentions to the sixteen-year-old middle sister, Margaret.[18] When Mary left Boston, where the Sanfords lived when he met them, for a trip to Newport, he had the opportunity to become better acquainted with Margaret. Apparently he was soon smitten, and it did not take long for Boston's courtly young patrician to "let the second sister know the wound she had given which she alone could cure."[19] The young suitor's visits to the Sanford household were soon more frequent and specific, and he married Margaret Sanford on May 16, 1734, he "being in his twenty-third year and she not completing seventeen."[20] It was exactly one hundred years since the first devoted Hutchinson couple had set foot in America.

Although his marriage was a typical provincial upper-class alliance, seeking to combine two complimentary fortunes and families of appropriate social standing, the union was indisputably a love match as well. Margaret and Thomas Hutchinson had almost twenty happy years together during which time they had twelve children, five of whom survived to adulthood.[21] Unfortunately, Margaret Sanford Hutchinson died prematurely on March 12, 1754, of complications resulting from childbirth. The loss devastated Thomas and years later he wrote movingly of his long-deceased marriage partner that, "such was his attachment that she appeared in body and mind something more than human."[22] He never considered re-marriage, which was highly unusual in the eighteenth century, and he chose to live out the rest of his days as a widower. Whenever the subject of marriage arose, he wrote passionately from his lonely exile in Britain, "the remembrance of her alone was sufficient to prevent him from all thoughts of another marriage."[23] For the rest of his life, although he was only forty-three years old when his wife died, he evinced no interest whatsoever in any other woman. Politics, gardening, and his children became the exclusive concerns of this emotionally self-contained individual.

Every year of his marriage, he celebrated their anniversary as "the happiest day of his life by making it a constant practice to invite his relations and dearest friends to dine with him on the occasion."[24] Given Hutchinson's obvious commitment and devotion to family life, coupled with his relative youth at the time of his wife's demise, it seems reasonable to conclude that the tragic loss left deep emotional scars that accompanied him for the rest of his life.

In 1734, however, as a young married couple, Thomas and Margaret appeared to have every worldly opportunity available to them. For their honeymoon they visited New York, and he carried a letter of introduction from Governor Jonathan Belcher which describes the condition of a very fortunate man. "He [Hutchinson] is a young gentleman of exact virtue," wrote Belcher, "of good natural sense and which he has improved by the best education this country affords." The testimonial continued: "He lately married a fine young lady of this town, with whom he has a fortune to the value of 5 or £6,000 sterling and is himself in good business as a merchant."[25] Like his father before him, he had significantly increased his wealth by marriage. Young, taller than average for his day, with a slim figure and elegant good looks, well-educated, exceptionally well-connected, and extremely rich, his circumstances seemed exceedingly favorable by the time he entered the political arena in his own right in 1737.

The documentary record of Hutchinson's early life is sparse. We are forced to rely on a single autobiographical essay written by the deposed ex-governor while in exile in England. This source, however, used in combination with reflections about him by contemporaries, yields a portrait of the young man as a hard-working and earnest representative of the commercial bourgeois élite of eighteenth-century Boston. His main priorities in life appeared to be to provide for his family, to conduct a successful business, and to discharge his public duties honorably. Wealthy, bookish, refined, courteous, and unrebellious, the young Hutchinson accepted without much reflection or doubt the obligations of his social class. He knew he was born to govern, as his antecedents Thomas, Elisha, and Edward had established before him. He bore this responsibility as a natural fact, just as he joined the family business and acknowledged his role as the custodian of the interests of his relatives and friends. By the time he set foot on Boston's political stage in 1737, he had already internalized the values of the bustling seaport's ruling class. Although only twenty-six years old, he was a fully formed gentleman who expected gratitude and deference from more common folk in exchange for his willingness to provide enlightened political leadership. As the archetypal representative of the Anglo-American patrician governing class, Hutchinson, more than any other individual in British North America, came to bear the brunt of the forthcoming political revolution that turned his world upside down.

In the spring elections of 1737, Hutchinson secured the position of selectman for Boston and as a member of the lower house of the General Court.[26] He took over the seat formerly occupied by the prominent country party advocate Elisha Cooke, Jr. Despite his youth Hutchinson proved to be an aggressive participant in Bay colony politics. Although these were his first public offices, almost immediately he became mired in acrimony, controversy, and divisiveness. Throughout these initial arguments he displayed the self-assured attitude of the eldest son of privilege.

At first Hutchinson concerned himself with relatively trivial matters. He supported a request by Peleg Wiswall's school for an usher and endorsed plans for draining nearby marshland. Soon, however, provincial currency reform emerged as a major issue. His involvement in this confrontation provoked controversy and enmity that followed him for the rest of his life.[27]

When he entered the House in 1737, he was already widely known as a "hard money" proponent by virtue of his authorship of a pamphlet entitled, *A Letter to a Member of the Honorable House of Representatives on the Present State of the Bills of Credit.* He originally published this pamphlet anonymously in 1736. He intended the tract to assist his father's protests against a rival campaign to employ inflationary paper money as a medium of exchange. The political forces that aligned themselves behind the effort to continue the distribution of paper money and eventually inaugurate a Land Bank came to despise him for his rôle in the currency dispute. In this confrontation resided the origins of a significant strand of opposition to Hutchinson that persisted throughout the remainder of his public life. Especially Samuel Adams, Jr.,the critically important future revolutionary leader, resented his "hard money" stance. The up-and-coming lawyer from Braintree, John Adams later recognized Hutchinson's expertise and bestowed grudging praise on him for his role in the currency fight. Samuel Adams, however, felt no such gratitude. The currency reform debates and the Land Bank crisis of 1740–41 marked the beginning of Adams's lengthy campaign of opposition to Hutchinson.

The underlying problem afflicting Massachusetts' currency in the late 1730s and 1740s was depreciation, or, in modern terms, inflation. The province had issued paper money since 1690 and secured its value through loans and future taxes. However, as the time period between emission and the redemption of bills of public credit gradually increased, creeping depreciation ensued. The continuing inability of the rocky Massachusetts countryside to produce a reliable and abundant agricultural product for export, along with the ever increasing demand for British consumer products, exacerbated the problem. To put the matter simply, Massachusetts lived beyond its means.

Debtors, of course, favored a depreciating currency and enthusiastically proposed more paper issues. Creditors, on the other hand, feared the longer-term consequences of a devalued currency, probably because they did not wish to be repaid for their credit in devalued bills. The Hutchinson family, owing to their prominent position as successful traders and creditors, favored currency reform. So, in his short pamphlet the young patrician proposed curbing inflation by employing private specie to retire public paper over a ten-year period. He concluded his pamphlet by promising to underwrite the project with donations from his own personal estate.[28]

In May 1738, Boston's voters instructed their selectmen to approve further emissions of paper money. In addition to citing economic competition with businessmen from Rhode Island, these instructions complained of the excessive tax burden carried by Bostonians. "If we continue to be heavily Taxed, whilst they [businessmen in Rhode Island] are free from Taxes, what Advantages are there that they will not have over this Province?" The instructions continued: "In order to increase Our Trade, We Apprehend, it will be absolutely Necessary to have a sufficient Medium, under good Regulations . . . and to lessen Our Taxes especially Our Impost."[29] Paper money appeared as an answer to both a sluggish economy and to the problem of tax relief.

Hutchinson elected to vote in opposition to these unambiguous instructions. He preferred instead to resist the introduction of more paper money. He "publickly argued against them [the instructions] as iniquitous, and declared that he should not observe them."[30] Very early in his political career the young selectman determined to act as conscience and breeding informed him, rather than heed the wishes of his constituents. This highly independent behavior characterized his future approach to many public matters. Secure in the truth of his own expertise, public opinion simply did not matter to him. Clearly he intended to perpetuate his father's imperious style of leadership and showed an unyielding commitment to a traditional notion of the stewardship of the élite with regard to public matters. He recorded proudly that his father "regardless of the frowns of a Governor or the threats of the people, spoke and voted according to his judgement."[31] Obviously he intended to do the same.

Displaying confidence exacerbated by the arrogance of youth, he believed he knew best concerning matters of business. This unilateral action, however, invited considerable criticism. Hutchinson himself recalled that in a subsequent town meeting shortly after the above vote, "Mr. Balston, a vociferous man, called out 'choose another representative, Mr. Moderator.'" Somewhat smugly Hutchinson observed, "but this was not seconded, nor could it be done."[32] Public opposition was reflected in the wages received by the young legislator in exchange for his maverick decision making. After disregarding his constituent's instructions he temporarily lost his seat as a representative from Boston in the lower house of the General Court in 1739. This defeat, however, did nothing whatsoever to temper the young man's future political independence.

With regard to depreciating paper currency values the two sides resolved little in 1739. Hutchinson secured re-election to the House in 1740, when once again debtors and creditors prepared to do battle on the currency issue. This time the confrontation occurred in the context of the

Land Bank debates. Throughout the 1740s, until the final retirement of paper money in 1749, this nettlesome currency problem provided a recurrent economic and political issue around which partisan groups coalesced. In important ways Hutchinson's future political fortunes would be intimately associated with the "hard money" position he adopted and articulated during these critical debates.

In the summer of 1739, while on a visit to a large social gathering at Castle William, Hutchinson contracted a nonspecific "putrid fever" which incapacitated him for several weeks. Some forty other people were similarly afflicted, including his brother Elisha, who eventually succumbed to the fever. At twenty-eight Hutchinson now endured the painful loss of a second brother. His aging father adored Elisha and took his loss particularly hard. Later that same year the older man died. The loss of his beloved father and brother in such a short time-span reminded the young man of the perpetual fragility of life and of the random nature of the universe. His response to these tragic events was to endeavor to shape and control events before fate surprised him again.

To counter his own illness his physicians employed their customary cathartic remedies. Not surprisingly their efforts weakened him. No doubt he began to worry for his life. After several weeks of persistent illness, with his typical self-reliance, he resolved to disregard the misguided "professional" advice. He decided to entrust himself to the care of John Taylor, a sympathetic country pastor and family friend.

Taylor lived in Milton, a small rural community about seven miles south of Boston. Here Hutchinson finally managed to convalesce. Eschewing his doctor's advice and "confining himself to [a] milk and vegetable diet," the patient eventually regained his strength.[33] Within a few days he was riding and walking again. For the rest of his life he remained convinced that a simple diet combined with regular exercise were essential for good health, and he maintained a regimen consistent with that conclusion. He also further confirmed his belief that his judgment was usually best and that listening to others often did not pay.

During this episode he became enamored of the verdant countryside around Milton. A few years later he decided to build a country seat for himself and his family here atop a gentle rise overlooking the farmland which surrounded this bucolic locale. This modest nine-room residence came to provide an oasis of quiet from an endless series of conflicts concerning its beleaguered owner. To his enemies this house in the country symbolized more than ever how badly Hutchinson wished to emulate the English aris-

tocracy. Much later the revolutionary couple James and Mercy Otis Warren gleefully occupied this residence.

After recovering from his illness, his next significant political involvement
came when he acted as a provincial agent in London. Ostensibly the purpose of this mission was to resolve a boundary dispute between Massachusetts and neighboring New Hampshire. He departed for England in November 1740, and returned to Boston in December 1741. During this time
he lived in London and awaited an audience with the Privy Council.

Scant correspondence has survived regarding this particular sojourn in
London. Consequently, we know little of his personal impressions of the
imperial metropolis in 1741, thereby rendering impossible a comparison
with his views of English life as an older man from the 1770s. Judging from
his political performance, however, he seemed intimidated by the pace and
sophistication of the ruthless competition for advantage among the man-
darins of Whitehall.

Hutchinson acted more as Governor Belcher's paid personal emissary
than as a general agent of the province. He received £300 in payment for
this brief visit to London and carried with him a power of attorney from
Belcher, who owned approximately one thousand acres in the disputed bor-
der region which he wished to maintain under Massachusetts' jurisdiction.[34] Belcher's correspondence suggested a second reason why Hutchinson in particular was chosen to go to London. This was to guarantee advancement of the interests of the Massachusetts "court" party in the Land
Bank dispute. Both men vehemently opposed the inflationary Land Bank.
It is probable that Hutchinson's primary purpose in London in 1740 was to
persuade British government officials "to put a stop to the great fraud and
iniquity of paper currency."[35] Belcher displayed great confidence in
Hutchinson and he wrote to the powerful Duke of Newcastle, secretary of
state for the colonies: "I gladly embrace the opportunity of writing on this
great affair [referring to the currency dispute] by the bearer Thomas
Hutchinson, Esq., . . . a gentleman well understanding in the affairs of his
country and particularly so in the business of the paper currency. . . . I think
your grace will get as good information and satisfaction from him as from
any gentleman whatsoever."[36]

In an enigmatic letter fragment sent to Provincial Secretary Josiah
Willard, Hutchinson hinted that not all of his activities while in London
should be openly reported. In July 1741 he wrote, "I made private application, a publick one being judged inconvenient."[37] Here we catch an

intriguing glimpse of the young Bostonian's proclivity toward secret negotiation and the dual nature of his agency to London.

Whatever his priorities during this shadowy episode, he resolved nothing concerning the boundary dispute with New Hampshire. By the time he
relinquished the agency to his friend and business partner, Eliakim Palmer,
negotiations between the two colonies had shown little progress. Aside
from having his portrait painted by Edward Truman and buying books for
his family, Hutchinson achieved little while in London. He was not particularly proud of his performance. In his later narrative of public affairs during this time period, published in 1767 as volume two of *The History of the
Colony and Province of Massachusetts-Bay*, he completely omitted any reference to his agency. One suspects that the straightforward provincial was too
inexperienced and naive to prosper politically in London. He probably
spent most of his time waiting in the antechamber at the Board of Trade or
exchanging polite but meaningless missives with England's harried and
haughty colonial administrators.[38]

Hutchinson's principal role in the complex series of events known as the
Land Bank affair was to submit a financial plan to the General Court seeking to alleviate the deleterious effects of Massachusetts' inflated paper currency. He proposed that the colony borrow silver in England in an amount
roughly equal to that of all the circulating paper money in the colony. This
would then be used to purchase (or redeem) every paper note that had been
issued by the General Court. Once this had been accomplished, the money
borrowed from England could be repaid over a period of several years. The
idea behind this plan was that the medium of exchange in Massachusetts
would eventually become entirely silver specie.[39]

The provincial legislature rejected this "hard money" plan. In Hutchinson's opinion the reason was because the lower house could not appreciate
the longer-term benefits which would have ensued despite the short-term
inconvenience.[40] In his view his fellow legislators were simply too myopic
to see the virtues of this plan. In reality, the issue encompassed more fundamental economic and political disagreements concerning the conflicting
interests of important competitors for power.

The General Court had already accepted an alternate private Land Bank
scheme which revived a plan first suggested in 1714 by John Colman. This
up-dated Land Bank proposal attempted to organize a private group of in-
vestors who would issue paper money primarily based upon mortgages of
land. Participants in the Bank created a fund of £500,000 which was to be
loaned out at 6 percent and repaid in paper money, silver, or produce. Some

of the profits went to encouraging manufacturing, school building, and other charities, while the bulk of the money would be divided among the directors. Approximately nine hundred individuals throughout the province subscribed to the proposal including Samuel Adams, Sr., and many prominent members of Elisha Cooke's country party. Supporters of the scheme comprised a rival group to the international merchants who prevailed in the "hard money" court party.

The "Land Bankers" and their supporters were small-scale, local traders, shopkeepers, and artisans. These businessmen did not necessarily need coin for their everyday business transactions. With an undisguised upper-class sneer Hutchinson observed, "men of estates and the principal merchants in the province abhorred the project and refused to receive the bills, but great numbers of shopkeepers who had lived for a long time before upon the fraud of a depreciating currency, and many small traders gave credit to the bills."[41] An unmistakable disdain for those who subscribed to the more inflationary theory of colonial currency pervaded his critiques of their position. Yet, however "low-class" they seemed, the Land Bankers could not be ignored.

One of these smaller, local traders was maltster and merchant Deacon Samuel Adams, Sr., who, along with his son Samuel, Jr., deplored Hutchinson for his rigid stand against the Land Bank.[42] To men like Samuel Adams, Sr., opponents of the Land Bank desired only to protect the established interests of the creditor upper class. For the Deacon and others like him, the deflationary proposals of the court party appeared as little more than élite plans to monopolize business and restrict opportunity for the less privileged.

Continued refusal by Boston's wealthiest merchants to accept Land Bank bills eventually drove the province to the edge of civil conflict. The Land Bank affair became so politically divisive throughout 1741 that Governor Belcher became convinced that his opponents were "combining in a body to raise a rebellion," and he even thought he might be driven to "apprehend some of the heads of the conspirators."[43] Although matters never reached a point of direct conflict, the affair contributed enormously to the definition of lasting class and political battle lines.

Parliament eventually suppressed the Land Bank in 1741.[44] This measure added another layer to the controversy by propelling the vital principle of Parliamentary sovereignty into the forefront of public debate in Massachusetts. Now the extent to which colonials should obey or defy British authority became an issue.

Hutchinson initially opposed direct Parliamentary intervention to re-solve the dispute. Later he changed his mind and concluded that, "had not the Parliament interposed, the province would have been in the utmost confusion and the authority of government intirely in the Land Bank com-pany." Similarly, Governor Belcher complained that "the common people here are targeted by their advisors to believe they are pretty much out of the reach of government at home."[45] For this reason, both Belcher and Hutchinson believed that on this occasion Parliamentary intervention was necessary to keep the peace. In spite of vocal and strident opposition from the country party, however, Hutchinson could still convince himself in 1741 that "the authority of Parliament to controll all public and private persons and proceedings in the colonies was, in that day, questioned by no-body."[46]

In fact some Bostonians clearly challenged this belief. The political bat-tle lines that were drawn during the Land Bank controversy indicated the presence of growing opposition to unrestricted Parliamentary sovereignty. Land Bank proponents represented the advance guard of a rising economic clique who subsequently dedicated themselves to replacing the "hard money" men in power.

In May 1741, warrants were issued "for apprehending and conventing the persons or some of the principal of them that are represented or con-cerned in a design to come in a tumultuous and seditious manner into Boston and force the Currency of Land-Bank bills."[47] Regardless of the warrants, and even as the leading "conspirators" were being jailed, Deacon Samuel Adams, Sr. retained enough support in the lower house to secure his reinstatement to a seat on the Provincial Council. Clearly widespread popular opposition existed to Belcher's and Parliament's demands on this issue.

Overall, public opinion favored an inflationary currency. In language which was often invested with religious intensity— revealing the impact of the Great Awakening on New England's political rhetoric—popular writ-ers frequently decried Boston's upper class as venal, immoral, and un-Godly during the Land Bank debates. Such denunciations contained the intellectual and moral beginnings of a deep-seated challenge to royal au-thority. Parliament's peremptory suppression of the Land Bank, as John Adams pointed out later, contributed just as much as the Stamp Act to en-gendering a sense of opposition to Parliamentary authority and to Britain's loyal agents such as Hutchinson.[48]

Young Samuel Adams agreed as he contemplated the financial implications for his family resulting from the suppression of the scheme into which his father had invested a substantial amount of money. It was no coincidence that he chose as the subject of his Masters of Arts degree at Harvard the affirmative position concerning "whether it be lawful to resist the supreme magistrate, if the Commonwealth cannot be otherwise preserved."[49]

The Land Bank dispute represented a profoundly important development in the evolution of opposition to royal government in Massachusetts. Since the expulsion of Edmund Andros in 1689 and the introduction of the new provincial charter in 1692, politics in the colony comprised three central competitive forces. First among these ranked the "old charter" adherents primarily associated with Elisha Cooke, Sr., and his friends. This group, based in Boston, represented organized economic and political opposition to royal officials. On November 15, 1692, Cooke held a "thanksgiving" dinner at his home to inaugurate the "old charter" party. His objective was to limit the growing influence of Governor William Phips and his supporters and to protect the traditional rights of self-government as embodied in the institution of the town meeting. Cooke's was the party of opposition, the outsiders, and the challengers for position and influence.

Those affiliated with royal authority had been empowered by the new charter in 1692. These men were dedicated to advancing the Crown's influence by manipulating patronage and exerting executive privilege. A third group comprised many among Boston's merchants who gradually enjoyed increased political leverage by virtue of their financial resources and attendant social standing.[50] Initially the merchants favored either court or country depending on the details of the issue of the day. Later, however, Boston's mercantile community would increasingly and more consistently favor the whig argument.

Throughout the first forty years of the eighteenth century the Boston community experienced a unique series of economic and social stresses that inevitably shaped the political alignments and behavior of these three active groups. The drive by Elisha Cooke, Sr., and later his namesake son and their popular or country party, to promote economic development for Boston, particularly during the period from 1700 to 1720, constituted one of the most significant of these developments.[51]

Following in his father's footsteps Elisha Cooke, Jr., led a group of aggressive, ambitious young businessmen who expanded salt manufacturing in Boston, built roads, developed land, and constructed the Long Wharf. A private land bank represented another business innovation connected with the Cooke faction. In 1714 the Boston Town Meeting rejected the private land bank suggestion, apparently fearful of the degree of economic control that would accrue to the Cooke group if the bank were approved. After this defeat, Cooke and his associates resolved to broaden their public appeal and abandoned attempts to curry favor with Massachusetts' royal authorities. In doing so they took another step toward permanent, organized opposition to the status quo. This decision constituted a conceptual turning point for the history of popular politics in Massachusetts. Rather than try to co-operate with the court party, from 1714 onward the Cooke group constituted a permanent opposition faction. After 1714 Cooke's popular party cultivated public opinion as a means to power. They operated in the vanguard of the modern political paradigm whereby economic élites compete for power in the name of popular sovereignty.

Meanwhile, the decade of the 1720s was a difficult period for Bostonians generally. Population grew rapidly as did crime and pauperism. New England's leading seaport experienced perpetual currency shortages, an adverse balance of trade with Britain, and a devastating smallpox epidemic in which more than one thousand people perished. Life was hard for people of limited means. In addition, a continual chorus of clerical moralizing emanated from many of Boston's ministers as they enjoined the troubled citizens to search their souls for the origins of their misfortunes.

During this period of uncertainty Elisha Cooke, Jr., and his supporters constructed the nucleus of the "popular" party in the form of the Boston Caucus. This political institution became increasingly effective in shaping, framing, and popularizing issues, choosing acceptable candidates as Boston selectmen and for General Court seats, and organizing opposition to royal authority. From 1719 onward, Elisha Cooke, Jr., succeeded in using the Caucus to mount a series of challenges to royal government. By the time of the Land Bank dispute in 1740 the Boston Caucus had become a well-established political agency that met privately in smoke-filled rooms to chose candidates before elections and to orchestrate votes in support of its proposals.[52]

During the economically depressed decade of the 1730s, a group of young "reformist" merchants appeared on the political scene in Boston. Led by Andrew Oliver and Thomas Hutchinson, this group argued that the seaport's Town Meeting was outmoded and too inefficient to address effectively the new challenges presented by Boston's struggling economy and pressing social problems. This "reform" group championed an agenda of structural and institutional political and economic changes that included redefining the powers of the selectmen, regulating the town's marketplace, and even suggesting the abolition of the town meeting in favor of a mayor and alderman system of municipal government.[53] As the "reformers" and the "popular" party engaged these concerns, important and lasting battle lines appeared. Hutchinson and Oliver determined that the gentleman-politicians who knew how best to govern should do so through the exercise of the royal prerogative, plural office-holding, and economic monopoly. On the other hand, Boston's popular party concluded that government by the traditional town meeting and an open marketplace should be protected at all costs. Inflationary currency reform and free trade also comprised key elements of their agenda. Eventually these two factions became permanent competitive political rivals.

The Land Bank dispute of 1740 and 1741, when cast within the context of these broader historical and political developments, appears as an important milestone in the progression toward more clearly defined partisan political alignments. By forcefully opposing the Land Bank scheme, and thereby affiliating himself with royal authority, Hutchinson presented himself as an enemy of the popular party. To the Land Bankers his opposition represented far more than a mere disagreement on economic theory. His position seemed freighted with larger moral concerns. To the heirs of Elisha Cooke, Jr., such as Deacon Adams, Sr., and his son Samuel, Hutchinson's intractable animosity toward the inflationary currency scheme constituted a dangerous threat to traditional popular government. Following the vituperative Land Bank fight many Bostonians came to regard Hutchinson's elitist notion of the gentleman-politician to be increasingly disconcerting, undesirable, and potentially dangerous.

The Great Awakening in Boston coincided with the Land Bank dispute and exacerbated the new popular mood of anti-authoritarianism.[54] Awakening preachers encouraged people to reconcile themselves to rapid social change, economic hardship, and confusing political conflict by investing in themselves. To New Light divines, God's will could be understood through individual examination far more readily than by conforming to the outmoded demands of a stifling intellectual and social élite. Every man, woman, and child could gain God's spiritual acceptance through a conversion experience. The shared enthusiasm to be reborn would produce a new community of the converted, a new brotherhood of man. Here resided the universal appeal of evangelical revivalism that found a particularly receptive audience in the economically troubled Boston community of the 1730s and 1740s.

George Whitefield came to Boston in September 1740, and before several large crowds directly enjoined ordinary individuals of any social background to "become the instruments of their own salvation." Gilbert Tennant took over after Whitefield departed, reiterating and reinforcing an evangelical message critical of the status quo and antagonistic toward the upper class. Tennant's leveling rhetoric deeply offended Boston's clerical establishment and their gentlemen supporters. By the time James Davenport arrived on Boston Common to hurl his thunderbolts at the community's "finest men," Boston's upper class detested New Light proselytizing. The *Boston Evening-Post* referred to Davenport's audience as "idle or ignorant Persons, and those of the Lowest Rank." It was said that he had "few admirers among the sober and judicious Part of the town." Eventually, when his rabble rousing became too much, in traditional New England style, Davenport would be deported from Boston.

The seaport's unique receptivity to New Light social radicalism resided in the knowledge among the working population that all was not well. Laborers, seamen, the impoverished, slaves, and the young and insecure all responded positively to the egalitarian and empowering messages of the preachers of the Great Awakening. As these exhorters appealed to the oral traditions and emotional enthusiasm of ordinary people, Boston's élite shuddered.

This message of greater social equality provided an important additional psychological dimension to the Land Bank debate. As Boston's wealthiest merchants vowed not to accept Land Bank bills, Davenport denounced the upper class and urged his audience to "Pull them down, turn them out, and put others in their Places." Soon opponents of the Land Bank would be referred to openly as "carnal Wretches, Hypocrites, Fighters against God, Children of the Devil, cursed Pharisees."

The revival years raised political consciousness among the lower orders, filling them with suspicion about their alleged superiors and preparing them for independent action when the next challenge appeared. Boston's lower-class awakening found further expression later in street politics. Riots against impressment occurred in 1747. A flood of denunciation accompanied the retirement of paper money in 1749 as Boston's upper classes were characterized as men driven by such base motivations as, "Lust of

Power, Lust of Fame, Lust of Money." These self-interested "Birds of Prey" were increasingly cast in the public mind as detrimental to the well-being of the general community. Eventually, Boston's popular party leaders would tap into these emotions to mobilize ordinary people against Hutchinson.

Despite these latent concerns, in the years immediately following the Land Bank dispute Hutchinson's political career flourished. He learned quickly to co-operate with the ambitious new governor, William Shirley, who succeeded Belcher in 1741. He secured election to the powerful position of speaker of the lower house of the General Court in 1749. From this prominent political platform he successfully engineered the retirement of devalued paper money according to a plan which was very similar to the one that he had suggested earlier.

In June 1749, Britain reimbursed Massachusetts in silver specie in the amount of £180,000 for the colony's expenditures in the military campaign against the French at Louisbourg in 1745.[55] Hutchinson utilized his influence to advance his resolution to use this money to retire the existing paper money. This measure provoked considerable popular anger, and Bostonians verbally harassed and insulted him in the streets. It was even suggested that a guard be placed at his house in Milton to protect the speaker from popular reprisals. Hutchinson himself recalled that "a great part of the people were extremely incensed."[56] Despite these threats and rumors the measure remained unchallenged and his self-assurance impregnable. The displays of popular antagonism soon passed and he seemed to be vindicated. Before long the currency was stable, trade brisk, and the people apparently satisfied. Many years later even John Adams wrote candidly of Hutchinson, "as little as I revere his memory, I will acknowledge that he understood the subject of coin and commerce better than any man I ever knew in this country."[57] By 1749 Hutchinson could proudly conclude that, "I can rightfully claim to be the father of the fixed medium."[58] Nevertheless, unspoken resentments percolated and invisible scars remained. The rivals of the court party remembered the defeats suffered during the Land Bank dispute and the subsequent retirement of paper money. Many Boston businessmen nursed their grievances against him and plotted their revenge.

Over the next several years, Hutchinson consistently held a seat in the Massachusetts General Court as a representative from Boston. At the same time he enjoyed the life of an aristocratic gentleman-politician. He had considerable persuasive skill as one contemporary admirer observed: "he had the charms of oratory beyond any man in the assembly. There was equal fluency and pathos in his manner; he could be argumentative and smooth. He was active, diligent, plausible and upon all occasions seemed to be influenced by public spirit more than selfish considerations."[59] To some he thus appeared to be an effective, energetic, and talented community leader.

Throughout the 1740s he worked hard on a variety of public matters and consolidated his reputation as a respectable manager of provincial political affairs. In 1742 he assisted in negotiating a treaty with the neighboring Penobscot, Norridgewalk, St. Johns, Saco, and St. Francis Indians. In 1745 he managed the province lottery. Even during this period, however, he was not free from rebuke. In the time of King George's War (1744 to 1748) New Englanders eagerly fought against the French to prove their loyalty to Britain and to demonstrate their martial prowess. Colonial soldiers gained a noteworthy victory in 1745 when they occupied the forbidding French fortress at Louisbourg at the mouth of the St. Lawrence River. At one point Hutchinson's opponents accused him of selling axes to a Frenchman during the Louisbourg campaign. Later he recalled, in the third person, that "from 1742 to 1749 some and generally all of the Town members were considered as of the country party and he [Hutchinson] of the court. Mr. Allen and Mr. Tyng particularly were very opposite to him."[60] Partisan politics clearly influenced how men such as James Allen and William Tyng behaved toward Hutchinson since both of them had been partners in the Land Bank. James Allen had been expelled from the House in 1748 for his overzealous defense of paper money. Shortly following this expulsion "a report thereupon spread that he Hutchinson had supplied the Frenchman with the tomahawks."[61]

By virtue of his life in daily politics, Hutchinson made important and lasting enemies. Many aspects of the political process and management of public affairs generated friction with other men. The root cause of this growing animus remained the Land Bank affair. As he recalled years later, "nothing made him more obnoxious to a great part of the people than his stand with paper money."[62] Throughout the 1740s, Hutchinson appeared to be accompanied every step of the way by an ominous Greek chorus of implacable and irreconcilable critical observers.

In the uncertain days of King George's War he served as a trusted diplomat and ambassador for his colony. In October 1745, he was one of the Bay Colony's delegates to the Albany Conference with the Six Nations. Some in the Massachusetts deputation, although not Hutchinson, wanted to cajole the Iroquois into fighting the French. "Bring in some French scalps," they urged the Indians, to exchange for clothing, powder, and shot. The Iroquois wisely resisted these trouble-making demands. For other reasons, Hutchinson regarded the delegation as a failure and his main accomplishment was to accumulate valuable political experience with the Indians, and in dealing with representatives from other colonies.[63]

Given his family's losses in fighting with the Indians, Hutchinson remained surprisingly sympathetic toward Native Americans. In 1749, he headed a delegation to Casco Bay in Maine to update a peace treaty first formulated by William Dummer in 1726.[64] He was accompanied on this business by both James Otis, Sr., and Jr., two men who would later be among his worst enemies. At this point in their careers both Otises were staunch supporters of William Shirley's administration. As New England's negotiators chatted away the hours on the way to their meetings, important personal impressions, likes and dislikes, inevitably established themselves. The refined Hutchinson, the earthy elder Otis, and his impressionable son became better acquainted with one another as they conducted the colony's official business. When their friendship-in-patronage fell apart later, their enmity was all the more vehement owing to their previous familiarity.[65]

While the negotiators were in Falmouth (later Portsmouth, Maine), some English inhabitants from Wiscasset killed one Indian and wounded two others. After the apprehension and trial of the murderers it became clear that no jury would convict them, and the perpetrators were acquitted. This miscarriage of justice appalled Hutchinson and he wrote later, "many of good people at this time lamented the disposition, which they thought was discovered, to distinguish the guilt of killing an Indian, and that of killing an Englishman, as if God had not made of one blood all the nations upon the face of the earth."[66]

He evinced an unusual sensitivity toward the plight of New England's Native Americans. On the perennial problem of continued encroachment by English settlers upon Indian lands, he could write, "I should think that measures for encouraging a large and extensive trade with them [New England's Indians] were to be favoured rather than for extending settlements into their country. I think British America seems large and populous enough for their own benefit as well as the benefit of Britain."[67] To the fair-minded Hutchinson, there was enough land for everyone in New England, regardless of ethnicity. His breezy and earnest eighteenth-century optimism in the civilizing properties of trade prevailed even in the treatment of Indians.

In 1749, Hutchinson attained a seat on the Provincial Council, the upper house of the General Court. It was from this prominent position that he gradually emerged as a key adviser to the ambitious and imperialistic Shirley.[68] As his career developed throughout the 1750s, Hutchinson seemed to recover from his undoubted unpopularity as the organizer of Massachusetts' return to a specie currency. He negotiated boundary disputes with neighboring New York and extended his degree of political and social influence though the acquisition of two judgeships in 1752. Although he was not a trained lawyer, he secured appointment to judgeships on the Suffolk County Probate Court and the Suffolk County Inferior Court of Common Pleas. In this latter position he filled a judgeship previously occupied by his uncle Edward, who had died in March 1751.

In 1754 he attended the Albany Congress as a representative from Massachusetts. Here he collaborated closely and amicably with Pennsylvania's Benjamin Franklin, someone else who, like the Otises, had a devastating influence upon the course of his later political career. By his own admission Hutchinson did not significantly shape the Plan of Union, as some scholarship has suggested, and the record remains unclear as to what degree he endorsed Franklin's nascent plan of colonial unification.

Following his mother's death in 1752 and the tragic loss of his wife in 1754, Hutchinson threw himself into his political career with almost obsessive dedication. His objectives during this phase of his life were to lose himself in hard work devoted to frenetic public service, and to advance the mercantile interests of his family. His great-grandson, Peter Orlando Hutchinson, later wrote perceptively of his infamous ancestor, "his attentions to these parts [mercantile business] and the business of the General Assembly was the only relief from the distress of his mind upon the death of his wife."[69] For the next twenty years Hutchinson maintained an extremely high work output. The combination of a pronounced sense of familial duty along with the emotional damage at the loss of his wife produced an individual possessed of clear workaholic tendencies. In rigorous application to public business he derived a sense of self-worth and well-being.

Although he was ambitious and industrious, he appeared, nevertheless, to have always been capable of empathetic and humane decision making. Despite the fact that his political enemies often caricatured him as selfish, cold, haughty, aloof, and aristocratic, several examples exist in the documentary record of his genuine concern for the plight of others.

Benjamin Franklin's sister, Jane Mecom, wrote, "may God protect and preserve him still" after Hutchinson as a probate judge demonstrated considerable clemency while settling her intestate claim.[70] Similarly, although much later in his career, he wrote to Robert Wilson concerning financial reimbursement for the family of a missing military casualty, "I am the patron of these people who cannot help themselves and this obliges me to ask another favor of you for a poor widow who supposes her husband has money due to him in England."[71] His life-long opposition to naval impressment indicated his real concern regarding one of the most vexing problems confronting ordinary people in Massachusetts.

He demonstrated genuine and even unique humanity in providing for a group of destitute Acadian refugees who were stranded in Boston during the Seven Years' War. With his usual indifference to public opinion, he disregarded how unpopular rendering assistance to these French Catholic refugees undoubtedly was in Protestant New England. He "personally cared for a group of ten" impecunious individuals while simultaneously using his influence to petition the British authorities to assist materially these unfortunate refugees of war.[72] During the same war he demonstrated unusual compassion while providing for many returning veterans. Acutely aware of the physical difficulties associated with providing food, clothing, and shelter for often impoverished and wounded soldiers, he "skillfully administered" this "tedious task" with great dedication and genuine concern.[73]

Finally, in 1773, he went out of his way to endeavor to improve the circumstances of an obscure and nameless "black man," who had "been brought to the Province by a whaling vessel from one of the Western Islands and has been sold as a slave."[74] Willing to write to the secretary of state for American Affairs Lord Dartmouth himself, a man who probably cared little for the misfortunes of an unnamed "black man," Hutchinson directly sought "an Action to recover the man's freedom and to punish any persons who may have been guilty of so atrocious a crime."[75]

These episodes indicate that if he appeared occasionally coldly ambitious, he also behaved empathetically and kindly and seemed a competent caretaker in public matters. Whether motivated by a desire to get ahead or by genuine humanity, or, as is more likely, some combination of both, from the 1750s onward he clearly emerged as a trustworthy and reliable steward

of the public interest. He appeared a compassionate and conscientious public figure whose status and sense of noblesse oblige qualified him for political office-holding and high public esteem. It is equally clear from these
episodes that public sentiment mattered little to so independent-minded a
figure who was certain at all times of the rectitude of his decision making.

His most important political relationship of the 1750s was with John
Campbell, 4th Earl of Loudoun, the British military commander-in-chief
in North America during the early years of the Seven Years' War. Whether
these two men were like-minded, no-nonsense, political achievers, or
whether their mutual passion for horticulture provided a particular personal basis for friendship, they shared a close professional relationship
throughout the initial stages of the critical Anglo-French struggle for dom-
inance in North America. Loudoun was not well-liked in America but this
mattered little to Hutchinson. Initially chosen because "his rank and personal qualities" were perceived in England "to commend him to Americans," Loudoun soon impressed people as annoyingly arrogant. For the
aristocratic Bostonian, obedience to authority apparently came first in this
relationship. No matter how unpopular Loudoun was, Hutchinson resolved to serve him because he was the superior individual and could help
him in his campaigns for higher office.

The two men first met at Albany in 1754 and remained in touch with
one another until at least the middle of 1757.[76] When Governor William
Shirley left Massachusetts for England in 1756, the decrepit lieutenant
governor, Spencer Phips, temporarily assumed gubernatorial responsibilities, despite the fact that his "age had now rendered him less fit for it than
ever."[77] Hutchinson viewed this particular development as an opportunity
for advancement and began to cultivate Loudoun as a patron. With a view
to succeeding Phips since the latter's demise was obviously imminent,
Hutchinson wrote on the subject of a replacement, "no recommendation
can be more effectual than your Lordship's."[78] Phips died later in 1757. On
this occasion, Hutchinson failed to acquire the governorship, despite having received Loudoun's endorsement.

Hutchinson prepared an important speech for Loudoun, which the latter delivered in Boston on January 20, 1757. He spoke to a meeting of New
England War Commissioners and dealt mainly with the mechanics of raising and provisioning troops. This speech, in which Hutchinson dutifully
"endeavored to express your Lordship's own sentiments as I received them
at Albany," amounted to a rather peremptory demand for more commitment to the war against the French on behalf of New Englanders.[79]

Loudoun criticized the New England war effort, and enjoined: "I hope, Gentlemen, that under the guidance and blessing of Divine Providence the plan of operation for another year will be better prosecuted." He contin- ued, "I must recommend to you the giving better encouragement to your Officers than you have formerly done. . . . I think more encouragement should be given to the men by allowing necessary cloathing [sic] than what has generally been your practice."[80] The speech contained the rather con- descending message to the colonials that although Loudoun could apprise them of his military plans, he chose not to, and that New Englanders should raise more troops anyway. He concluded his message with a veiled threat that should his requests be rejected, "you would never be able to atone for a refusal."[81] It is doubtful whether the proud, parochial, and pa- triotic commissioners welcomed these hectoring words of disparagement. Eventually Loudoun raised the troops he had requested, although with some financial restrictions. Following this collaboration, Hutchinson de- veloped a closer relationship with the irritable military commander who often required a more reasonable colonial interpreter.

Hutchinson's relationship with Loudoun illustrated his considerable skill in manipulating the patronage system. This remained the essential mechanism for power and advancement in the eighteenth-century envi- ronment of the gentleman-politician. Public life in Colonial America tran- spired according to a firmly established paradigm of personal connection, flattery, and consistent application to influential people for the reward of higher office. As a veteran of some twenty years as a public servant, Hutchinson had thoroughly mastered the intricacies of this complex and highly subjective managerial model. He commanded great expertise in the art of self-advancement and it was not without validity that his whig antag- onists later despised him as a monopolist of significant positions of power. Essentially, he lobbied Loudoun for assistance in acquiring either the gov- ernorship or the lieutenant governorship.[82] For reasons beyond his control, he failed in his bid to acquire the governorship in 1757 when Thomas Pow- nall was named as Phips's successor. However, analysis of Hutchinson's cor- respondence from this time period is instructive in demonstrating his pol- ished and sophisticated political style.

The Loudoun-Hutchinson correspondence of 1757 showed the Bostonian's ability to combine dedicated public service with self-interested advancement according to the rules of the hierarchical system of eigh- teenth-century British America. His letters invariably contained useful and practical advice for his patron. He offered suggestions regarding how to raise and utilize troops, as well as how to acquire adequate supplies of tents, knapsacks, and ammunition. He helped Loudoun understand how local taxation practices influenced military appropriations and how local factional politics affected general strategic military decisions. Nevertheless, he invariably couched these informative and important details in the subtle political prose of the ambitious man on the move.

In early 1757, for example, he wrote to the British commander analyzing the problems of keeping track of how many troops had been raised, where they had served, and the drawbacks of a politicized muster-master. Woven into the text was a mild criticism of Phips: "the Lieutenant-Governor is a very worthy gentleman but at his years vigor and close application cannot be expected."[83] This comment would certainly have registered in Loudoun's mind that his young, competent correspondent was circumventing a moribund and ineffectual superior.

Hutchinson often appeared as the master of the subtle suggestion. In addressing the problem of a politicized muster-master, he wrote, "I have no acquaintance with military affairs My Lord, and am at a loss what to propose." The very next sentence was, however, a proposal: "I fear it would be impracticable for any one person to act as muster-master general otherwise I should think it best such a person should be appointed from among the Officers who served last year before your Lordship left the Province and who should be approved by your Lordship."[84]

Similarly, he offered a four-page synopsis of his views on attacking Quebec, despite his self-professed lack of military knowledge.[85] He was not above occasionally making more direct suggestions. For example, in June 1757, he requested that his brother's snow, which was a small vessel like a brig, not be discharged from military service owing to the expense which had been incurred in fitting it for this purpose.[86] More usually, however, his correspondence contained greater delicacy in advancing his personal agenda.

His letters always concluded with a seemingly endless variety of disclaimers and flattery. These were often finely nuanced according to the perceived importance of the recipient. In 1757 Loudoun was indubitably a connection of paramount significance. Hutchinson wrote, "I send these thoughts to your Lordship in writing to save your Lordship time more of which would be taken up in a personal attendance and as I have only the public service in view I know your Lordship will excuse me."[87] On another occasion he wrote, "I have had too much experience of your Lordship's goodness to think it necessary even to make an apology for this freedom."[88]

Finally, he produced a letter after Loudoun had returned safely to Britain in July 1757, containing the following remarkable phrases: "I am, my Lord, as far from delighting in matters of form and compliment as any person in the world and I thought I would never trouble your Lordship with a letter except when I had facts to communicate which might be of public service, but I cannot help expressing the gladness of my heart on this occasion. . . . I have scarce ever waited with more impatience for any event than your Lordship's arrival."[89] Even as he prepared to begin a new relationship with Loudoun's successor, General James Abercrombie, Hutchinson demonstrated his deep commitment to the gentlemen's system of personal flattery and encomium which characterized the style of the Anglo-American gentleman-politician.[90]

His correspondence with Loudoun was invariably obsequious and self-serving. Occasionally he even over-stepped the usual boundaries of eighteenth-century standards of fawning and falsity. When Her Royal Highness the Princess of Hesse died he exclaimed hysterically: "Every good subject and especially every good servant of the Crown must feel the repeated melancholy Providences which grieve so good a King and Master; and they are ungrateful to heaven if they are insensible to its favor in continuing the health of His Majesty upon whose life the public happiness so much depends."[91]

His style of flattery was decidedly unctuous and even distasteful to the modern reader. His efforts, however, usually advanced colonial interests. He apprised Loudoun of the heavy tax burden carried by Massachusetts during the war and cautioned him against expecting this situation to continue. He urged the British military commander to place colonial troops in camp sites close to home so they would be protecting their own families and friends. He also requested favorable treatment for people in Massachusetts who resided in a disputed area with New Hampshire. On another occasion, he lobbied for a relaxation of the war-time trade embargo, since Bostonians worried about grain shortages.[92]

The nature of his relationship with Loudoun occasionally hinted at a conspiratorial and even clandestine style. In March 1757 he wrote, "I am much obliged to your Lordship for expressing yourself with so much caution to the Lieutenant-Governor as that he has no suspicion of my communicating our proceedings to your Lordship."[93] Notwithstanding this desire for secrecy, however, it is difficult to view the contents of his letters as anything but beneficial to the troops and the general public of Massachusetts. If he was secretive or manipulative he was also a competent and diligent administrator. The conclusion that he was merely working his way up the political ladder by accepted eighteenth-century methods appears unavoidable.

Until the appointment of Thomas Pownall as governor in 1757, Hutchinson's political power and influence grew steadily. At the same time, despite the demands of public service, he remained an active participant in Boston's mercantile community. Late in 1751, he was probably in business alone, advertising for sale in the Boston press a consignment of Irish beef and salt from Cadiz.[94] Busy as he undoubtedly was with his official functions, he was never so preoccupied that he neglected his family financial interests. Unfortunately, the documentary record regarding his mercantile activities during the 1750s remains extremely limited. When Hutchinson took over the position of chief justice of the Massachusetts Superior Court in 1760, he relinquished direct management of the family business to his sons Thomas and Elisha. However, he maintained a financial interest in the East India Company and probably continued to be available as an adviser to his sons. By all accounts he appears as the archetypal gentleman-politician who was still occasionally active in business while serving the public interest out of a sense of personal responsibility and obligation.

Hutchinson's political fortunes temporarily waned with the arrival in Massachusetts of Governor Thomas Pownall in 1757.[95] The new governor favored the whig point of view over that of the court group. This brief fall from favor, partly at least, resulted from his close association with the Shirley administration and the "prerogative" faction. In particular Hutchinson supported the provincial agent and relative by marriage to William Shirley, William Bollan, when Pownall tried to replace him. When Hutchinson later reflected on this period of his career, he bemoaned that "I really am of less consequence than I have been these twenty years," adding that, "many things which used to fall to me go into other hands and I am oftentimes wholly at leisure. . . . It does not suit me."[96] He also complained that Pownall expected him to perform menial and unpleasant tasks such as rounding up deserters and obtaining housing for returning veterans.[97]

Thwarted during Pownall's tenure as governor, despite having successfully secured the lieutenant-governorship in 1758, an appointment that testified to his enduring weight as one of Boston's leading political figures, he determined to wait matters out. During these lean years he witnessed the increased influence of the country party as wartime profiteering and office-holding among his enemies expanded.[98] Despite his differences with the new governor, Hutchinson, nevertheless, remained secure as a powerful and well-respected gentleman-politician. In addition to his work in the General Court, his performance as a fair-minded probate and common pleas judge contributed considerably to his reputation as a distinguished and worthy citizen of Boston. There was little reason to doubt that, given a more congenial governor, his hitherto successful political fortunes would not soon recover.

In August 1760, Francis Bernard arrived as Pownall's replacement. This new appointee proved far more well-disposed toward the court party than his predecessor. Hutchinson's career began to prosper again, and his degree of influence and power increased to unprecedented proportions.

CHAPTER TWO

"The Butt of a Faction"

T homas Pownall departed from Massachusetts on June 3, 1760. During the brief interlude before the arrival of his replacement, Francis Bernard, chief executive responsibilities fell temporarily to Lieutenant Governor Thomas Hutchinson. At forty-nine years of age the aristocratic Bostonian had at last climbed to the apex of political authority. Although he relished this achievement, the next few years were not good ones for his reputation. Between Pownall's exit and the end of the Seven Years' War, Boston's radicals made critical inroads into his seemingly solid position of authority.

A corrosive family quarrel with the Otises began in 1760 that eventually damaged profoundly his image as an impartial and public-minded steward of the people. His support for William Bollan as province agent exposed him to charges of favoritism. His clumsy advocacy of general writs of assistance, as discussed later, alienated him from an important constituency of opposition merchants and smugglers who would continue to assault him in the future. Finally, whig newspaper attacks effectively articulated his growing untrustworthiness as a public servant in the eyes of his opponents. By challenging his plural office-holding and willing nepotism, and by disrespecting his high social standing, determined radicals discovered a virulent critical vocabulary that undermined the foundations of his continued acceptance by the community. James Otis, Jr., and Oxenbridge Thacher especially represented a new whig challenge determined to demonize, stigmatize, and eventually eliminate Hutchinson. The steady erosion of his reputation began around 1760, ironically just as his political fortunes appeared to be most favorable.

In July 1760, Acting Governor Hutchinson directed his efforts toward securing reimbursement from the British Parliament for the Massachusetts war effort. He understood the sacrifices, both personal and financial, made by many members of the general public during the Seven Years' War. Although a devoted member of the British imperial administration, he was also a colonial; he clearly demonstrated a firm commitment to having the war-time contributions of his province fairly recognized, appreciated, and compensated. With this patriotic objective in mind he requested reimbursement for equipment lost at Fort Oswego. He submitted financial claims on behalf of seamen from Massachusetts who had fought in the war, and for the cost of keeping garrisons at Louisbourg and Nova Scotia throughout the previous winter. Hutchinson claimed to know the people's inclinations. He recorded that if their efforts were not recognized, they would be less willing to support future military endeavors. In July 1760 he reminded the British that "the people hitherto have cheerfully submitted to an amazing burthen of taxes every year and seem disposed still to exert themselves" but, if Parliament refused to recognize their efforts, "I fear they will be disposed to avoid doing more than in proportion to others."[1]

While Francis Bernard, Pownall's successor, enjoyed a leisurely trip to Boston from New Jersey and contemplated the "tolerable musick and other amusements" awaiting him at his new home, Hutchinson busily immersed himself in the difficult daily details of fighting the war and representing colonial interests to the British government.[2] His competence, industry, and ability with regard to the vital concerns of the colony were indisputable. These positive qualities contributed to making him a formidable opponent of the radical contenders for power.

Francis Bernard arrived in Boston on August 2, 1760, brimming with optimism for the future. "I have the pleasure to inform your Lordship," he wrote to his friend and patron Lord Barrington, "that I have a very fair prospect of an easy Administration from the Assurances of All persons concerned in it that I have yet seen."[3] He concluded, "I am assured that I may depend upon a quiet and easy administration." The new appointee apparently believed that in Massachusetts, "the People are well disposed to live upon good terms with the Governor and with one another: and I hope I shall not want to be directed by a junto or supported by a party; but that I shall find . . . that plain-dealing integrity and disinterestedness make the best System of policy."[4] Hutchinson later recalled the confident mood of the earliest days of Bernard's administration when he wrote, "The people had conceived a very favorable opinion of him [Bernard], and evidenced it by publick marks of respect as he travelled through the Province, and upon his arrival at the seat of government."[5] Time would show these to have been mere courtesies ritually extended to an incoming executive officer and not at all the affirmative expressions of affection that they appeared to be.

Before long Bernard's administration began to encounter serious political difficulties, and the new governor's initial optimism turned out to be wildly misplaced. He quickly came to experience the highly competitive and partisan nature of Massachusetts politics. Soon Bernard became hopelessly lost in the maze of family and personal rivalries from which there would be no escape. Hutchinson remembered that, in only a few short weeks the new governor "found himself under the necessity either of making a particular family, and its connections, extremely inimical to him, or of doing what would not have been approved of by the greater part of the province."[6]

The lieutenant governor played a central role in the political troubles of the Bernard administration by virtue of his involvement in one dispute after another with his whig critics. In September 1760, Hutchinson accepted the position of chief justice of the Superior Court of Judicature. This controversial decision unleashed a chorus of constant criticism from powerful opposition forces for the fledgling government. Talented and determined individuals led by James Otis, Jr., and Samuel Adams, systematically, consistently, and ruthlessly criticized Bernard and his colleagues during the next decade. As these critics mobilized and coalesced, Hutchinson increasingly emerged as the primary target for their attacks.

James Otis, Jr., was an especially noteworthy opponent of Hutchinson and of the royalist regime. Born in Barnstable, Massachusetts, on February 5, 1725, the younger Otis attended Harvard and then trained as a lawyer under Jeremiah Gridley. From 1746 to 1750, he practiced law in Plymouth before moving to Boston where the political scene was much more lively and his considerable ambitions could be realized more effectively.

He quickly earned a reputation as an eloquent spokesperson for the opposition on the issue of general writs of assistance. He also articulated the first radical fears of plural office-holding by the Hutchinson-Oliver oligarchy. This latter issue especially emerged as a crucial avenue of attack for the whigs, down which they marched their followers time and again throughout the next decade to embarrass their prominent opponent.

Otis, the eager provincial lawyer, secured election to the lower house of the General Court for the first time in May 1761. He was later chosen as speaker in 1767 although Governor Bernard vetoed this appointment. His most creative period of leadership of the opposition to the royalists ended in 1770, although he remained active in politics well into the Revolutionary War. Reports of his emotional instability date from 1762 and his behavior became increasingly erratic over time. In September 1769, he sustained a blow on the head after provoking a tavern brawl with a customs officer named John Robinson. It was not unusual for Otis to be drunk in public, and he soon became an object of local ridicule. The next year he had to be restrained after getting into a "mad Freak" and breaking many windows in the Town House. On April 22, 1770, "Mr. Otis behaved very madly, firing Guns out of his Window that Caused a Large Number of People to Assemble about him."[7] Before his logorrhea drove him to such acts of madness, however, his talents as a pamphleteer and orator secured for him a central position as a framer of opposition to the Hutchinson faction.[8]

In Otis's opinion, Hutchinson's place on the Superior Court had been promised to his father by the erstwhile governor William Shirley. James Otis, Sr., had already been passed over for this appointment once, and the family determined that this disappointment would not recur. When the younger Otis discovered that Hutchinson was being considered for the post, he declared openly that "if his father was not appointed Judge, he [Otis, Jr.,] would set the whole Province in a flame, tho' he perished in the attempt."[9] When Bernard announced his choice, James Otis, Jr., proved to be as good as his word. He immediately turned against the rival appointee and the administration. "From this time," Hutchinson wrote, "they [the Otis family] were at the head of every measure in opposition, not merely in those points which concerned the governor in his administration, but in such as concerned the authority of parliament; . . . From so small a spark a great fire seems to have been kindled."[10]

No direct evidence exists to demonstrate that Hutchinson personally solicited his appointment to the chief judgeship. Moreover, Governor Bernard never explained his reasoning for this divisive decision. There is compelling evidence that James Otis, Sr., actively petitioned for the position. Little doubt remains, however, that acquisition of the post remained consistent with Hutchinson's *modus operandi*. He certainly saw nothing wrong with collecting offices and securing influence through multiple of-fice-holding. On this particular occasion he probably did nothing whatso-ever to ask for the position but was simply awarded it by the neophyte gov-ernor. When he accepted this new appointment, however, he secured for himself a future of personal enmity and criticism from the Otises, both fa-ther and son. From this point onward, whenever other political conflicts emerged, the Otises functioned as influential, articulate, and dedicated op-ponents of Hutchinson and the Bernard administration.

Here we see personal competitive politics in its most naked form. Al-though they had been close political allies in the Shirley and Pownall ad-ministrations, Otis, Sr., and Hutchinson were now rivals. The aggrieved Otis family now deeply resented the defeat and swore revenge against him. This overt personal animus, similar to that harbored by Samuel Adams after the Land Bank fight, represented an important source of energy for the early whig campaign against Hutchinson's career and reputation. Hell hath no fury like an Otis scorned.

Another intriguing dimension to the feud with Hutchinson concerns the strained emotional relationship between the Otises, father and son.[11] James Otis, Jr., was never consistent in his politics and his unpredictable opinions often infuriated his whig allies. He remained ambivalent toward authority, swinging wildly from a posture of deference to defiance. The only really consistent aspect of his behavior in the 1760s was his obsession with Hutchinson. Certainly the younger Otis seemed to despise his aristocratic rival but precisely why this should be requires explanation.

Most of Otis's accusations leveled at Hutchinson, portraying as they did an ambitious and shameless office-seeker, apply most plausibly to his own father. The father-son relationship between the Otises was not close but, instead, characterized by competitiveness, rejection, and anger. The elder Colonel Otis was overbearing, tyrannical, and penny-pinching in his deal-ings with his son. Part of the reason why young James left Plymouth was because, owing to his father's influence, he could not accumulate enough clients to sustain a viable law practice. As the younger Otis matured, his lit-erary tastes and intellectual turn of mind came to resemble more those of the refined Hutchinson than the blatant provincial striving typified by his father. Probably the younger Otis admired Hutchinson as an exemplar of colonial polish and dignity and was compelled to face a deeply painful emo-tional question of loyalty when Bernard rejected his father for the chief jus-ticeship appointment.

In the end the younger Otis was perhaps ashamed of his father's grubby maneuvers for advancement and, beginning in the writs of assistance conflict, transferred his anger toward a replacement father figure, that of Hutchinson. This hypothesis explains why the thrust of Otis's attacks on the chief justice stressed a mean-spirited self-seeking person obviously in pursuit of more power, far more descriptive of his father's petitioning for the place, not Hutchinson's. Overly aggressive plural office-holding in Barnstable was precisely the charge against James Otis, Sr., in the corridors of power in Boston. This was one of the reasons why Hutchinson had broken off his political friendship with Otis, Sr. Now, driven by the powerful psychological imperative of family loyalty, the younger Otis projected his embarrassment at his father's behavior onto an authority figure upon whom he could take out his resentments. Hutchinson thus became, unwittingly, the surrogate father figure of whom James Otis, Jr., deeply disapproved and yet felt obliged to support because he was related by blood. Here, of course, also reside the origins of his later mental instability. Resolution of the nagging ambivalence toward a nonfamilial authority he respected, and a father whom he wished was different, and thereby provoked rebellion in his heart, proved impossible for the unfortunate younger man.

Family animus was not the only basis for whig opposition. Other country party supporters disapproved of this appointment to the Superior Court. John Adams, for example, denounced the decision. Initially, Adams confined his criticisms to Hutchinson's age and lack of professional qualifications as a lawyer. He asserted in 1760, referring to the rigors of the law:

> A man whose youth and spirits and strength have been spent in husbandry, merchandise, [and] politics . . . will never master so immense and involved a science; for it may be taken for a never-failing maxim, that youth is the only time for laying the foundation of a great improvement in any science or profession, and that an application in advanced years, after the mind is crowded, the attention divided or dissipated, and the memory in part lost, will make but a tolerable artist at best.[12]

In other words, the aging gentleman-politician was too old and too much of an amateur to merit this judicial appointment. Adams, who regarded himself as the spokesperson of a new generation of youthful professionals eager to advance their views, strenuously objected to the obvious favoritism demonstrated by this appointment. Youth and professionalism, especially when associated with law and medicine, were two qualities Boston's radicals repeatedly stressed as antidotes to the poisonous politics of connection and patronage associated with the older generation.

Later, Adams recorded criticisms of the chief justice that betrayed a more personal level of commentary. He resented Hutchinson's introduction of English-style wigs into the courtroom. Adams regarded the innovation as "so showy and so shallow, so theatrical and so ecclesiastical of scarlet and sable robes, of broad bands, and enormous tie wigs, more resembling fleeces of painted merino wool than any thing natural to man and that could breathe with him."[13] Furthermore, he disliked the new chief justice's "gravity and subtlety, that artless design of face." Hutchinson irritated him by his prominent status as the powerful, yet unqualified, amateur legal patrician.[14] Undisguised personal dislike thus played a role in the unfolding drama. Co-existing alongside the substance of whig criticisms of Hutchinson were simple human envy and distaste. As Ralph Waldo Emerson once enjoined, in analyzing history do not be too profound, for often the causes are quite superficial. Adams and Otis, and eventually many other pro-whig critics, merely disliked Hutchinson and resented his high status and position of influence and prestige.

The documentary record reveals no reliable explanation of Hutchinson's motivation for accepting the chief justice's position. Years later, Adams argued that "Bernard, instead of fulfilling the promises of two of his predecessors, Shirley and Pownall, to give the next vacancy on that bench to Colonel Otis, appointed Hutchinson, for the very purpose of deciding the fate of the writs of assistance, and all other causes in which the claims of Great Britain might be directly or indirectly implicated."[15] This may well have been the case. In 1760, however, the Bernard administration demonstrated a pronounced desire for political harmony, which renders this explanation unlikely.

It is far more plausible to interpret the judicial appointment in 1760 as evidence of the considerable power of the Hutchinson-Oliver family oligarchy as an effective and organized patronage machine. Governor Bernard, as an incoming administrator, would probably have been unable to resist any solicitations for appointment which may have been advanced by this influential political circle. The new governor probably concluded that to secure co-operation for his policies from the colonials he should reward the most important of them with the judgeship so as to secure their loyalty.[16]

There were no organized, coherent, and permanent political parties in pre-Revolutionary Massachusetts. Instead, groups of friends dispensed patronage according to the power and influence of competing oligarchies. Although these alliances were not parties, they practiced virulent partisanship. Hutchinson, along with his life-long ally Andrew Oliver, controlled an entrenched oligarchy of office-holders and office-seekers, variously referred to by their enemies as "the court party," "prerogative men," or "the junto." This group of royalist lawyers, customs officials, and merchants usually belonged to the Anglican church, were often related by blood or marriage, and subscribed to the political assertion that "the best men" should govern. In 1760 this group included Hutchinson, Andrew and Peter Oliver, Eliakim Hutchinson, Timothy Ruggles, Daniel Leonard, Charles Apthorp, Robert Auchmuty, Benjamin Lynde, Samuel Waterhouse, Charles Paxton, Thomas Flucker, John Irving, Jr., Edmund Trowbridge, and Chambers Russell.[17] These men comprised an established plural office-holding oligarchy which came under increasing attack after the controversial judicial appointment in 1760.

The opponents of the court party were, of course, a competitive potential oligarchy. James Otis, Jr., Samuel Adams, and their country party supporters coveted power for themselves, and traced their origins back to the days of Elisha Cooke, Sr. The problem for them was that the Hutchinson group stood in their way. If the whigs were ever to prevail, they had to eject the court party oligarchy. In order to realize this objective, new political methods had to be employed. One of the most important of these would be the utter demolition of Hutchinson, who represented the keystone in the court party arch. Discrediting him afforded the whigs the opportunity to define and legitimate their own claims to governance.

Hutchinson wrote nothing on the subject of plural office-holding. However, his upper-class notion of government by "the best men" who were endowed with a natural birthright to rule explains his proclivity for assembling an office-holding oligarchy.[18] To him such an arrangement appeared completely normal. Additionally, the difficulty of recruiting willing servants to the royal cause may have increased his reliance on friends and family. This élitist view of politics naturally desensitized him to the growing animosity which his acceptance of yet another office engendered among his political rivals. This extended oligarchy and the entrenched power it wielded irritated, antagonized, and offended his political enemies. The distinguished and learned whig lawyer Oxenbridge Thacher often

referred in print to Hutchinson by the derogatory nickname *"summa potes-
tatis"* or, more usually, simply *"summa."*[19] Thacher's colleagues and readers
had little difficulty knowing whom he had in mind.

The first major political controversy that engaged Chief Justice Hutchinson, other than the appointment itself, was the case of the general writs of
assistance. The Superior Court argued the matter in February, and rendered a decision in November 1761. During this important dispute James
Otis, Jr., an erstwhile government attorney, emerged as the lawyer for a
group of Boston merchants whose objective was to weaken enforcement of
the laws of trade and challenge the authority of the Hutchinson-Oliver oligarchy. The chief justice did everything he could to uphold the existing
legal structure of customs enforcement. By approaching the writs of assistance dispute from a rigidly traditional and legalistic perspective, Hutchinson came to be regarded as the political enemy of a very important group
of dissident Boston merchants.

This commercial group constituted a key collection of enemies for the
upper-class gentleman-politician. By the end of 1761, following the writs
of assistance controversy, Hutchinson's enemies included those who personally disliked him; those who envied and resented his plural office-holding and the power of his family oligarchy; and those merchants, represented by lawyer Otis, who increasingly perceived him as an obstacle to
their business. It was not without some justification that many agreed with
John Adams, who claimed after hearing Otis's performance before the
court in February 1761, that "American independence was then and there
born."[20]

In the writs of assistance dispute James Otis, Jr., and Oxenbridge
Thacher argued against the legality of general search warrants by the customs service and challenged the authority of the Superior Court to issue
such writs. General writs allowed customs officers to break open and search
homes and warehouses for contraband without specifically naming the
place to be searched, the goods to be seized, the names of the informants,
or the reason for the search. The merchants, "some of whom had been affected by these forfeitures," detested the writs and opposed them in court
shortly after William Pitt had ordered their employment in August 1760.[21]
Hutchinson, in his first major case as chief justice, made a legal ruling upon
the applicability of this general writ principle.

From the point of view of many merchants the writs of assistance issue
was more than simply one of formal legality. "A Fair Trader" pointed out

in the *Boston Gazette* that competition with businessmen in Rhode Island played a vital role in the argument against these measures. In addition the hated use of paid informers by such energetic customs officials as Charles Paxton contributed to the opposition. Finally, unequal enforcement of general writs affected traders' livelihoods and factored into the political opposition to this legal policy. Many traders regarded smuggling with impunity as essential for the maintenance of a healthy business environment.[22]

James Otis, Jr.'s, impassioned arguments against the writs employed a broad-ranging and emotional rhetoric which cast the case in terms of a serious challenge to colonial liberties. Otis argued, "Reason and the constitution are against this writ," further claiming that "no acts of parliament can establish such a writ," and appealed for the abolition of this "monster of oppression," that "remnant of Star Chamber Tyranny."[23] To the opponents of general writs of assistance, the case involved critically important economic and constitutional considerations. Otis's elevated rhetoric introduced a new level of intensity to the radical language of high principle that became characteristic of whig polemics for the next sixteen years. By abstracting resistance to general writs away from self-interest into the realm of a defense of liberty, he articulated a new vocabulary of opposition.

After he had heard Otis's impassioned criticisms of the general writs, Chief Judge Hutchinson deferred ruling on the case until he could write to England for advice. "I prevailed with my brethren to continue the cause [Hutchinson secured a continuance of the case] until the next term, and in the mean time wrote to and procured a copy of the writ, and sufficient practice of the exchequer there."[24] Then, on November 23, 1761, he made his decision. He announced that general writs of assistance could legally be issued by the Superior Court and would be issued in the future. On December 2, 1761, customs officer Charles Paxton received the first general writ issued after this controversial ruling, which was prepared in Hutchinson's own hand.[25]

The chief justice's analysis of the issues were, characteristically, far less emotionally charged than those of Otis and the merchants. He conceptualized the case in a formal, legalistic context, and eventually ruled in favor of the existing practice of the continued application of general search warrants. His lodestar in arriving at this decision had been existing practice in England. In upholding general writs, however, he incurred the lasting enmity of a vocal and powerful group in the Boston mercantile community.

This defeat for Otis as the attorney for the merchant's organization, now known as the Boston Society for Encouraging Trade and Commerce, had lasting consequences. He secured re-election to the lower house of the General Court in May 1761, largely on the basis of his performance as the outspoken critic of general search warrants. Hutchinson sarcastically recalled, "Mr. Otis's zeal in carrying on these causes was deemed as meritorious as if it had sprung from a sincere concern for the liberties of the people."[26] The Boston Society for Encouraging Trade and Commerce was a political club that reflected mercantile opposition to most British trade regulations.

Obviously he believed Otis and the merchants to have been motivated entirely by material self-interest. Many undoubtedly were, of course, since the B.S.E.T.C. was not a philanthropic organization, but Otis's motives were different. Here Hutchinson seriously underestimated his opponent. Otis's principal objective was power and respect rooted in a psychological imperative to prove himself before those he esteemed as authority figures. Not all whigs were driven by the familial demons which propelled Otis's hatred of Hutchinson. Nevertheless, his high-minded assault on the older generation reached a sympathetic audience among many young men of Boston. His style of opposition was an emotional rhetoric which, however disdainful it appeared to the older man, represented the preliminary vocabulary of the new politics—republican appeals to popular sovereignty as the basis of power. Otis represented the advance guard of a powerful opposition movement that was determined to replace the Hutchinson-Oliver oligarchy with a new governing élite. Another court party supporter, Timothy Ruggles, presciently declared that "out of this election will arise a d——d faction, which will shake this province to its foundation."[27]

Antagonism between Hutchinson and Boston's incipient popular party continued in the confrontation which intended to make gold legal tender and in the dispute regarding the replacement of province agent William Bollan by Jasper Mauduit.

Conflict over these two ostensibly insignificant issues instructively demonstrates the purely political dimension of the struggle that characterized Bay Colony public life between those out of power and those in search of more. In assessing the respective positions of the antagonists no clear ideological division emerges. Instead, within the continuum of power exercised by a socioeconomic élite, two competing positions emerged. Rich and privileged men vied for decision-making power in matters of money and politics.

With respect to the currency question of 1761, Hutchinson's condescending approach to his opponents and his elevated view of himself can be seen in the following words: "I stood in the front of the opposition," and, referring to a renewed proposal to devalue the currency by allowing gold as well as silver to become legal tender, "if it should succeed I look upon it to be the first step of our return to Egypt."[28] He saw himself as an omniscient fiscal Moses, who, having led the colony out of Egypt in the 1740s when he had retired paper money from the Massachusetts economy, was not about to countenance a return to the fiscal uncertainties of the days of the Land Bank dispute. In his opinion provincial currency should comprise silver only. The suggestion to introduce gold represented a dangerous attempt to inflate the medium of exchange and should be resisted regardless of how popular the new measure appeared to be.

Ever the fiscal conservative and proponent of "hard money," Hutchinson wrote a series of articles which appeared in the *Boston Evening-Post* defending silver as the only reliable means of maintaining a stable currency. In the same series he warned against the inflationary threat of the introduction of gold as legal tender.[29]

Almost immediately Oxenbridge Thacher and James Otis, Jr., responded to his arguments in the pages of the pro-whig *Boston Gazette*. These writers did not engage the plausibility or cogency of his arguments on the currency question. Rather, they criticized the chief justice for the impropriety of expressing his views in public. Additionally, they assaulted Hutchinson's status within the "leviathan in power," counting him among "those other overgrown animals whose influence and importance is only in exact mathematical proportion to their purses."[30] The overwrought language here indicates the psychological reference point of the whig writers. Rather than attack the economics of the dispute, radical writers targeted the chief justice's social prominence and position of authority.

Hutchinson retaliated by stating that his opponents wrote out of "whimsical conscience," were "wrong headed," and failed to treat him with the requisite "delicacy and politeness" that someone of his social status should expect.[31] In their respective responses both Otis and Thacher registered unwillingness to listen to Hutchinson purely by virtue of his social standing. In January 1762, Otis wrote: "no man carries the atmosphere of his commission or public character into a disputation; if there was any rule of logic in favour of that, the very name of a justice of the quorum would be as effectual to strike a poor plebeian dumb as the *ratio ultima regnum* of a Lewis the XIV."[32]

Thacher too employed a deliberately disrespectful tone in his prose, suggesting that Hutchinson's personality, social standing, and multiple office-holding were more irritating than his views on the currency. He wrote sarcastically: "it would be a great affront to his Honor to suppose that he demanded implicit belief from his readers, and that when he proposed his projection to the public consideration he should be offended at, the freest discussion of it."[33]

During this dispute, in Boston's newspapers and in pamphlets usually emanating from the printing shop owned by Benjamin Edes and John Gill, emerged an emotional vocabulary of opposition to Hutchinson's position of political prominence and his upper-class social status. In these important exchanges of 1761 and 1762, Thacher and Otis began to erode the general validity of one of Hutchinson's core political assumptions: that he should be listened to and respected primarily because of who he was. Such anti-authoritarian rhetoric proved to be a crucial prerequisite for the development of a revolutionary mentality. It would take a long time for Hutchinson to comprehend fully the implications of this new, more egalitarian tone that was creeping into the arena of political discourse in 1761.

Similarly, Hutchinson's emerging role as the unique symbolic target of a vital opposition group slowly came into focus in the tone and tenor of the debates of the early 1760s. In questioning his social status and authority as a qualification for leadership, Otis and Thacher took a critical first step toward legitimizing a more general challenge to his dominant political position. Before he could be replaced, enough people had to be convinced of the real danger to their interests posed by his continued enjoyment of authority. Such an argument could never rest on a purely economic foundation. Nobody would ever hate Hutchinson because he was a currency expert. He had to be presented as a symbol of too much power in the hands of too few people before the public would fear him. Otis and Thacher thus employed the print medium to articulate their attack on him as the embodiment of Boston's dangerous establishment. These audacious and unprecedented attacks constituted an important psychological foundation for change by preparing the public, and to some degree the writers themselves, for the dawn of a new political day.[34]

In his dispute with Boston's popular party concerning the province agency in London, Hutchinson again appeared unconcerned with popularity. At the same time, however, political competition and criticism insulted and irritated him. William Bollan was a member of William Shirley's inner circle. He had come to Massachusetts in 1740, established himself as a lawyer in Boston, risen to the status of province agent, and eventually married Shirley's daughter. He secured election to the provincial agency in 1746, and remained in power protected by the influence of the court party.[35]

As a councilor Hutchinson had been a key member of "the Shirlean faction" and remained a long-standing personal and political friend to Bollan. During the Pownall administration, in which an attempt had been made to build a greater degree of consensus between country and court interests, Bollan's position had been temporarily weakened. When Francis Bernard acceded to the governorship in 1760, however, Bollan's political fortunes began to rise accordingly, as did those of the prerogative or court party advocates more generally.

In 1762 the Massachusetts popular party decided to attack the Hutchinson-Oliver oligarchy by targeting Bollan's position as province agent. Boston's radical opponents of the court party hoped to replace Bollan with someone more congenial to them. They demanded an appointee who was willing to report directly to the speaker of the lower house of the General Court and not to the Council and House combined, which had been the usual practice. In so doing they hoped to secure an independent channel of communication with England that would enhance the power of the lower house. Boston's newspapers and the country party in the legislature predictably denigrated their opponents in the establishment.

Hutchinson determined to fight to retain Bollan; in March and April 1762 he assured him that he "did everything in my power, more I am sure than any other member of the court to prevent your [Bollan's] dismission."[36] During the struggle over the agency Hutchinson seemed untroubled by his unpopularity. In a typical statement from his correspondence of the spring of 1762 he declared, "I shall make no complaint under this cloud but please myself."[37] Ascribing merchant opposition to Bollan entirely to partisanship and personal politics, he observed, "we have more violent parties in our little mock Parliament and some times the publick interest gives way to private picques."[38] His tone was supercilious and scathing. For example, he recorded that he was "glad to be out of the way," fulfilling his Eastern Circuit court duties in April, disappointed and annoyed by "the influence of Mr. Otis and men of his disposition."[39] There was no doubt that Hutchinson regarded Otis as far beneath him in social standing. Elsewhere he wrote that while men of the upper class should marry women of similar background, people like Otis could wed their mother and nobody would be shocked.

While Hutchinson disapproved of the criticism directed toward him, he did not deliberately seek isolation and unpopularity. His behavior was by no means pathological as the historian William Pencak has asserted.[40] No perverse, irrepressible martyr complex drove Hutchinson inexorably toward his own demise. The self-assured gentleman-politician simply believed himself to be superior to his opponents in terms of his leadership qualities, education, overall social standing, and competence as a public figure. He imagined himself as more suited to govern and judge others than his political opponents, even to the point where he accepted a high degree of popular criticism. As he wrote in a revealing letter during November 1762, "I have been so often ill-used by the people when I have endeavored to do service . . . I am tempted to take for a motto '*odi profanum vulgus.*' When the popular mind changes I am little cooled. I fancy at last that they turn to me and not I to them."[41] To his radical opponents this deeply felt superiority must have been profoundly irritating. From Hutchinson's standpoint, he did not expect wisdom from the public. He remained unmoved by either acceptance or rejection, although there is no reason to assume that he courted the latter out of some personal perversity.

By 1762, he demonstrated a political personality that had crystallized into a perception of himself and his class as the only true advocates of the public interest. In his opinion the popular party spokespersons, who increasingly appealed to qualified members of the public for ratification and support for their views, were self-interested participants in the political process. The future virtually guaranteed that he would pay heavily for this remarkable condescension as the era of popular sovereignty gradually superseded the defeated world of the gentleman-politician.

Popular party proponents of a new province agent favored Jasper Mauduit, a London wool draper and prominent religious dissenter, as Bollan's replacement. While Hutchinson described Bollan's recall as "an ill-judged proceeding" motivated by personal animus, popular party leaders voiced other more substantive reasons for their actions.[42] Jonathan Mayhew, for instance, a prominent Boston Congregational minister, raised religious concerns and suggested that Mauduit would be "much more likely to serve the Province in its most essential Interests, than a Gentleman of the Chh. of England tho' this is by no means the only objection that has been made against Mr. Bollan."[43]

Other more secular objections included James Otis, Jr.'s, criticism that Bollan was "little more than agent for his father-in-law," and his supporters "a motley mixture of high church men, and dissenters who, for the sake of the offices they sustain, are full as high in their notions of prerogative as the churchmen."[44] Bollan squandered public money by traveling too often between Boston and London. His critics accused him of pocketing £6,000 of a Parliamentary grant to Massachusetts, and he had made little progress in the long-standing boundary dispute with New Hampshire. He had antagonized Otis and others by forwarding a copy of an English writ to Hutchinson during the writs of assistance dispute in 1761. Finally, he remained too tight-lipped and secretive for the radicals. In James Otis, Jr.'s, direct words, "one of the articles against Mr. Bollan, among many others, was, that they [the lower house] could never get any intelligence from him, even when he did condescend to write them."[45]

Hutchinson, characteristically, insisted on supporting Bollan's continued agency despite these specific and substantive criticisms. In doing so, he further antagonized his country party opponents who, by 1762, were already beginning to feel that they "have groaned under his Tyranny twenty years already."[46] In retrospect Hutchinson would perhaps have been well advised not to support Bollan although it is likely that had he not fought here the radicals would have found some other grounds upon which to engage him. The real significance of the Bollan squabble was that it demonstrated that the whigs followed a deliberate, if largely tacit, strategy of confrontation toward Hutchinson with the objective of loosening his grip on power. Every future issue of provincial business provided the whigs with an opportunity to assail Hutchinson's position as the preeminent figure of authority.

Throughout 1762 and 1763, Hutchinson, multiple office-holder, gentleman-politician, prerogative advocate, and Anglican high-churchman, became increasingly frustrated. Offended and angered by partisan attacks in the newspapers and on the floor of the House, he endured a barrage of scathing public criticism. Seemingly insignificant matters triggered vigorous personal attacks, and the pugnacious James Otis, Jr., was usually the initiator. The increasing frequency of these assaults led him to reflect that "for two or three years I have been the butt of a faction." He comforted himself with typical self-assurance, however, by noting that "they have missed their aim and have not hurt me in the esteem of the best people in the Province."[47] Eventually he would be forced to recognize that he had been mistaken by engaging in such whistling in the dark. Every newspaper attack added another brick to the wall of whig patriotism. By denigrating Hutchinson in the print media the radicals steadily constructed an "imagined community" of Massachusetts unity and uniqueness which represented an essential precondition for mobilizing people for revolution.[48] Before long it would be utterly irrelevant what "the best people" in the Province thought of him. "I have been out of humor this fortnight," he complained "by an infamous piece in one of the papers wrote by young Otis."[49] Irritated as he was by these attacks, he did not perceive them to be harbingers of serious political trouble for himself or his supporters. So long as "the best men" ignored Otis's poisonous barbs, he seemed willing to tolerate them with good grace.

Elsewhere, Otis wrote the following remarkable passage about Hutchinson: "At one time he appears in the character of a fine gentleman, kindly greeting, softly soothing, sweetly pleasing and plainly courting. Divers ladies, both maids and matrons, have taken him for an angel of light. . . . I have seen him twice or thrice in the pomp and puff of an American barrister. Nay, his cloven foot has peep'd from under the summer flowing black, white and grey, and the gorgeous winter scarlet."[50] Here Otis plainly invoked the language of demonization and elevated Hutchinson to a symbolic level of opprobrium. By hinting at an association with the devil Otis appealed to an enduring New England emotional tradition which continued to have profound cultural resonance in the public mind. This inventive language represented the beginning of a sustained attack on Hutchinson's position and person that culminated in his eventual rôle as the singular and unique enemy of liberty in Massachusetts.

Despite these colorful and vicious attacks on his character, in 1763 Hutchinson attributed the criticisms he received either to suggestions by outsiders from England or merely confusion on the part of his attackers. He wrote to Richard Jackson in London, "our *Boulefeus* take the advantage of the licentiousness in England and their partisans vindicate them by saying they do not go to the lengths that Wilkes does."[51] He interpreted opposition attacks on his status and position as primarily imitative of the English political scene. He wrote again to Jackson, claiming that "a faction by which I have been treated with great virulence has been an obstruction. It seems at present to be in a declining state but in our little affairs we imitate the people of England."[52]

By minimizing indigenous dissatisfaction and attributing James Otis, Jr.'s, attacks to mere imitation, he seriously miscalculated both the degree of animus harbored toward him by Boston's whigs and the deleterious effects their journalism had on his reputation among the readership of the *Boston Gazette*. Eventually, in August 1765 when an angry crowd attacked his house, the supercilious lieutenant governor paid a very high price for discounting the virulence of his opponents' hatred.

Hutchinson offset his occasional anger by occupying himself with judicial responsibilities, compiling the first volume of his *History of Massachusetts-Bay*, and relaxing with his family at his country home in Milton. Politics took a back seat to history and horticulture for most of 1763. In September, he wrote to David Cheseborough, his friend and land agent in Rhode Island, that preparing his *History* filled up "a winter's vacation from the courts morning and evening. In the daytime I have generally other employments."[53] He demonstrated more goodwill toward Otis than the latter had a right to expect when he wrote to Ezra Stiles and joked, "I threaten Mr. Otis sometimes that I will be revenged of him after I am dead," by virtue of writing history.[54] This good-natured tolerance and jocularity proved misplaced in the long run. He did not see that his attackers pursued a comprehensive strategy of character assassination in the name of establishing a new governing élite. Furthermore, in Otis's case, his deeply felt need to challenge authority in the symbolic figure of Hutchinson represented a dire threat to the older man's reputation. Profound political change percolated in the substratum of the Bay Colony. In 1763 Hutchinson remained unaware of the central role he was to play as events developed.

His obvious unawareness of the deeper meaning of radical strategy cannot be attributed to dullness. Hutchinson may have had a prosaic personality but his mental acuity and attention to detail were faultless. Even while on vacation he appeared driven and meticulous. In his dedication to horticulture he demonstrated considerable fastidiousness. He wrote to a nephew who was on vacation in England: "procure me three larch trees about as large as a small walking stick and 6 or 7 feet high and half a dozen mulberries about the same size."[55] To another correspondent he explained at length how to ship pear trees to England "before the buds begin to open or swell. . . or there will be a danger of their putting out on board."[56]

The same exhaustive attention to detail suffused Hutchinson's correspondence in other areas of his life. His instructions were extraordinarily exact, for example, when ordering clothes from England. "I desire you to send me a suit of cloathes," he wrote to his tailor, Peter Leitch, "half dressed of a drab coloured broad cloath of a strong mixture not dark nor very light, a deep gold thread button basket if worn holes on both sides the coat and waistcoat either Gold binding or, if it will not cost more or but a trifle more, a Gold [wa...?] or slightly embroidered hole." He continued laboriously, "I want it to travel in in the summer upon the Circuits to serve instead of black under a robe the Breeches lined with thin leather also a black waistcoat lapelled, the forebodys only either of Satin or Corduroy which will wear the best."[57]

Occasionally his sartorial instructions contained the telling phrase, "not to be singular." Nevertheless, he concerned himself with fashion trends as set by George III and by his English peers. "I am told the judges and lawyers upon the circuits wear a fine camblet surtout cloth colour when they travel in over their black, if so, send me one," he wrote in 1764.[58] Obviously he did not want to be left behind in the projection of his place and status. In leisure, recreation, and in the conduct of mundane daily life, just as in business and politics, he appeared painstakingly meticulous, earnest, pedantic, and serious. Above all, acceptance, recognition, and respect mattered to him as did certainty, order, and continuity. When combined with his public life, these observations confirm a conventional personality. Quite a leap of imagination is required to comprehend how Boston's radical whigs transformed such a mundane character into the unique and extraordinary villain of early American history.

Until 1764 and the vicissitudes associated with the news of the Sugar Act, Hutchinson primarily occupied himself with boundary disputes concerning Nova Scotia, Maine, and Connecticut. He also resolved the administrative details of the General Court's grant of Mount Desert Island to Governor Bernard. When he was not preoccupied with the public business of the colony, in his private correspondence he sometimes pondered James Otis, Jr.'s, virulent attacks. To David Cheseborough, he wrote in a slightly mystified tone that Otis was "indeed the strangest in the world, says a hundred things I do not deserve in all company as if he designed to raise my character and as soon as goes home sits down to libel me."[59] He seemed genuinely confused by Otis's inconsistencies. This is perhaps not surprising, however, given Otis's subsequent mental problems.

Peter Oliver, Hutchinson's relative and political ally, shared his view of Otis as erratic and unreliable. Oliver allegedly told John Adams, "I have known him [Otis] these twenty years and I have no opinion of his head or his heart. If Bedlam[ism] is a talent, he has it in perfection. He will one time say of the Lieutenant-Governor, that he had have him, than any other man he knows, in office; and the next hour will represent him as the greatest tyrant and most despicable creature living."[60] Hutchinson confided to his old college friend Israel Williams that Otis "professes to have buried the hatchet every 3 or 4 months. As soon as ever any body affronts him be it who it will he wreaks all his malice and revenge upon me."[61] When Otis finally did go mad, around 1770, his irrational criticisms and confusing ambivalence became far easier to explain.

Smuggling was another issue that Hutchinson wrote about in 1764. He advocated reform of the system of revenue collection by the simple expedient of paying customs officials more. He wrote to Richard Jackson in England that "the real cause of the illicit trade in this province has been the indulgence of the officers of the customs and we are told that the cause has been that they are quartered upon far more than their legal fees and that without bribery and corruption they must starve."[62] This simplistic answer to a complex problem indicated his straightforward and rational intellectual style. Such an uncomplicated approach, however, omitted the crucial consideration that, in Daniel Leonard's telling phrase, "whigs and smugglers are cousin Germans."[63] Behind the smuggling issue resided an important power struggle. No matter how much economic common sense Hutchinson's suggestion contained, his analysis ignored the important political implications of smuggling. Later, when this issue dominated provincial politics, his views demonstrated far more sophistication.

Regarding his business interests in 1763 he asserted that "the place I have in the Government renders it inconvenient for me to be concerned in factorage businesses."[64] He did not have the time to attend effectively to both politics and commerce. Therefore, the family business passed into the hands of his eldest son, Thomas, Jr., who was later assisted by his brother Elisha. Busy as he was with politics, throughout his career, the family patriarch made himself available to comment on business. In late 1762 he wrote to Edward Lloyd, a business associate in London, "it sometimes happens that Irish butter is as cheap in Bristol as Ireland," and advised his sons on "the sale of yard goods, butter, cheese and especially bohea teas."[65] One suspects that he could not conquer the life-long instinct to trade with a view to coming out ahead. However, very few intelligible references to business by Hutchinson have survived in the documentary record.

In February 1763, the Seven Years' War ended, concluding an era of considerable social and financial strain in Massachusetts. Even James Otis, Jr., appeared to have been temporarily carried away by the euphoria of the peace settlement. At the first Town Meeting following the announcement of the peace Otis, having been chosen moderator, delivered the following words: "we in America have certainly abundant reasons to rejoice. . . . And we may safely conclude from His Majesty's wise administration hitherto, that liberty and knowledge, civil and religious, will be co-extended, improved, and preserved to the latest posterity. . . . The true interests of Great Britain and her plantations are mutual, and what God in his providence has united, let no man dare attempt to pull asunder."[66] Despite these loyal words, powerful and divisive political impulses lurked to jeopardize future harmony. In 1763 though, even someone as radical as James Otis, Jr., went out of his way to articulate loyalty to the King. At the conclusion of the war with France Hutchinson wrote "there does not appear to be any special cause of dissatisfaction with the administration of government."[67] The only political difficulties that he anticipated were the perennial problems of competition for office and the steady incitement of dissatisfaction within the colonies that emanated from England. As he wrote in his History in 1763 "at all times, there are many out of place who wish to be in it."[68] Moreover, radicals in Massachusetts copied the disturbances and criticisms advocated by the followers of John Wilkes from England and that helped explain the cutting criticism that his enemies directed toward him.

Both Otis and Hutchinson turned out to be mistaken in their optimism for the future. As the forthcoming years were to show, James Otis, Jr., and Thomas Hutchinson shared common ground only in their mutual miscalculations regarding the degree of political harmony that was possible in Massachusetts. It would not be very long before Boston faced political convulsions unprecedented since Sir Edmund Andros's ignominious exit in 1689.

CHAPTER THREE

Enter the Crowd

W hen the Seven Years' War ended in February 1763, Thomas Barnard, a Boston minister, optimistically predicted that "now commences the Aera of our quiet Enjoyment of those liberties, which our Fathers purchased with the toil of their Lives, their Treasure, their Blood."[1] Unfortunately, this was not to be an era of tranquility. Shortly following the conclusion of the War, the Massachusetts political scene was soon convulsed and divided. The acrimony generated by the British intention to collect revenues in the American colonies provided the backdrop for this new round of conflict. During the turbulent disputes of 1764 and 1765 Thomas Hutchinson found himself repeatedly at the center of controversy on the floor of the General Court, in the pages of the *Boston Gazette*, and eventually in the streets of Boston. Although he had nothing to do with the formulation of the unpopular Sugar and Stamp Acts, he found himself in the unenviable situation of being compelled to defend them. As such he became the target of radical attacks on his position and character.

With the introduction of the Sugar Act of April 1764, the British government explicitly announced the desire to collect revenue in America. The act was a renewal of the Molasses Act of 1733, and scheduled to take effect on September 29, 1764. The preamble to the new law stated quite unequivocally, "that a revenue be raised, in your Majesty's . . . dominions in

America, for defraying the expenses of defending, protecting, and securing the same; we . . . the commons of Great Britain . . . being desirous to make some provision . . . towards raising the said revenue in America, have resolved to give and grant unto your Majesty the several rates and duties herein after mentioned."[2] The act authorized naval commanders and customs house officers to seize vessels and cargoes suspected of violating the Acts of Trade and Navigation. The Sugar Act lowered the import duty on foreign molasses into Boston from six-pence to three-pence per gallon.

This particular feature of First Lord of the Treasury and Chancellor of the Exchequer Sir George Grenville's new legislation gave many Boston merchants immediate cause for alarm.[3] According to the provisions of the Molasses Act of 1733, the duty owed by importers of foreign molasses was six-pence per gallon. Usually, however, this tax had not been collected. For many years Boston's merchants had been able to smuggle in molasses from the West Indies under the noses of corrupt customs officials. Bostonians manufactured rum from the smuggled molasses, which was then traded by local fishermen "for export to the southern colonies for naval stores, which we send to Great Britain, and for grain; and to Africa to purchase slaves for our own islands in the West Indies."[4] The new Sugar Act, by reducing the duty and by promising stricter enforcement, threatened this complex triangular trading network. The financial interests of Boston's smugglers came under direct attack as a result of this legislation. Not surprisingly, many merchant-smugglers opposed the new regulations. Oxenbridge Thacher summarized well the concerns of Boston's illicit traders with this observation on their business. Trade, he said, was a "nice and delicate lady; she must be courted and won by soft and fair addresses. She will not bear the rude hand of a ravisher."[5]

Hutchinson, lifelong merchant that he was, agreed with Thacher's criticisms of the Sugar Act. In July 1764 he recorded that "taxes and duties will lessen the advantages which the nation [Britain] has for so long [a] time received by having the colonies for their customers." He continued to argue that "greater benefit must accrue by diverting rather than restraining them [the colonies] from manufactures and branches of commerce interfering with the national interest than can arise from taxes and duties."[6] Later he confided to Richard Jackson that Britain would be better off encouraging trade and consumption in North America and not introducing more excises and duties.

Elsewhere he expressed his opinion that the three-pence duty proposed by the new legislation was too high. In his view, if the Grenville administration was serious about enforcing its molasses duty, then the amount should be reduced to one penny or three-halfpence. If this were the amount he averred, "it would have been acquiesced in by the merchants."[7] Governor Bernard concurred when he wrote to the Lords of Trade, "if it is meant to be an Act of Revenue, the best means to make it effectual, that is to raise the greatest Revenue by it, will be to lower the duties in such proportion as will secure the entire collection of them and encourage the importation of the goods on which they will be laid."[8] So, in 1764, when Massachusetts' political leaders confronted Grenville's new commercial legislation, Hutchinson agreed in principle with the criticisms of the legislation advanced by his country party counterparts and Boston's merchant-smugglers.

To formulate an appropriate response to the measure represented a serious problem for Hutchinson. The great political chasm that eventually developed between him and Boston's radical whigs hinged upon the central question of Parliamentary sovereignty and to what degree the General Court could constitutionally resist unpopular or unwelcome legislation. The origins of this conflict can be seen in the debates following the news of the introduction of the Sugar Act and in the politics surrounding the framing of a response to Grenville's provocative legislation. During the course of hammering out an answer to the Sugar Act, and the proposed Stamp Act, Hutchinson offended Boston's popular party advocates in two major ways. First, he engineered the dilution of an important and forceful protest petition from the House and Council to Parliament, thereby weakening colonial resistance to the new imperial policies. Second, he consistently urged the General Court to comply with British policy, no matter how unpopular or uncomfortable this was. In so doing, he incurred the lasting wrath of important merchants and whig activists who wanted to force Parliament's hand. Later, by the time of the Stamp Act crisis, in the summer of 1765, many active players on the Boston political scene perceived Hutchinson as an annoying, gentleman-politician, cosseted by virtue of his lifetime of privilege, and blind to the growing threats to colonial freedom of action that British policy increasingly represented. He became an obstacle to whig ambitions, a figure that must be removed.

In July 1764, Hutchinson recorded his view of how best to protest the Sugar Act and the proposed Stamp Act. Predictably he counseled reasonable, deferential opposition. He wrote, "I never was of [the] opinion that any good could come of a sturdy and sullen behavior by the colonies. The only ways in which I thought they could be served was by humble representation of their claim submitted to the wisdom and justice of a British Parliament in whose determinations British colonies must always acquiesce."[9] He hoped that Boston's opponents of Grenville's legislation would resist the temptation to insult the ministry in print. "No good can come from such a spirit," Hutchinson opined, "but the individuals who are most active in stirring it up care not for the consequences to the publick provided they can make themselves popular and conspicuous."[10]

The individuals he had in mind were his old enemies James Otis, Jr., Oxenbridge Thacher, and the editors of the *Boston Gazette*.[11] James Otis, Jr., whom he referred to as "a great incendiary," particularly irritated him. In Hutchinson's view, pure personal vindictiveness motivated Otis who headed a faction which relentlessly reviled the unfortunate royal official. "Upon my coming into the place of chief justice," Hutchinson wrote accurately of Otis, "and encouraging the due execution of the laws of trade he set up in opposition, made himself the head of a party and has been scattering fuel thro' the province ever since."[12] Personal hatreds aside, he believed that bombastic and critical arguments directed toward British policy or self-righteous moral posturing would achieve little. He preferred a less public and more diplomatic approach.

Throughout most of 1764, Hutchinson worked to articulate low-key, nonconfrontational resistance to the Sugar Act and the proposed Stamp Act. At first the General Court called upon him to travel to London in the capacity of special provincial agent to personally protest the new legislation. Some indication of how eager Boston's whigs were to get rid of him appeared in the *Boston Gazette*. Writers in this important pro-whig organ informed their readers that they hoped he would go to London, thereby vacating his numerous offices, so that "they must be divided among a number [of other men]." The newspaper continued, "in this case there will be little or no danger of any ONE man's arriving to such a degree of power and influence as to become the object of either dread or envy."[13] The influential and persistent Gazette could not resist an opportunity to criticize his plural office-holding.

Hutchinson refused this appointment, citing his advanced years as his reason for declining the assignment. He declared himself to be "distressed to death" by the prospect of going to England at his age. He opted to remain in Boston and engineer a political response from inside the General Court.[14] Eventually his opposition to British policy appeared in two forms: one, privately, in a long letter to Richard Jackson in the summer of 1764;

the other, publicly, in a petition from the General Court to Parliament in November 1764.

Richard Jackson, a merchant from Weasenham in Norfolk, participated enthusiastically in the political and commercial affairs of North America during this time period. Although not particularly ambitious as a politician, he acted as an agent in London for Massachusetts, Connecticut, and Pennsylvania, and served as secretary to George Grenville when the latter was the chancellor of the exchequer. He appeared particularly sensitive to American concerns throughout the 1760s. He opposed the Stamp Act in 1765, and supported the Pennsylvania petition that protested taxation without representation in December 1767. His last recorded speech in the House of Commons, delivered on April 19, 1769, endorsed Thomas Pownall's motion to repeal the Townshend Duties. Overall, Jackson was friendly to whig political interests; he was a large landowner in the colonies, and an important colleague of Benjamin Franklin and Thomas Hutchinson.[15]

Hutchinson wrote to Jackson in June and July 1764, to articulate his opposition to the Sugar Act and the proposed Stamp Act.[16] In this private correspondence he demonstrated that his objections to Grenville's new imperial legislation were not significantly different in principle from those of his whig opponents James Otis, Jr., or Oxenbridge Thacher. Moreover, in this important letter, he provided some of the central arguments advanced later in the House of Commons by such leading critics of Grenville and the Ministry as Sir Isaac Barré and Sir Henry Conway. Basically he agreed with the radical whigs as to the shortcomings of the legislation.

On the matter of Parliamentary taxation, for example, Otis and Hutchinson together rejected the distinction made between internal and external levies. Both men thus challenged the Sugar Act as a legitimate means of raising revenue in the colonies. Otis declared flatly: "There is no foundation for the distinction some make in England, between an internal tax and an external tax on the colonies."[17] Similarly, when contemplating the alleged difference between the two types of taxation, Hutchinson asked rhetorically, "are the Privileges of the People less affected [by an external tax] than by an internal Tax. Is it any difference to me whether I pay three pounds ten shillings duty for a Pipe of wine to an officer of Impost or whether I pay the same sum by an excise of nine pence per Gallon to an excise Officer."[18] In his opinion, as this rather clumsy example attempted to articulate, impost duties levied externally and excise duties levied internally amounted to the same thing.

He also believed, like Otis and Thacher, that Parliament, as a legislative body, was supreme and that the colonies ought to acquiesce in its decisions. All three agreed that American colonists were Britons and, therefore, retained all the rights of subjects in England. Finally, he accepted that there should be no taxation without representation. Only their vocabulary differed. Otis and Thacher invariably referred consistently to colonial "rights" while Hutchinson alternated in his use of the words "rights" and "privileges," using these terms synonymously.[19] Comparison of these three opinions from 1764 indicates a considerable degree of harmony between the establishment gentleman-politician and his popular party opponents Oxenbridge Thacher and James Otis, Jr.

Eventually Hutchinson's letter to Jackson found its way into the hands of General Henry Seymour Conway who was His Majesty's Secretary of State for the Southern Department. Jackson later informed the Bostonian that Conway, and his parliamentary colleague Sir Isaac Barré, utilized ideas and arguments furnished in this letter to attack and eventually defeat the Stamp Act. Jackson wrote to Hutchinson: "I have intrusted Mr. Conway Secretary of State with a copy of the manuscript piece you sent me last year. . . . He has been a Principal Assistance to us in procuring the Repeal."[20] It was thus highly ironic that Hutchinson had his house destroyed by a crowd, who allegedly believed that he had participated in formulating the Stamp Act, when in reality he had acted diligently and effectively behind the scenes to secure the Act's repeal.

Hutchinson's intransigent public reticence undoubtedly contributed to this misunderstanding. Whig partisan rumormongering alleged that he had shared in authorship of the proposed Stamp Act. His failure to respond to their allegations reinforced this ludicrous impression. At this point in his career Hutchinson still refused to recognize any need to state his position clearly and publicly. Public declarations of decision making by the rightful stewards of colonial well-being were unnecessary, demeaning, and even vaguely insulting. As the consummate insider and prime mover within a complex oligarchy, Hutchinson contented himself with making his point to Jackson in private, confident that his upper-class peers would listen to his view and act upon it accordingly. In contrast with the raucous and public protestations of disapproval contained in Thacher's and Otis's pamphlets, he opted to lobby from behind closed doors. As such Boston's general public remained uncertain and uninformed as to Hutchinson's degree of involvement in, and level of opposition to, the Sugar Act and proposed Stamp

Act. He soon paid a very high price for neglecting to cultivate a more favorable public perception of his activities.

In addition to privately communicating his thoughts on Grenville's legislation, Hutchinson labored assiduously in 1764 to influence the wording of a protest petition from the General Court. In keeping with his belief that inoffensive, diplomatic, and reasonable language would be the most effective with British legislators, he successfully sought to ameliorate the language of a remonstrance to "His Majesty in Parliament" concerning the Sugar Act and the proposed Stamp Act. He spent ten days persuading a committee of the General Court to address their remonstrance to the House of Commons and not to "His Majesty in Parliament" and to protest, specifically and explicitly, only external taxation as a matter of "privilege" and not "right."[21] From Hutchinson's perspective, these were small tactical concessions to British pride, well worth the effort if they yielded legislative reform. He succeeded, however, against the wishes of Boston's popular party leadership and their merchant-smuggler supporters who advocated a far more confrontational approach. Even after the General Court approved the more moderate protest petition, many of Boston's whigs were still not satisfied. Later a joint committee of the House and Council, which included the ubiquitous James Otis, Jr., and Oxenbridge Thacher, drafted a letter to Jasper Mauduit that adhered to the original and more stringent version of the petition.

Especially in August 1765 when an angry crowd demolished his house, Hutchinson would be made to regret his pursuit of this cautious and prudential path of resistance. By choosing to influence politics through discreet and private channels, and by opting for moderation in opposition, he exposed himself to future criticism. When the Massachusetts opposition received word of the far more radical New York protest petition against the Sugar Act and the proposed Stamp Act, they were "ashamed of their own conduct and would have recalled what had been done if it had not been too late."[22] Boston's whigs wasted no time in blaming Hutchinson for this and they again accused him of endorsing and even authoring the hated Stamp Act. His aristocratic refusal to publicize his views in 1764 and answer his critics helped to perpetuate the credibility of this unfounded assertion.

Between 1761 and 1765, party politics in Massachusetts crystallized around a series of issues. On the floor of the Assembly and in the pages of Boston's lively newspapers, Boston's public servants argued about whether to use gold as legal tender; they disputed the appointment of Jasper Mauduit as province agent; the parties clashed over implementation of the trade laws, the wording of protest petitions, plural office-holding, and who should rightfully pay the governor's salary.

Partisanship had always influenced the political scene in Massachusetts. As James Otis, Jr., honestly observed: "The world has ever been, and will be pretty equally divided between those two great parties, vulgarly called the *winners* and the *losers;* or, to speak more precisely, between those who are discontented that they have no power, and those who never think they can have enough."[23] However, it was not until the Stamp Act crisis of 1765 that Boston's popular party discovered the correct combination of offensive tactics that would enable them to prevail in this long-standing struggle for power with the Hutchinson-Oliver oligarchy.

During the Stamp Act crisis, Boston's popular party successfully combined organized, violent crowd action, sustained personal vilification of government officials, especially of Hutchinson, and a plausible popular justification of opposition. In so doing they crafted a powerful critique of British management of colonial affairs.

In Boston, as in any urban setting in the Anglo-American world of the eighteenth century, crowds of working people occasionally massed to make their feelings known. Sometimes crowd action appeared associated with specific political grievances. More often, however, marching and rioting conveyed a ritualistic or recreational objective. In 1710 a Boston crowd protested Andrew Belcher's selfish hoarding of grain in a time of relative scarcity by damaging the rudder of his ship so the product could not leave the port. In 1747 Bostonians collectively challenged a hated British impressment gang. Every November in Boston and apparently for recreation, Guy Fawkes Day celebrations provided the backdrop for the North End crowd to battle the South Enders with fists and clubs.

Prior to the Stamp Act crisis, direct crowd action was only sporadic. With the introduction of George Grenville's detested new tax measure, however, Boston's whigs effectively formalized and politicized the crowd. During the crucible of the Stamp Act crisis, opponents of royal authority successfully fused their drive for political power with the awesome capacity for intimidation contained in mass crowd mobilization.[24]

Boston's leading whigs personally disliked Hutchinson. Now, in 1765, Samuel Adams, James Otis, Jr., and the other leading challengers to the royal administration had an army of sorts through which they could give voice to their private and public resentment of Hutchinson.

Early in the morning of August 14, 1765, two effigies appeared hanging from Deacon Eliot's elm tree in Boston's South End.[25] Daily work came to a halt as the residents of the city congregated to examine the images of "stamp master" Andrew Oliver, and a large boot, a pun on the Earl of Bute's name, with the devil protruding from inside. John Stuart, the third Earl of Bute, was a ministerial favorite of George III but widely despised and distrusted in America. Offended by this display, Lieutenant Governor Hutchinson requested that Sheriff Stephen Greenleaf remove the effigies. However, successive organized guards, and the rumor that the images would be buried at nightfall anyway, dissuaded the authorities from taking this action. Boston's patriots removed the effigies at dusk, placed them on a bier, and carried them, as in a funeral procession, to the town house, accompanied by the cries of "liberty, property for ever," "No Stamps" and, "No placemen."[26]

After protesting briefly at the town house, the demonstrators continued to Kilby Street where Andrew Oliver was erecting a new building rumored to be used as a prospective stamp office. Very quickly the crowd attacked the edifice until not a brick remained in place. As if to reiterate their protest, the crowd ritualistically "stamped" each brick and beam as they dismantled the building.

Next, the crowd headed for Fort Hill to conclude their demonstration with a celebratory bonfire. This conflagration was to have been, in the words of a contemporary newspaper, "a burnt offering of the effigies [of Oliver and Bute] for those sins of the people which had caused such heavy judgements as the Stamp Act etc. to be laid upon them."[27] On the way to the bonfire site, the crowd broke several windows in Oliver's mansion and appropriated parts of his fence for kindling.

Later, on Fort Hill, after the liquor bottles had circulated and the more genteel leaders of the activities had gone home, crowd discipline apparently evaporated. The crowd returned to Oliver's mansion and stoned the place for half an hour. Then some of the more enthusiastic members of the gathering entered the house—after having "tore down his privy," and "ruined his flowers and fruit trees"—and began to drink the "stamp master's" liquor, while "throwing chinaware, silver, and furniture about the house."[28]

As the evening's festivities drew to a close, Hutchinson courageously appeared to face the crowd, accompanied by the redoubtable Sheriff Greenleaf. His hope was to persuade the rioters to disperse peacefully. However, his presence seems only to have further annoyed Boston's protesters. Later he recalled, "the cry was God damn their blood here's H . . . with the gov.

stand by my boys and let no man give way. The cry was suc[c]eeded by a volley of stones and bricks," and Hutchinson wisely disappeared into the night.[29]

So transpired the first Stamp Act riot in Boston. Andrew Oliver and his family had escaped personal injury, although he had incurred substantial property loss. However, the would-be stamp distributor's personal unpopularity had been firmly established. Governor Bernard issued a proclamation against the rioters, offering a reward of £100 for information concerning those involved in the activities of August 14. His answer came in the form of a rather defensive anonymous note asserting "that the persons at the head of the late insurrection are in all respects as good and respectable as the Governor and Council."[30]

The Boston crowd acted again on the very next evening. The perplexed Governor Bernard, from the relative safety of Castle William in Boston harbor, remembered that, as he sat in his candlelit room he looked up and, beyond the water, "I saw a bonfire burning on Fort Hill; by which I understand that the mob is up and probably doing mischief."[31]

None of the drama of the previous evening was to be repeated that particular night. This time the crowd simply assembled at the bonfire to celebrate collectively the news of Oliver's resignation as stamp distributor, which had been publicized earlier that day. As the evening wore on, however, a section of the crowd determined to question Hutchinson as to his role in the passage of the Stamp Act.

He had been the object of a persistent rumor circulating among Boston's popular party, that he had assisted Grenville's administration in drawing up the Stamp Act. We have no historical evidence as to the provenance of the rumor but it is reasonable to conclude that it came from his whig enemies. Hutchinson wrote in April 1765 that "I found it whispered about I had some private intelligence" with regard to the Stamp Act.[32] This rumor of his collaboration became especially persuasive, since he had played a prominent role in convincing the Massachusetts House of Representatives to use less inflammatory language in a petition against the Sugar Act and the proposed Stamp Act, published in November 1764. Furthermore, his behavior in defense of the besieged Oliver did not endear him to the crowd. Oliver, like Hutchinson, represented the older generation of pro-British gentlemen-politicians whose multiple office-holding and social superciliousness irritated ordinary Bostonians. Nevertheless, there is no evidence above and beyond the whispering campaign originating with the *Boston*

Gazette that Hutchinson had any input into the formulation of the Stamp Act. The opposite was the case.

The crowd reached Hutchinson's house at about 9:00 P.M. His family had already been evacuated, and the doors and windows were barricaded. He listened in silence as the leaders of the congregation pounded on the door demanding that he come out and deny that he had written to England in favor of the Stamp Act. It was a tense moment for both the crowd leaders and for the embattled Hutchinson. Members of the crowd had already begun to dismantle his fence while others were asking "whether they should begin with the coach house or the stables."[33] Meanwhile, inside the dark house he debated with himself whether or not to answer. In the end, characteristic of the true gentleman-politician, he remained silent. "He did not chose to be 'catechized' by them [the crowd]," for, "my answers must either have enraged them or encouraged them. If I had been obliged to answer their questions I must either enrage them or else give them a handle to justify their extravagant behavior." Eventually, after "about an hours siege," the tension subsided. One of his neighbors persuaded the crowd that their quarry was not in the house. When he heard the crowd leaders' order to "move," he slipped out to his sister's house, only returning later that night. The next day he moved his family to his country house at Milton for safety.[34]

Despite this narrow escape, his troubles with this activist segment of the Boston populace were not over. On August 26, rumors circulated throughout the town "that there was to be a mob in Boston that night with intent to pull down the Lieutenant-Governor's house, and that their ships crew was sent for."[35] By early evening, according to the Town Records, an unusual number of people from neighboring communities were on their way toward Boston.

The evening's activities began when "about dusk a number of rude fellows were gathered upon the Exchange—they quickly began to be very noisy and their numbers increased so fast as to create fears in the minds of the inhabitants that the consequences of their tumultuous assembling would be mischievous."[36]

After having set a bonfire in King Street, disregarding the protestations of the fire warden, the crowd then divided into two groups "to attack the houses of two gentlemen of distinction."[37] These two gentlemen were William Story, deputy registrar of the Vice-Admiralty Court, and colony comptroller Benjamin Hallowell. The crowd sacked both men's houses, drank their liquor, broke their china, pocketed their sterling, demolished their furniture and, most significantly, destroyed their files and burned their official papers. The crowd targeted these men since their official actions ran counter to the interests of Boston's whig-smugglers. Story and Hallowell, of course, were staunch enforcers of British commercial legislation. Story, even though he was a member of the Boston Caucus, stood rebuked for allegedly writing letters to England critical of the merchant group. Significantly, the crowd stole documents belonging to the Vice-Admiralty Court from Hallowell's dwelling, an action which plainly suggests that they operated in the name of people who were in trouble with the customs service.

After this the two crowds united and proceeded to Hutchinson's house. There, "with hellish fury" and "like devils loose," "they totally ruined the house and destroyed or carried off everything in it."[38] "The destruction was really amazing," recorded the laconic Josiah Quincy, an eyewitness to the event.[39] Hutchinson described the event in the following terms:

> The hellish crew fell upon my house with the rage of devils and in a moment with axes split down the door and entered my son being in the great entry heard them cry damn him he is upstairs we'll have him. Some ran immediately as high as the top of the house others filled the rooms below and cellars and others remained without the house to be employed there. . . . Not content with tearing off all the wainscot and hangings and splitting the doors to pieces they beat down the cupola or lanthorn and they began to take off the slate and boards from the roof and were prevented only by the approaching day light from a total demolition of the building. My garden fence was laid flat and all my trees and &c broke down to the ground. Such ruins were never seen in America. Besides my plate and family pictures household furniture of every kind my own my children and servants apparel they carried off about £900—sterling in money and emptied the house of everything whatsoever except a part of the kitchen furniture not leaving a single book or paper in it and have scattered or destroyed all the manuscripts and other papers I had been collecting for 30 years together besides a great number of publick papers in my custody.[40]

Nobody in authority called for help to counteract the riot from the soldiers and sailors who were stationed on a British man-of-war anchored in Boston harbor. Similarly, though there must have been hundreds of spectators, there is no record of anyone coming to the defense of Hutchinson or his property. Governor Bernard was nowhere to be seen, and all accounts agree that the lieutenant governor was fortunate to have had enough time to get himself out of harm's way before the crowd arrived.

Even after his mansion had been reduced to a shell, the night was not quite over for the mob. Hutchinson again recalled:

> Without the least remorse at these execrable facts, they determined still to go on and bent their course southward with an intent it is said to attack the house of Charles Paxton, Surveyor and Searcher of His Majesties Customs, but thro' the entreaties of the inhabitants and perhaps as it may reasonably be thought, having spent all the rage that the human breast is capable of, they retired without doing further mischief.[41]

The day after the demolition of his home, Sheriff Stephen Greenleaf arrested the shoemaker and riot leader Ebenezer Mackintosh. It was common knowledge that Mackintosh had led the assault on Hutchinson's property. Nevertheless, he was released shortly after his arrest upon the insistence of Nathaniel Coffin, a future tory, who was the leader of a security force engaged to protect the city against further rioting. Either Mackintosh would escape prosecution or there would be no security guards and presumably more rioting. The leader of the riot seemed to be protected from punishment. In Hutchinson's opinion, Mackintosh knew who had ordered the riot—probably the Loyal Nine—and presumably would tell the authorities who these men were unless he went free.

Little reliable documentary information is available on the organization known as the Loyal Nine. Consequently the group has remained something of a historical mystery. The group appears to have acted as a liaison between radical policy makers, such as Samuel Adams and James Otis, Jr., and street-level activists, especially Ebenezer Mackintosh and Samuel Swift. The Loyal Nine included, John Avery, a distiller and club secretary; John Smith and Stephen Cleverly, both braziers; Thomas Crafts, a printer; Benjamin Edes, who along with John Gill produced the important *Boston Gazette;* Thomas Chase, a distiller; Joseph Field, a ship's captain; George Trott, a jeweler; and Henry Bass, a merchant who was related to Samuel Adams. This political organization acted in the tradition of Elisha Cooke's Caucus, playing a vital role in formulating, coordinating, and implementing country party opposition to royal authority. The attack on Hutchinson's house in 1765 represented an important coming of age for cooperation between the Loyal Nine and patriot street-level activists led by Mackintosh.[42]

Ebenezer Mackintosh was born in Boston on June 20, 1737. His family was very poor, but he managed to acquire the trade of cordwainer or shoemaker. He lived in Boston's South End and, following military service in the 1750s, affiliated himself with fire company number nine as a result of the reforms instituted after the great fire of 1760. He emerged as an acknowledged crowd leader after his arrest in connection with the death of an infant in the annual Pope's Day fight with Samuel Swift's North Enders in 1764. Following his arrest and subsequent release he assumed the title of "captain." Despite being arrested for leading the attack on the Hutchinson mansion, he secured election to the position of leather sealer (whose responsibility was to judge the quality of the leather offered for sale in Boston's market) several times between 1765 and 1768. He married Elizabeth Maverick on August 7, 1766, and thereafter his crowd-leading activities diminished until he reappeared in the Boston Tea Party crowd in 1773. Part of the explanation as to why he again involved himself in street agitation was that one of his relatives by marriage was killed in the Boston Massacre on March 5, 1770. After the tea party he left Boston and moved to Haverhill, New Hampshire, where he lived out his days as an itinerant shoemaker. He died in 1816. Following the attack on Hutchinson's house, William Bass wrote that the Loyal Nine were "not a little pleased that Mackintosh has the credit for the whole affair."[43]

On August 28, six more individuals linked to the rioting were arrested and imprisoned. However, again in the words of Hutchinson, "the people did not intend that they should be tried."[44] Five weeks later, as a final indignity to Hutchinson:

> A large number of men entered the house of the prison keeper, compelled him to deliver the keys; opened the prison door; and set every man free who had been committed for this offense. They also absconded for some months; after which, finding that no authority had taken any notice of the prisoners or of the persons concerned in their rescue, they returned; appeared openly, and were very active in other irregular proceedings.[45]

Boston's forces of opposition clearly were not willing to allow their riotous operatives to be held accountable to the law. In Governor Bernard's opinion, "the real authority of the government is at an end; some of the principal ring leaders of the late riots walk the streets with impunity; no officer dares attack them; no attorney general prosecute them, no witness appear against them and no judge to sit upon them."[46]

With the destruction of Hutchinson's residence, organized political crowd violence in Boston reached a new level of intensity. From August 26, 1765, onward, any advocate of British policy, or royal official, would be forced to consider seriously the risks he was taking. Fear of personal retribution and property destruction penetrated the ranks of Boston's would-be loyalists as never before. In a sympathetic letter of commiseration to Hutchinson, for example, court party supporter John Osborne felt compelled to add, "I trust my letter will not be so expos'd as to bring me . . . under the Rables Resentment etc. Would it not be best to destroy this?"[47] From now on Boston's supporters of royal authority feared for property and even their lives. The radicals' innovative organization and utilization of the crowd had successfully tipped the balance of power in their favor.

On August 27, the Boston Town Meeting announced its "utter detestation of the extraordinary and violent proceedings of a number of persons unknown."[48] Hutchinson noted later, however, with obvious disapproval and indignation: "Persons unknown! Mackintosh who is now a town officer and no doubt with other leaders of the mob was at the town meeting expressed their abhorrence the next day of what they themselves had done the night before."[49] In his opinion his property had been attacked by the same people who now officially disavowed the action. He remained shocked by this display of hypocrisy.

In October 1765, Hutchinson reflected on the possible reasons why he had been singled out for attack. He cited a series of incidents from the past as contributing to "the causes of my being the object of this fury." Among the affairs listed he included his hard money position from 1749, his role in the writs of assistance controversy, his plural office-holding, and his role in ameliorating the language of the petition against the proposed Stamp Act in 1764. In addition, he recalled advocating submission to the supreme authority of Parliament and enforcement of the Stamp Act after its passage as potential reasons for the attack on his home.[50] He was aware that during the course of his long political career, he had accumulated many enemies. What he did not seem to appreciate, however, was the depth of hatred that Boston's leading radical activists had generated.

Governor Bernard more clearly understood this fervent hatred and correctly perceived that a combination of economic and personal animus toward Hutchinson had precipitated the attack. James Otis, Jr., according to Bernard, fomented

> a malicious, virulent and unrelenting animosity against the persons employed in the government, among which the Governor and Lieut. Governor are principal objects, as well from the Supereminency of their Station, as from particular offence taken at their conduct upon private and self-interested considerations. Without this union of popular politicks with private

vengeance, it is impossible to account for the ruin which was brought upon the Lieut. Governor.

He continued, "opposing the Stamp Act has been made a Mask for a Battery, a stalking horse to take a better Aim at the Royalty of the Government."[51] In Bernard's opinion, Otis especially had conspired in smearing his administration with complicity in formulating the hated Stamp Act. It was an impression that would prove impossible to dislodge from the public memory.

Aside from purely personal motivations, economic factors contributed to the particular vehemence with which the Boston crowd registered its disapproval of the alleged proponents of the Stamp Act. Since the conclusion of the Seven Years' War, Boston's economy had experienced a persistent recession. Renewed English measures to restrict Boston's West Indies trade, along with a credit contraction after 1762, precipitated bankruptcies and a drastic reduction in the number of vessels employed in that trade. Dockside laborers found work more difficult to secure and steady berths for seamen became far less numerous. Boston's rate of pauperism increased significantly during the postwar depression. Food and firewood prices rose as did tax rates, while war refugees, injured veterans, and impoverished widows and children swelled the ranks of the indigent and destitute.

Meanwhile, the French and Indian War had provided accelerated opportunities to make money for a fortunate few. The increased economic stratification did not escape the attention of Boston's working populace. John Adams was not alone when he remarked that the house of a wealthy merchant was "the most magnificent of any Thing I have ever seen."[52] If a house containing furnishings that cost more than £1000 impressed John Adams, it is easy to understand how those on the margins of survival could envy and resent such opulence. This increased gap between the rich and poor jeopardized New England's historical concept of social harmony and community co-operation. Now Boston's working men began to question their life of hard work and struggle when compared with the overwhelming wealth of their more fortunate neighbors. With the growing economic distress of the mid-1760s Boston's working people reasserted their anti-authoritarianism learned during the fiery revivals of the Great Awakening.

It did not help matters that Hutchinson had already publicly demonstrated little sympathy for the plight of Boston's poor. In an unfortunate phrase which appeared in a newspaper article on the subject of currency devaluation he had claimed that "the common people of this town and coun-

try live too well."[53] His whig detractors delighted in repeating this sentiment, often quoting the words out of context to make their author appear
unacceptably callous. Now, in the Stamp Act riots, popular resentment at
these recent, unequal economic developments and Hutchinson's apparent
indifference to the hardships they produced could be expressed.

By August 1765, Boston's whigs had clearly targeted Hutchinson for removal from office. The Stamp Act crisis provided a catalyst that accelerated
the attack by Boston's popular party. In the words of John Adams, men of
Hutchinson's type were motivated by a "ravenous sort of ambition and
avarice," and they "ought to be avoided and dreaded as the plague." In another diary entry dated December 30, 1765, Adams criticized Hutchinson
for monopolizing "almost all the power of the government to himself and
his family; and . . . [for] endeavoring to procure more both on this side and
the other side of the Atlantic."[54] The destruction of his home showed that
many Bostonians, rich and poor, agreed with the substance of this por-
trayal. The older generation of gentlemen-politicians, as exemplified by
Hutchinson, seemed to Boston's popular whig partisans, to be élitist, excessively powerful, and egregiously unaccountable for their actions. Consequently, beginning in earnest with the Stamp Act crisis, Boston's radicals
determined that they would topple Hutchinson from power, whatever the
cost and by whatever means necessary.

A powerful combination of factors coalesced during the stormy days of
the Stamp Act crisis in Boston. These included unresolved personal quar-
rels and business rivalries between highly competitive individuals, un-
healed political wounds and the settling of old resentments, a growing sentiment of personal autonomy among people who hitherto would have taken
a back seat in political matters, increasing hostilities between the very rich
and the rest, and organized crowd action. Colonial Americans crossed a
mental Rubicon when they approved and endorsed the demolition of
Hutchinson's house. Even those who did not participate in the event, or
even residents of other colonies, believed themselves to be involved emotionally in these momentous events by virtue of the "imagined community"
of "the provincial creole printmen" who, in their newspapers, pamphlets,
and pictorial imagery, encouraged all colonials to think of themselves as
linked to the rioters in Boston.[55] In 1765 American radicals were not yet
ready to reject the King directly. However, in the Stamp Act riots Boston's
country party demonstrated unequivocally its willingness to denounce his
most prominent colonial minister. After 1765 Hutchinson's future status as
the indispensable symbol of colonial treachery burgeoned proportionately

as the challenge to royal authority became more direct. As many Bostonians of all social classes ritualistically prepared themselves for the role of revolutionaries, Hutchinson's designated status of the unique and singular enemy became ever more permanent. In a profound emotional sense, Hutchinson, after 1765, became an essential and integral component of the radical argument against British rule, since the budding revolutionaries could not hope to vindicate the new order until the old one had been proven moribund. In the conflicts ahead, he increasingly became the most important standard of political and personal venality against which whig virtue would be repeatedly measured and tested.

CHAPTER FOUR

"An Ill Temper and a Factious Spirit"

F
ollowing the August rioting against the Stamp Act, Boston's political factions anxiously awaited November 1, 1765, when the measure
was officially due to take effect. Hutchinson knew sometime in October 1765, by virtue of his correspondence with province agent William
Bollan, that a repeal of the odious legislation was imminent in Parliament.
Bollan wrote explaining how he had met with the Marquis of Rockingham.
"I said a few things to satisfy him [Rockingham] that the colonies were not
in a taxable condition." He further recorded that Rockingham was unhappy
with the legislation.[1] His advice to Hutchinson during this tense waiting
period was to maintain "decent conduct and proper representation of all
your grievances," since "every minister has a bucket in each hand to extin-
guish those flames which the mistakes of some and the madness of others
are daily encreasing." He continued with the reassuring words: "The Marquis said that His Majesty and his present ministers were enclined to relieve
the American trade in general in all points wherein it was improperly
curbed and put the whole upon the best foot for the common good of the
kingdom and the colonies."[2]

Hutchinson adopted a cautious and noncommittal approach to the
Stamp Act during the late summer and fall of 1765. His stance at this time
may be characterized as limited, passive acceptance of the legislation. He
did not advocate the use of stamps in Boston. Rather, he did everything he

75

could to prevent their usage. At the same time, he steadfastly upheld the principle of Parliamentary sovereignty and gave every indication that, if compelled to, he would support the ministry and implement the act. He supported Governor Bernard's conciliatory approach to the General Court. Finally, he resigned his position as judge of probate for Suffolk County so that he would not have to conduct legal business with stamps and thereby attract more attention to himself as an apparent advocate of the hated Stamp Act.[3] By January 1766, he received the news from Bollan that "the Stamp Act will certainly be repealed."[4] On the basis of this knowledge, he hoped to avoid controversy and concentrate his efforts on his personal priority, which was to secure compensation for the considerable property damage he had sustained on August 26, 1765.

Hutchinson's conciliatory approach did little to avert new attacks against him and Bernard from Boston's whigs. Popular party criticism continued even after the official repeal of the Stamp Act on Friday, March 16, 1766. It was not difficult to see why; he had already become the primary target of incessant radical denunciation.

Governor Bernard observed "the repeal [of the Stamp Act] occasioned no relaxation in the disposition and designs of the Faction which had raised itself by the Act." He continued that this opposition group "believe themselves, and [to] persuade others, that it is in their power to displace any Governor against whom they can raise a popular cry. When once the flame is made to burn, it is easy to supply it with fresh fuell, & blow it up with popular breath." He concluded by neatly summarizing the royalist point of view; "it signifies nothing whether the Governor is good or bad, faulty or blameless; if it can but be contrived to make him appear obnoxious to the People, his business is done." He continued, "Truth & Justice, Innocence and merit must be sacrificed to what shall seem to be the voice of the people. This is the political System of the present faction by which it directs its operations against the Government."[5] Hutchinson, above all others, became the preferred object of radical criticism. In the immediate aftermath of the Stamp Act debacle his political enemies attacked him in two specific areas: first, on his role as chief justice of the Superior Court, and second, on his position as a Councilor.

As chief justice of the Superior Court for Massachusetts, Hutchinson suggested that his colleagues comply with the Stamp Act. He believed that those in the government had no choice. Although personally opposed to the measure, he concurred with Parliament's legal right to introduce the act. Moreover, he declared that "the oaths I had taken bound me to discharge of my public trust to conformity to it."[6] Nevertheless, he was not enthusiastic in his compliance. His chosen tactic was to keep the law courts closed for business until properly stamped papers could be used or until Parliament formally repealed the act.

His opponents, especially the trio of whig lawyers James Otis, Jr., Jeremiah Gridley, and John Adams, disagreed with this passive resistance and demanded that the courts be allowed to re-open immediately.[7] These popular party leaders enthusiastically employed the pages of the *Boston Gazette* to advance and publicize their point of view. Writing as "Freeborn Armstrong" in January 1766, James Otis, Jr., for example, again eagerly grasped the opportunity to broaden the challenge to Hutchinson by invoking the familiar issue of plural office-holding. The chief justice's criticism of a house resolution to re-open the courts summoned forth a blast of personal vituperation from Otis that quickly became a blanket denunciation of the Act, Hutchinson, and royal government more generally.[8]

Eventually the question of whether to proceed without stamps or remain closed had to be faced by the five justices of the Superior Court. When the court met on March 11, 1766, for the first time since the House had introduced its demand in December for the court to meet, they arrived at no firm decision. Consequently, no substantive business transpired. Chief Justice Hutchinson sagaciously boycotted the meeting, thereby guaranteeing that the proceedings would be noncontroversial.[9] Apart from settling some minor matters that did not require stamps, the court simply deferred any real decision until its next session. By the time the court reconvened, news of the repeal of the Stamp Act had already reached Boston.

Hutchinson had undoubtedly waited for this news, since his correspondence with Bollan assured him that repeal was imminent. Regarding the Superior Court, his tactic had clearly been to temporize until his awkward predicament could be ameliorated by the Act's repeal that he knew was coming. In April he wrote: "We have some Crown business and before it is finished I hope we shall have advice of the repeal of the fatal act, if not, I shall be unwilling any other business shall go on."[10]

His deft handling of the Court during the period prior to the repeal of the Stamp Act garnered him little respect among his popular party opponents. He had averted more controversy; however, conflict was exactly what the whigs wanted. The struggle for power would founder if Hutchinson could not be presented as the originator of further division. To Boston's radicals, no matter what he did, he remained the hated symbol of British authority and of compliance with the Stamp Act. They continued to advance the position that he had to be eliminated as a political force. With this objective in mind the opponents of royal government commenced an attack on him that culminated in his removal from the Council in the May 1766 elections.

The Massachusetts Council comprised the upper house of the General Court. It usually contained twenty-eight members who were elected by the House of Representatives and subject to gubernatorial approval. The Council existed primarily as an advisory body to the governor and as such became an important institution that the increasingly organized radicals targeted for control. Councilors mainly assisted in the execution of the law and approved or disapproved civil appointments. The Massachusetts Charter of 1692 granted legislative powers to the Council similar to those held by the House of Representatives. Prior to 1766, however, the Council rarely exercised these powers and governors exercised control through the use of the veto and patronage. Later, as the crisis of royal government developed and radical influence grew, the Council became increasingly independent of the governor.[11]

In the wake of the Stamp Act crisis the character and behavior of the Massachusetts Council began to change significantly. As James Bowdoin, Jr.'s, influence within the body increased, radical critics of the government came to regard the Council as a positive force for the elimination of royal authority from Massachusetts. Securing Hutchinson's removal from the Council in 1766 constituted an important milestone in the evolution of the upper house from the governor's rubber stamp to a persistent thorn in the side of royal government.

James Bowdoin, Jr., like Paul Revere, was descended from French Huguenot stock. A long-time ally of the country party, his background was in trade and real estate speculation. His family was one of the wealthiest in Boston. Bowdoin had sat on the Council since 1757 and developed a strong record on free-trade issues. His formal and consistent opposition to the Bernard administration dated from the Stamp Act crisis. Hutchinson's view was that Bowdoin's dissatisfaction with the government after 1765 had more to do with a personal disagreement with John Temple, the surveyor general of the customs. It is more likely, however, that Bowdoin's political and business interests clashed with those of the court party oligarchy. James Bowdoin eventually came to represent another enthusiastic opponent of Hutchinson.[12]

In Hutchinson's opinion, the motivation to remove him from the Council was purely personal and vindictive. As he wrote to Israel Mauduit, "I have thirty years past delivered my sentiments freely, and sometimes upon very unpopular points, and yet have always retained a majority of the Province in my interest until the present year. . . . This is owing to the junction of the father, [James Otis, Sr.] who was negatived last year as a counsellor, with the son [James Otis, Jr.] in the House of Representatives and both of them make me their object and made every concession upon every other point provided they could take off every member from my interest."[13]

In Hutchinson's view all opposition to him was the product of personal animus. Those who attacked him during the Stamp Act crisis were "base," "villainous," and "criminal." He described his enemies as "collective bodies of the worst of men, who under pretense of reforming the state leave no safety in it for the best."[14] He readily agreed with the court party judge John Cushing who wrote with obvious disgust that in 1766 "a spirit of levellism seems to go through the country and very little distinction between the highest and lowest in office."[15] Finally, in 1766, he referred to those who had replaced him and other members of his oligarchy on the Council as "little better than scum."[16]

Personal dislikes and old grudges definitely informed and influenced popular party opposition to Hutchinson. However, in addition to these motivations two other related factors contributed to his removal from the Council in May 1766. First, Hutchinson's correspondence demonstrates a profound contempt toward his opponents. Often he proved to be a skillful political operator who balanced self-interest and public concerns. In 1766, however, he appeared unable to accord his whig opponents the same qualities, thereby denying them their just measure of respect. The radicals became more organized after the Stamp Act crisis. They represented a competitive political party determined to eradicate him from the scene. This was their ideology. Certain individual whigs despised him personally. But, in addition to these motives, the larger enterprise of controlling the government existed. Hutchinson underestimated the innovative and unprecedented lengths to which the whigs were prepared to go to diminish his influence. This miscalculation occurred in part because he over-personalized their dislike of him, and failed to comprehend the radical commitment to eliminate him, as a symbol and as an institution, and not just as a rival.

Second, deriving from his condescending refusal to respect his opponents' motives, Hutchinson's opposition to the Stamp Act (although not to Parliamentary supremacy) was never clearly understood by the wider public. He made no serious attempt to explain his position on the Act so that ordinary Bostonians could comprehend his point of view. Consequently, in the popular mind, the whig conceptualization of him as a secret proponent of the hated measure easily prevailed. Working-class Bostonians, who stood to gain little by removing Hutchinson from office, had willingly destroyed his house and accepted without question the rumors that he was the author of the Stamp Act. Even his impassioned statement to the House denying any involvement in authorship of the Stamp Act, which he delivered the day after his house had been destroyed, fell on deaf ears. His refusal to represent himself and his views in public while the political pot simmered cost him dearly when the crisis reached boiling point in the 1770s.

Similarly, when the *Boston Gazette* lambasted the court party and instructed the townspeople how to vote in 1766, many Bostonians believed the worst of him. The aristocratic and genteel gentlemen-politicians of Boston's past, among whom Hutchinson remained the exemplar, were incrementally losing their power to a new generation of more aggressive office-seekers. This new group, led by Samuel Adams and James Otis, Jr., were far more willing to mobilize and manipulate public opinion via the print media to collect support. Hutchinson, shrewd political manipulator that he was, took too long to realize this. As a result, radical opinion prevailed among voters in the lower house and he lost his seat on the Council in May 1766.[17]

The whig attack in the newspapers went unanswered by the court party which proved to be a fatal mistake. Typical of the whig style from this period was "J. R." in the *Boston Evening-Post*. This particular polemicist argued that anyone who had "discovered an approbation of the *Stamp Act*, and manifested a willingness that it should take place in this province;—then, without doubt they are justly to be accounted *enemies to their country* and, according, their names ought to be *hung up*, and exposed to contempt." Inevitably the court party came to be associated with incumbency, unreliability, and corruption. The *Boston Gazette* urged its readers to vote only for "such as you have Reason to think prefer the Happiness of the whole and would not be bribed, or bought, or coaxed, or wheedled, or threatened out of a sense of Duty to God and their Country."[18] These words represented the formulation of a collective consciousness that appealed to emotional abstractions vital to building nationalist sentiment. The eventual symbolic sacrifice of Hutchinson as the Great Traitor became a critical ingredient in articulating this important pre-Revolutionary impulse. Eventually the court party joined the newspaper wars, but by then, in both form and content, their efforts proved inadequate.

Following the Stamp Act crisis, Hutchinson pursued compensation for the damages he had sustained on the night of August 26, 1765.[19] Boston's popular party had every intention of opposing this endeavor, despite their passionate disavowal of the riotous and wanton demolition of his property.

In the *Boston Gazette* an anonymous writer urged representatives to "make no grant of the public money or property, to make up the loss any person or persons have sustained in the late tumults (raised by means of the Stamp Act) until we your constituents are made certain that the mob or mobs who have committed any outrages, were not raised on purpose to counteract and bring into disgrace the true born SONS OF LIBERTY, and put a stop to their commendable proceeding."[20] The writer clearly had Hutchinson in mind, and it serves as a measure of popular party vindictiveness that the author suggested that he may have destroyed his own property so as to discredit his opponents. Although the whigs divided the August riots into the first one which was "justifiable" and the second which was not, they remained implacably opposed to restitution for Hutchinson.

His quest for compensation soon became a partisan struggle within the lower house of the provincial legislature. At first he considered going to England to lobby personally for reimbursement. He decided to remain in Massachusetts, however, when the possibility arose that Bernard might travel to England to brief his superiors on the state of affairs in New England. Hutchinson welcomed the possibility of being left in command and hoped that it would help him eventually accede to the governorship.[21] In time he sent his son Thomas to England to represent his claim, although not without first making elaborate and fastidious preparations.

The elder Hutchinson's refined and genteel approach to public business was inherent in his advice to his son as Thomas prepared himself for Great Britain. "It will be a good general rule to say and do everything you can with a good conscience," instructed the elder man, "to obtain everyman's favor and to avoid as far as possible giving offense."[22] The lieutenant governor continued with the following words of advice to his son: "Especially be very careful of using any freedom in these times with the characters or late actions of any of your countrymen as many of them may happen to have connexions there which you may know nothing of."[23] The elder man expected his son to be discreet in the company of strangers. Clearly he appreciated how readily loose talk in the wrong ear could precipitate damaging rumors that would spread rapidly throughout the small world of Anglo-American politics.

His campaign for restitution came to a head in June 1766, when the General Court received instructions from Sir Henry Seymour Conway, the secretary of state for the Southern Department in England, to make "full and ample" compensation to the riot sufferers. The lower house responded to this order by agreeing to the appointment of a committee of inquiry to look into the matter and then abruptly dissolved, leaving the proceedings incomplete. The legislators took no immediate action and seemed committed to moving as slowly as possible on the issue.

When the General Court reconvened in October 1766, an additional personal and partisan dimension was injected into the debate. Joseph Hawley, a country lawyer from Northampton and a member of the General Court who usually allied himself with the popular party, succeeded in attaching a rider to the compensation bill which indemnified all those who had been convicted of rioting under the Stamp Act.[24] This maneuver represented a part of Hawley's overall effort to damage Hutchinson.

Hawley had taken a personal dislike to Hutchinson during the "Berkshire Affair," and subsequently welcomed any opportunity to challenge his authority or position.[25] Earlier Hutchinson had successfully prosecuted Seth Warren, one of Hawley's clients, for rioting in the town of Lanesborough in Berkshire County. During the Stamp Act crisis Hawley protested the loss of this case and in the process insulted the court. Some of Hawley's later clients in Boston included the prominent whig merchants John Hancock and John Rowe. In the wake of this conflict Hutchinson wrote of Hawley that he was "an ill-natured man." To future tory Israel Williams, Hawley appeared "much altered from what he was" prior to the Stamp Act disputes. Now he appeared "more haughty, self-sufficient, obstinate and less disposed to suspect himself than formerly, owing I imagine to the flattery and applause he had [from] below, which though he pretends to despise, is fatally caught by it."[26] Here again court party proponents were content to attribute opposition to nothing more than personal perversity.

Eventually, on December 6, 1766, the compensation bill, including Hawley's rider, passed both the House of Representatives and the Council. Governor Bernard approved the measure, and Hutchinson received his money. The decision pleased Boston's patriots which ensured that no one would ever be publicly held accountable for the Stamp Act riots. Later that month, Hutchinson resumed his residence in the renovated family mansion on Garden Court Street.

*

The difficulty of the struggle for compensation had taken its toll. Hutchinson was beginning to tire of the constant vicissitudes of public life. "I often think how quiet and contented I was before I quitted my mercantile life for a political one," he confided to an unknown correspondent. He continued that "it adds to my misfortune that from my present station I cannot return to my former condition with honor."[27] For Hutchinson, enlightened steward of the public interest that he felt himself to be, compensation for the loss of his house was more an affair of honor than a matter of money.

On February 20, 1767, Hutchinson wrote to Francis Bernard: "I will avoid all occasion of further controversy with the present House of Representatives by wholly absenting myself from the Council Chamber."[28] These words reflected a spirit of conciliation and cooperation on behalf of the governor, Hutchinson, and their court party supporters toward a combative lower house.

When the new legislative session opened on January 28, 1767, Bernard delivered what he considered to be a deliberately friendly speech and invited Hutchinson to attend. Limiting his comments to only four sentences, Bernard innocuously recommended that "the Support of the Authority of the Government, the Maintenance of the Honour of the Province, and the Promotion of the Welfare of the people, may be the chief Objects of your Consultations."[29]

In the governor's opinion, his speech represented little more than a series of harmless platitudes. Predictably, however, this was not the point of view of the committee organized by the lower house appointed to respond to Bernard's address. In a rejoinder issued on January 31, 1767, this committee objected to Lieutenant Governor Hutchinson's presence in the Council chamber, since he had not been elected as a member of that body. The committee of the lower house, which comprised some of the popular party's most enthusiastic supporters, suggested that his presence afforded "a new and additional instance of ambition, and a lust for power, to what we have heretofore observed."[30] The house committee self-consciously denied the existence of "an ill temper and a factious spirit," despite "the malignant whispers of its enemies." Ominously, however, the committee stressed that it could not promise the governor "that there shall be no disagreement or diversity of sentiments in matters of importance that may come before the General Court."[31]

From Bernard's perspective, this unnecessarily combative statement in response to his conciliatory speech constituted one more example of the sustained and "unrelenting acrimony" demonstrated by the popular party toward his administration. He had already concluded in 1766 that Otis and the popular party would find ways to oppose him regardless of whatever policy he endorsed. He wrote with some justification to Richard Jackson that "everything I say is put into Otis's hands to be answered and the fairest honestest professions are to be perverted with a Chicanary that would disgrace an English pettyfogger."[32] On this occasion the popular party's primary personal target was again Hutchinson.

Governor Bernard had personally invited Hutchinson to attend the speech in the Council chamber. To the opponents of the administration, this action, not unjustifiably, appeared to have the effect of including him in Council affairs, despite his defeat in the elections of the previous May. Consequently, Boston's whigs moved to exclude the lieutenant governor, despite the fact that, before him, every holder of this office except one had attended Council sessions without complaint. Notwithstanding this precedent, in January 1767, the House of Representatives had no compunction in characterizing Hutchinson's presence as a further example of his hunger for power.[33]

This challenge to his presence in Council deliberations constituted another personal attack. Despite archival evidence that precedent endorsed the lieutenant governor's attendance as a nonvoting participant, on February 10, 1767, the lower house passed a resolution preventing the practice. On February 20, Bernard received Hutchinson's letter promising to stay away from Council meetings in the interests of conciliation. Following this correspondence the perplexed Bernard sent to England for instructions.

This time-consuming approach satisfied neither the House nor the Council, however, and both insisted on taking further action immediately. In the end the Council voted unanimously that Hutchinson had no right to attend Council meetings according to their specific reading of the Massachusetts charter. The lower house enthusiastically concurred and Hutchinson gave up the fight, recognizing the partisan nature of the dispute "at a time when union and harmony were more than ever to be desired."[34] He blamed Joseph Hawley for this initiative against him, concluding that he was mentally unstable. He believed that Hawley had simply replaced religious excess to become an "Inthusiast in Politics stuck in with the Party in opposition to Government" and "made me his mark."[35] Again, personal political grudge-bearing provided Hutchinson with a sufficient explanation to comprehend the motives of those who moved against him. Nevertheless, he remained sufficiently flexible to give ground to his opponents rather than to engage the whigs on what he considered to be a relatively trivial matter. His miscalculation, of course, was to underestimate the dangers of such incremental concessions. Behind these obvious personal rivalries resided a much larger threat, the overall whig objective, which was inexorably taking shape, to smear him forever as a threat to the public interest.

Hutchinson's struggle with the lower house of the General Court over the Council exclusion issue constituted only one aspect of his busy public life in 1767. In addition to his duties as lieutenant governor, he continued to serve as chief justice of the Superior Court and resumed the probate judgeship previously relinquished to his brother Foster in 1765.

Simultaneously, he served as one of three commissioners chosen to negotiate another important boundary dispute with neighboring New York. The Massachusetts delegates met with those from New York at New Haven, Connecticut, in September 1767.[36] Despite Hutchinson's impression that both sides wanted a resolution, they settled nothing and the dispute dragged on until 1773. In addition to these public duties, he labored privately to produce a second volume of his *History of the Colony and Province of Massachusetts-Bay*, bringing the story up to 1750.[37]

Even with all of his public obligations and private activities, Hutchinson complained of a lack of influence. His defeat in the Council seat dispute took its toll. "I am at present a meer cypher" he lamented, "and deprived of what used to be the Lieutenant Governor's right to a seat in the Council. . . . A year has passed without the least notice taken of it."[38] During this time he complained of "a nervous disorder" which adversely affected his ability to work. In correspondence to Richard Jackson he attributed this bout of ill-health to the "great slights and injuries" that he had suffered at the hands of his "own countrymen."[39] Nevertheless, regardless of his dubious health, he seemed eager for more political responsibility.

By the end of 1767, Hutchinson was fifty-six years old, and beginning to refer to himself as "an old man." "Send me a couple of pocket glasses for my old eyes," he wrote to his son in England. He asked his English tailor to "trim the waistcoat . . . according to the fashion for old men."[40] Despite his feelings of impending old age, however, he craved more political activity. Regardless of the loss of his personal property suffered during the Stamp Act crisis, the insults endured in the press, and his declining political influence and advancing years, or perhaps because of these, he demanded more public responsibility. He seemed to anticipate with relish the next fight. He still believed that he could rescue the citizenry of Massachusetts from themselves, by exercising his personal stewardship, predicated on his unyielding belief in the historic and social validity of his qualifications for leadership.

Parliament provided the basis for yet another confrontation for Hutchinson during which the philosophy of the gentleman-politician would again be tested with the introduction of the Townshend Duties in 1767. For the whigs, the new legislation represented another convenient pretext for renewing their assault on the leadership of the Boston establishment in general and Hutchinson in particular.

Like many Americans in the summer of 1767, Hutchinson was not pleased regarding the rumors of a new tax. Nevertheless, however ill-timed or impolitic he thought the Townshend Duties were, he never questioned the right of Parliament to levy these taxes. Instead he hoped that tax measures which were acceptable to the colonies could be arranged. "I really wish that no new attempt of the nature of the Stamp Act be made," he wrote to an unknown correspondent in June 1767, continuing, "but that rather we may be tried by acts of a different nature the force of which has from the beginning been allowed and acknowledged in the colonies."[41]

Judging by the response of Boston's organized radical opposition, it soon became clear that no such measures "allowed and acknowledged" could exist in America. The Townshend Duties were scheduled to go into effect in America in November 1767, the product of the flamboyant Charles Townshend's appointment as chancellor of the exchequer in July 1766.[42] News of the impending legislation, however, circulated in Boston from June onward. In response to these rumors, many of the anti-tax arguments familiar from the Stamp Act period re-emerged in the radical press. As Bostonians contemplated the specter of the proposed new tax legislation, it soon became clear that the new measures would not be tolerated.

Boston's popular party rejected the argument that the new duties were "external" tax measures and therefore constitutionally justified. An anonymous writer who employed the pseudonym "Benevolus" reprised the now familiar assertion that since "the declared intention of the Act is to *raise the revenue* . . . is it a groats matter whether it be by a tax on ships, merchandise, lands or anything else?"[43]

Other writers challenged the Townshend Duties on the more straightforward grounds that the new levies constituted a tax that Parliament had no right to impose. Boston's popular party reiterated the contention that as British subjects they could only be taxed by representatives of their own choosing. The British Parliament contained no American members;

therefore, any taxation in the colonies was illegal. One perplexed Boston writer requested: "Is it not apparent these duties will entirely render fruitless all our noble efforts for the support of our rights in the times of the late Stamp Act?"[44] This proposition, that Parliament had no legal right to tax Americans under any circumstances, eventually provided the central argument of the Massachusetts Circular Letter which was published in February 1768.[45] This important document of colonial resistance that was engineered by Samuel Adams clearly articulated the principle that many Americans would not accept the imposition of unsolicited taxes while avoiding any explicit negation of overall Parliamentary sovereignty. This latter expression of loyalty constituted a particularly crucial factor in the growth and development of opposition to British government in Massachusetts. Although firmly opposed to the Townshend Duties and to the legal principle on which they rested, Adams and his group were unwilling to countenance independence. Since they could not, or simply would not yet, express overt revolution by rejecting British government entirely, they focused their opposition on His Majesty's representatives in Boston. Hutchinson, the embodiment of this royal authority, became their target and attracted most criticism. He became the symbolic object of the pre-Revolutionary impulse that the radicals were as yet unwilling to express. As a native son of Boston and as a most distinguished member of the seaport's establishment, Hutchinson attracted all the negative attention that should more properly have been directed toward Parliament and Charles Townshend.

The issue of representation constituted a critical variable in the formulation of Boston's opposition to the proposed Townshend Duties. Hutchinson contemplated this subject in some detail in early 1767, and concluded that even if Parliament permitted Americans to send representatives to Parliament, "I doubt whether they would [go]." He remained highly skeptical of whig complaints that they were inadequately represented in England. He believed that American radicals would never be satisfied with any plan of representation. He asserted: "Let us suppose that all the colonies send 100 members which no doubt would be a full proportion, every measure not approved of by the colonies would nevertheless cause murmuring and discontent and perhaps opposition and resistance as great as it would do in our present state." In his opinion: "I think the colonies must either be separated from and independent of Great Britain or subject to the Supreme authority there." Here was a lucid expression of how clearly he foresaw the future course of the radical challenge to royal government.[46]

Extrapolating from this view of representation Hutchinson speculated as to the colonial future. He continued that since "no man whose passions have not deprived him of his reason . . . supposes it possible for the colonies to subsist independent of or without protection from some state or other in Europe, and a British colony . . . must always desire that this state should be Great Britain," arguments for colonial representation made little sense. From his standpoint the contentions of the whig opposition that there should be "no taxation without representation" were dishonest and concealed ulterior political motivations. His position echoed the one he adopted during the Stamp Act crisis; to urge compliance while simultaneously laboring to ensure that Parliament respected colonial rights. "Tender and indulgent I should hope the Parliament always will be of the rights of the colonies," he concluded, at the same time enjoining that "all reasonable men must allow that as the colonies cannot subsist without the protection of Great Britain and desire for the sake of enjoying it to be considered as part of the same Empire submission to the Supreme authority of that Empire will necessarily follow." Writing of his fellow citizens in 1767 he stated tersely that "it behoves them to acquiesce."[47]

Boston's popular party radicals also objected to the Townshend Duties on the grounds that the revenues raised might be used to pay the salaries of executive magistrates, customs officials, judges, and other civil officers appointed by the Crown. The radicals reasoned that, if Parliament established a civil list in Massachusetts, then crown officials would be independent of the legislature and thus able to "subvert the principles of Equity and endanger the Happiness and Security of the subject."[48] Hutchinson, as the Bay Colony's most ubiquitous crown official, became an obvious and immediate magnet for radical opposition on this matter. Eagerly following up on the attacks made on him in the Council, writers in the *Boston Gazette* enthusiastically referred to him as the "Grand Pensioner" in anticipation of his being the recipient of money from the proposed colonial civil list.[49] These criticisms eventually formed the basis of virulent popular party assault on him that succeeded in the defeat of his candidacy for the Council in the elections of May 1768.

Immediately prior to the implementation of the Townshend Duties, Hutchinson worried about the possibility of further rioting in Boston. This time, however, one of the leading Sons of Liberty assured him that a new tactic of resistance would be introduced. Instead of rioting "there would be a combination to eat, drink, and wear nothing of any sort imported from Great Britain and that it would be universal and include all ranks of people."[50] Nevertheless, Hutchinson remained unconvinced and, regardless of this supposed reassurance that the civil peace would not break down again, he gloomily recorded that "I expect another crisis upon the first seizure of contraband goods."[51] He worried that the radicals would effectively combine the introduction of an embargo with crowd action to destabilize the political scene.

In April 1768, Lord Hillsborough, Great Britain's new secretary of state for American Affairs, wrote to Bernard instructing him to demand that the Massachusetts House of Representatives rescind the resolution affirming the Circular Letter.[52] This document further instructed Bernard to prorogue the Assembly if it refused his demand to disavow the offensive statement. Hillsborough thus introduced an important new variable into the complex calculus of resistance; that of insensitive and inappropriate instructions issued from London.

Hillsborough's imperious demand arrived after a particularly vituperative series of political exchanges between Massachusetts' court and country parties. Bernard and his supporters among the Hutchinson-Oliver oligarchy had been engaged in an intricate series of battles with the popular party throughout 1767 concerning a variety of issues. Chief among these were secretary of state Lord Shelburne's letter, which praised the governor for the use of his veto in the Council elections of 1767, Hutchinson's alleged recommendation for an appointment to the American Board of Customs Commissioners, and persistent rumors of the introduction of a civil list along with troops to enforce this measure. The parties also clashed over the effort, advanced by the popular party, to implement a nonimportation agreement. Hillsborough's demand thus arrived in Massachusetts at a particularly sensitive juncture and provided Boston's popular party with a peculiarly effective issue with which to assail the ministry.[53]

When the General Court met on May 25, 1768, Boston's popular leaders rebuked Hillsborough's request and risked executive dissolution to make their point. On June 30, 1768, in a landmark vote of 92:17, the legislature opted to stand by their Circular Letter. At the same time the House passed a petition to remove Bernard as the governor of Massachusetts.[54] The degree of virulence directed toward Bernard by the radicals can be seen in Joseph Warren's audacious words in the *Boston Gazette*. He wrote: "Nothing has ever been more intolerable than your insolence upon a late Occasion, when you had by your Jesuitical Insinuations, induced a worthy Minister of State, to form a most unfavorable opinion of the colony in general, and some of the most respectable inhabitants in particular. You had the

Effrontery to produce a letter from his Lordship, as a proof of your success in calumnating us." Other articles by pseudonymous authors "Hyperion," "Vaspasian," and "Conciliator" echoed these sentiments.[55]

Hutchinson observed these political developments with disbelief. In May, he wrote that "there is such an absurdity in American principles of Government that I should be ashamed to own them." With reference to the popular party, he continued: "They call themselves British subjects and admit the Parliament to be the supreme authority and yet claim an exemption from all Acts of Parliament which do not please them."[56]

The chief difficulty, from his point of view, was that Boston's popular party leaders claimed too much for themselves. He wrote, "If only they [Boston's whigs] would cease urging the point of Right and denying their obligation to submit to Acts when made and urge their peculiar circumstances which deprive them of their Rights of Englishmen as an Argument to induce the Parliament to leave them to their internal Legislatures. . . . I should have no scruple to appear in their behalf."[57] The traditional "insider" remained unshakably committed to resistance predicated upon cooperation and deference. Steeped as he was in the tradition of discreet diplomatic negotiation among society's "best persons," he conceived of no alternative to dealing with the ministry than the politics of conciliation and quiet compromise. He appeared utterly unaware that this was a basic reason why Boston's whigs resented him and came to see him as such a threat to their endeavors. In the struggle for power Hutchinson's diplomatic criticisms of British policy may have succeeded. His correspondence indicated that there was little substantive difference between his views and those of his radical opponents. The crucial difference with his opponents resided more in the form of his opposition to the legislation than in the content of his preference. Hutchinson's rivals wished to provoke the government into a confrontation and could not afford any semblance of effective representation by him.

By the end of May 1768, Hutchinson contemplated his chances of becoming governor. In reference to Bernard he noted that "the Governor has wrote for leave to go to England," and he was clearly thinking about a possible successor.[58] He believed that he deserved the governorship and resolved that if he did not succeed Bernard, he would resign as lieutenant governor. He was disappointed with his tenure as second-in-command of the executive and recorded with some pique: "No Lieutenant Governor since the Charter has done and suffered so much as I have done. Each of them except Povey, who was fired in a year or two, was a great part of the time commander in chief. In 11 years I have had a run of only two months."[59]

Hutchinson realized his life-long wish before very long. In the meantime, however, the Bernard administration experienced more divisive political and social upheavals. Nathaniel Rogers informed the lieutenant governor in July 1768, that many British gentlemen in Parliament, "are grown quite weary of American matters . . . they seem now really to despise us," and "they think our opposition to the present Act so unreasonable and ungrateful."[60] In February 1768, Rogers explained further that: "Our resolves and our instructions give the greatest umbrage here, and steady plans will be laid to distress our trade . . ." Elsewhere he wrote: "Manufacturers and commercial people so far as their interest is affected are on our side, but all the landed interest is against us."[61] Indicating deep-seated feelings of imperial envy and fear of colonial growth he concluded: "The House of Peers are not friendly; one of that house said sometime ago that in a few years he expected all of his old family pictures and furniture would adorn a hall in America."[62] This was the prevailing mood in Parliament when Lord Hillsborough decided to send troops to Boston following the rioting of March 18, and June 10, 1768.[63]

The series of events that triggered this response from Lord Hillsborough commenced on June 10, 1768. Commonly referred to as the *Liberty* riots after the seizure of John Hancock's sloop of that name, these disturbances serve as important indicators of the deteriorating state of relations between British customs officials and an influential segment of Boston's mercantile constituency.

The street action directed against certain leading customs officials and known as the *Liberty* riots represented a culmination of sorts of long-standing resentment between Boston's merchant-smugglers and royal revenue collectors. Especially at odds with the British customs officers were southern European and West Indian traders whose businesses had been most adversely affected by the new imperialism.[64]

Since the end of the Seven Years' War, and aggravated by Boston's sluggish economy through the 1760s, an important group of illicit traders competed with crown custom officials over matters of revenue. This antagonistic trend in the history of colonial economic relations represents an important thread in the Hutchinson story. As a leading crown official and, especially, as chief justice of the Superior Court he had often dealt with legal disagreements between the customs service and disgruntled local merchants.

A powerful group of seaport traders whose financial interests were diametrically opposed to those of the customs officials coalesced sometime in the early 1760s in an organization known as the Boston Society for Encouraging Trade and Commerce. This group contained many future patriot merchants who supported free trade and smuggling. Confrontations such as the writs of assistance dispute, court cases against particularly energetic revenue enforcers, and the resistance to the Sugar and Stamp Acts pitted whig smugglers against royal officials. As British trade regulations became more restrictive, a powerful political coterie of merchant-smugglers consistently and intractably opposed London's policies.

With the introduction of the nonimportation movement in response to the Townshend Duties the shape of this evolving political competition altered perceptibly. From 1760 until 1768 Boston's merchants had maintained a recognizable degree of unity. The inception of nonimportation, however, revealed that not all smugglers were created equal. Opposition to the Townshend measures ushered in an important new variable into the traditional antagonism over smuggling.

Boston's larger, wealthier whig merchants, who could afford to maintain larger inventories of goods, favored nonimportation as a means of eliminating competition. From their point of view, an embargo against British goods contained the dual virtues of rationalizing the excessively competitive nature of trade in Boston while at the same time advancing the cause of patriot opposition to royal regulation. Well-heeled merchant princes such as John Hancock readily endorsed nonimportation. However, other less wealthy members of the B.S.E.T.C. did not regard this technique quite so enthusiastically, since they possessed less extensive inventories than their larger competitors and, therefore, stood to gain less from suspending business with Britain. The result was a split in the unity of merchant opposition to crown policy.

Gradually, in order to advance nonimportation as the official policy of resistance to the new Duties, powerful whig merchants expanded the B.S.E.T.C. into a larger group entitled "the Body" or "the Trade." This enlarged voting group included more artisans and petty traders who wished to oppose the revenue forces but whose businesses were unaffected by the means of opposition. Eventually "the Body" became indistinguishable from the town meeting. The whig strategy here was to out-vote their more direct competitors, erstwhile colleagues in the smaller B.S.E.T.C., so as to ensure the adoption of nonimportation.

Boston's whig smugglers took the lead in colonial resistance to the Townshend Duties by unilaterally announcing nonimportation before their equivalents in New York and Philadelphia could do the same. In early 1768 the stage was set in Boston for a new round of confrontation between the smugglers and crown customs officials. The most egregious of these occurred in June in the form of the *Liberty* riots. Following these clashes came Hillsborough's momentous decision to send two regiments of British troops who landed in October.

Nonimportation fizzled out in Boston by 1770 and enjoyed only limited application as a means of resistance. However, those patriot-whig-smugglers behind the policy utilized the experience of nonimportation to tighten and discipline their organization, extend the numerical base of their support, and advance their agenda more aggressively. Crowd action particularly, as evidenced in the *Liberty* riots, increasingly emerged as the enforcement method of choice, not only to intimidate customs officers but also to exert pressure on other merchants who remained not quite as enthusiastic for nonimportation as the whigs believed they should. In the long run, the *Liberty* riots and the civil disturbances that they represented set into motion a inexorable chain of disturbances linked to resistance to revenue collection by customs officials that culminated in the Boston Massacre and the Boston Tea Party. For the time being, however, the most immediate consequence of the rioting was the injection of an obnoxious British martial presence into Boston life.

Parliament was not in session when Lord Hillsborough unilaterally made the decision ordering General Gage to send the soldiers to Boston. Governor Bernard had not requested troops, since he had been unable to secure the Council's approval for such an action. This decision eventually represented one of Britain's biggest blunders of the immediate pre-Revolutionary period.[65]

Hutchinson, despite the devastating losses he had endured at the hands of a crowd in August 1765, was not congenitally opposed either to mobs or rioting. In common with most eighteenth-century public officials, he accepted that from time to time rioting would occur. He considered such events as an inevitable component of the political process. He wrote to Richard Jackson in March 1768, observing that the mobs of that year were no worse and no more threatening or unruly than normally assembled every year on Pope's Day. On other occasions he indicated that colonial crowd actions were sometimes justified although not to be encouraged. In 1770 he stated: "It may justly be said of the people of this province, that they seldom, if ever, have assembled in a tumultuous manner unless they have been oppressed."[66] This could almost have been Samuel Adams speaking when he expressed embarrassment after the uncontrolled sacking of Hutchinson's house in 1765. However, on the specific occasion of the *Liberty* riots, Hutchinson interpreted the events as compounding the earlier harassment of customs officers, and he deplored the breakdown of law and order that the disturbances represented. His main concern was with the apparent dissolution of civic harmony as a result of popular party mass mobilization. On this basis he supported the arrival of troops in September. Although no militarist he wrote to Thomas Whately in England: "These redcoats make a formidable appearance and there is a profound silence among our Sons of Liberty."[67]

During the summer of 1768 Hutchinson expressed deep concern regarding the breakdown of law and order in Boston. He welcomed the troops in his own quiet way, but he knew that soldiers alone could not resolve Boston's difficulties. He wrote contemplatively that, as a result of the troops "I hope we are in a state of more security but whether people will be more content is a matter of doubt."[68]

He recognized that if the British authorities were ever going to govern Boston peacefully again, they must address the political difficulties attendant upon the effective prosecution of law-breakers. In the wake of the *Liberty* riots Hutchinson wrote: "It is Very natural to ask where the Justices and Sheriff are upon these occasions. The persons who are to assist the Sheriff in the execution of his Office are Sons of Liberty and determined to oppose him in everything wch. shall be contrary to their schemes." He continued his lament by recording that "some of the Justices are great favourers of them [the Sons of Liberty] and those who are not are afraid of being sacrificed by them and will issue out no warrants to apprehend them." Further, he complained "let an officer become ever so ill even if he was to abet the disorders he ought to suppress I do not think it would be practicable to remove him seeing it cannot be done without the advice of Council and they would be afraid to give the advice."[69] The political dimension to the rioting became one of his principal concerns for the future. He was clearly irked that, since 1765, Boston's popular party had organized rioting with impunity. From 1768 onward, he was resolute in his commitment to oppose the corruption of the legal instruments of power by the use of organized crowd intimidation.

Boston's popular party passionately opposed the British decision to send troops, and vocalized their rejection through the Boston Town Meeting. Hutchinson's view of whig resistance can be seen in his words: "Many extravagant notions were made as well may be expected from such a Rabble." He pointed out sarcastically that "they [the whigs] finally agreed upon a number of valiant resolves." He employed unequivocal condescension when he assessed how Boston's whigs had promised to resist the troops, but then how the same patriots had eventually appeared "frightened and impotent." He observed superciliously that "Men are not easily brought to fight when they know death by the sword or halter will be the consequence first or last."[70] Hutchinson clearly regarded popular party posturing to be little more than hot air. In the end the resolves of the town meeting amounted to little. The meeting agreed to request all townspeople to clean their firearms but proposed nothing further. The British redcoats disembarked from transport ships and entered the town unopposed.

Failure to confront the troops did not mean that the fight was over, however, and throughout the ensuing three years Boston's patriots employed a variety of means to resist British military force.[71] Easily the most effective of these was the steady drumbeat of denunciation carried in the publication *Boston Under Military Rule, 1768 to 1769 as Revealed in a Journal of the Times.* This document, written by Henry Knox, Benjamin Edes, William Greenleaf, and Isaiah Thomas, stressed that the military presence was illegal and only provoked the people by exposing them to insolent and abusive military personnel. A second theme in the *Journal* was that haughty, corrupt, mendacious, and ill-mannered British customs officials exacerbated an already delicate and potentially explosive relationship between the government and the public.

This important document was first published in New York and was widely disseminated throughout the colonies, ensuring denunciations of the British further afield than just Massachusetts. Anti-British publicity represented an important technique in establishing the imagined community among Americans that remained a vital prerequisite to fomenting revolution. Whig publicists everywhere encouraged colonials to associate and sympathize with Boston's misfortune even though they themselves had not suffered at all as a consequence of British actions.

Resistance to the troops included an initial refusal to find quarters for the unwelcome military visitors. Hutchinson recalled that "several weeks were spent in endeavors to persuade the Council to provide Quarters and they finally refused and the commanding officer was obliged to hire

Houses at very dear rates the weather growing so severe that the Men could no longer remain in Tents."[72] Eventually, however, Boston accommodated the soldiers, thereby allowing the customs commissioners to return to town and hold "their boards here to the great mortification of their Enemies."[73] Hutchinson feared a violent confrontation between the townspeople and the troops and believed that "we certainly have some bad enough to take every measure in their power" to challenge the troops openly.[74] Furthermore, he displayed little faith in the integrity of the Council to act as a restraint on the excesses of the lower house. His position was that "the backwardness of the Council has done more than anything to prevent the restoration of Government and order among us."[75] He perceived that control of the colony was slipping away from the royal authorities.

By the close of 1768, Hutchinson was not optimistic about the future despite the active response of the British government in sending troops to keep the peace. He observed, "the malcontents are awed by the troops." Nevertheless, he continued "the same black blood still runs through their veins and the false notions of Government which they have spread through the Continent still remain upon the minds of people in general." Making reference to whig publicity activities he noted: "For five or six weeks past they [the whigs] have been sending a Diurnal to be printed at New York. They know such infamous falsehoods could obtain no credit here but at that distance there is nobody to contradict them and they are inflaming the Government of New York and Pensilvania which for sometime past seem to have been cool."[76] Hutchinson now realized that for the British to re-establish political control in Boston successfully, a great deal more should be done than merely send troops.

Precisely what he believed such measures should be, however, is impossible to discern. His correspondence from the winter of 1768 is full of general news but contains almost no personal observations. A concern for security provides part of the explanation for his reticence. After updating Thomas Whately on the situation in Boston he concluded with the important words "if there be no necessity for it I think it best it should not be known that the intelligence came from me."[77] Whatever thoughts he had he appeared reluctant to write them down. It was not surprising that someone whose home had been destroyed by anti-Stamp Act partisans would be afraid that his letters should fall into the wrong hands.

Additionally, Hutchinson could now see his way clear to achieving his enduring ambition: the governorship of Massachusetts Bay. He believed that he had been bred for this position. This appointment would be the crowning glory, not just of his own lifetime of service, but that of the historic Hutchinson dynasty. His entire view of politics in theory and practice bespoke the certain knowledge that he was the best person for the post. Governor Bernard was clearly in trouble following the collapse of law and order in late 1768. Soon he would be on his way to England to salvage what was left of his political career. By patiently watching and waiting at this critical juncture, Hutchinson reasoned, he would at last assume the highest mantle. It was for this reason perhaps that, late in 1768, with Boston in turmoil, he held true to an earlier commitment not to "suggest any measure to restore us to a state of government." "Prudence must accompany firmness and resolution," he reminded himself as 1768 drew to a close.[78]

By early 1769 Hutchinson believed that consistent British force and a clear resolve to prevail would be necessary to retain firm control in Boston. He generalized that "A thirst for Liberty seems to be the ruling passion not of America but of the present age." He admitted that, under some conditions, "murmuring" and discontent by government's opponents might be appropriate. He did not, however, think this was the case in Massachusetts. He observed: "In Governments under arbitrary rule it [opposition] may have a salutary effect, but in Governments where as much freedom is enjoyed as can consist with the ends of Government, as was the case in this Province, it must work anarchy and confusion unless there be some external power to restrain it."[79]

From his perspective, the breakdown of law and order in 1768 appeared unjustified and unnecessary. He was grateful for the reassuring presence of the troops and recorded that "I have not slept in Town any 3 months these 2 years [with as] much tranquility as I have done since the Troops came."[80] Nevertheless, he remained convinced that "the Parliament will have a hard task to restore America to its former tranquil state."[81]

At this particular stage in his career he seemed bereft of new political ideas to reconcile Crown and country. His own personal agenda was not advancing either. He was unsuccessful in his effort to collect his stipend as chief justice from the Crown. The nonimportation agreement damaged the family tea business. Finally, he could see no way out of the growing impasse of the disintegrating British-colonial relationship. In January he reflected: "it is past my skill to project a way" to restore harmony to the political relationship between Boston and Britain.[82] Hutchinson, perhaps a little disingenuously given the alacrity with which he was soon to accept the post of acting governor, lamented: "I have been so unsuccessful as well in regard of the public as my own private Interest that I grow every day more and more weary of my political life. All I can expect will fall short of the additional Expense I must be at in Public life to Keep up a tolerable reputation . . . and my own private fortune will support me in a retired way which will be as agreeable to my turn of mind." He concluded: "This makes me wait without any raised expectations the Event of the late intentions of the Ministry and be it what it may I shall think it for the best."[83]

Despite this modest declaration of limited expectations, he remained eager for the excitement of high politics. He did not have to wait long. In April 1769, the Bernard administration effectively collapsed with the publication of a series of incriminating letters written by the governor to Hillsborough and others in 1768.[84]

Boston's popular party had already attempted to force Bernard to reveal the contents of his reports to the ministry, alleging that the governor had misrepresented their motives by suggesting that the province was in a state of rebellion. In February 1769, several heated exchanges occurred between Bernard and Boston's fractious selectmen on the subject of why he had allegedly considered it necessary to solicit troops to preserve law and order in peacetime.[85] The governor naturally resisted these solicitations but on April 5, 1769, six of his confidential letters to Lord Hillsborough arrived in Boston.

These letters had been written between November 1, and December 5, 1768, copied in England, and then returned to Massachusetts by Council agent William Bollan. By the end of April 1769, Bernard's "Six Letters" had been edited and published in pamphlet form by Edes and Gill. They were, not surprisingly, presented to the general public as proof of Bernard's perfidy in misrepresenting Boston to the ministry and thereby ensuring the presence of the hated "Lobster-backs."[86]

In Hutchinson's opinion, Bernard's letters to Hillsborough contained nothing inappropriate: "He [Bernard] infers the necessity of the King's taking the council chamber into his own hands," remembered Hutchinson, "or, in other words, of his appointing a royal council in the stead of that elected by the people; and of an act of parliament, to authorize the King to supersede all commissions which have been issued to improper persons." These suggestions were not new, since "he had been free enough in declaring his sentiments," and, in Hutchinson's opinion "there seemed, therefore, to be no reason for a fresh clamour against him."[87] Bernard's concerns as communicated to his superior had been distorted and traduced by the radicals.

Boston's whigs, of course, felt differently and effectively utilized carefully edited versions of the letters to undermine Bernard. These publications presented the governor as the originator of the decision to bring the hated troops to Boston. The permanent and long-term damage of the affair of the six Bernard letters resided in the disastrous effect it had on the credibility of royal government in Massachusetts. The governor's correspondence had come to light after having been publicized by Parliament. The ministry itself had undermined their own official and compromised the integrity of the lines of communication between government agencies.

For any future governor the danger of exposure to withering whig criticism would be great if English officials were not more careful in safeguarding official correspondence. Candid and truthful letters from royal officials could possibly lead to public vilification and humiliation. This threat produced the contingency that the letters of royal officials would be tentative and thereby misleading to British decision makers. Now, the possibility of public disclosure of confidential documents impeded severely the task of royal governors. Having observed the destruction of Bernard by evidence allegedly manufactured by his own hand, Hutchinson must have been aware of this danger.[88]

By May 1769, however, the ministry informed Hutchinson that he would be the acting governor when the moribund Bernard left for England. Whatever misgivings he had in mid-1769 regarding the integrity and trustworthiness of the British system of imperial communication, he remained silent on the subject. Later the deposed Bernard had the requisite leisure to ponder his unfortunate experience in Massachusetts:

> When I reflect upon my case, I cannot but consider myself as a martyr to the cause of Great Britain. For if the Parliament had not taxed the Colonies; or if I had not in the height of my zeal for my mother Country, and the Service of the King tho't it my Duty to support the authority of Parliament; or if the Parliament had thought it their business to support their own Authority, I should probably at this time have been in Ease, affluence, and Health.[89]

These miserable words, offered as an epitaph for Bernard's governorship in Massachusetts, could well have served as an introduction to Hutchinson's gubernatorial tenure.

CHAPTER FIVE

John Mein and Christopher Sneider: Two Martyrs

"Upon governor Bernard's leaving the Province, the administration devolved upon Mr. Hutchinson, the lieutenant-governor."[1] With these noncommittal words written in the third person, Hutchinson recalled the beginning of his tenure as Massachusetts' chief executive. In the new acting governor's opinion, pervasive and malicious partisanship and competition for office represented the primary stumbling block to a successful administration. He observed: "At all times there have been parties, *Ins and Outs* in the colonies, as well as in the parent state." He continued that, first in the House of Representatives, then in the Council, "exception to the constitutional authority of parliament was first taken, and principally supported, by men who were discontented."[2] Hutchinson's assessment proved correct as Boston's factions and personalities inexorably pursued their mutually antagonistic agendas through the first year of his gubernatorial tenure.

Hutchinson believed firmly that popular party discontent stemmed from the view that whigs remained powerless outsiders as opposed to influential insiders. Here was the main reason why in the acting governor's opinion, expressed again in the third person; "the lieutenant-governor, [meaning Hutchinson] therefore, entered upon his office under circumstances peculiarly difficult and discouraging." Hutchinson averred that "he was bound by a solemn oath, as well as by the nature of his office, to support an authority to which the body of the people refused to submit, and he had no aid from any of the executive powers of government under him."[3] On another occasion he recorded: "The Chair could not have fallen to me at a more difficult time. I must do the best I can . . . without any . . . scheme or great dependence upon any plan in England where measures are always fluctuating and where the minds of the people seem to be as distempered as ours are in America." He concluded plaintively, "God help us on both sides of the water."[4]

Hutchinson's recollection that the summer of 1769 was a most difficult time for him to assume the duties of the royal governor of Massachusetts was not mistaken. He inherited a variety of nettlesome problems. Britain's detested redcoats still "occupied" Boston. The nonimportation agreement continued in effect, its supporters occasionally employing crowd violence to advance enforcement. Boston's newspapers maintained an abusive attitude toward royal authority. The aggressive Virginia Resolves of July 1769 acted as a competitive incentive for even more radical action from Massachusetts patriots who did not wish to be superseded as America's most assertive opponents of royal government. This southern pronouncement claimed the sole right of taxation for the House of Burgesses, the right to petition the King, and the right to join with other colonies in so doing. In addition, Virginia's planters adamantly declared themselves against the proposal to try Americans in English courts and ordered their proceedings to be published in the *Virginia Gazette*.[5] In response to the colonial challenges, British decision making remained amorphous and inconsistent.[6] Finally, Hutchinson, the gentleman-politician schooled in the arts of deference, humility, and compromise remained a hated figure among the ranks of Boston's opposition forces.

Hutchinson, nevertheless, believed optimistically that he could succeed in orchestrating the re-establishment of firm British control in Massachusetts, where his predecessor had failed. He regarded himself as the pre-eminently qualified person to govern the colony. By birth, class, training, and experience, no one else could execute the monumentally difficult task of reconciling British and American political interests. Moreover, he believed his opponents to be wicked, bad, designing individuals, who could only comprehend self-interest and power. To him Boston's whigs were incapable of dutiful, selfless, and honorable public service. In the end, he thought that the people, misguided as they had been between August 1765 and August 1769, could be made to understand the error of accepting the mistaken notions of government of James Otis, Jr., Samuel Adams, and the rest of

Boston's radicals. In August 1769, despite his characteristically understated demeanor, Hutchinson appeared eager to engage his opponents in a political battle which he considered to be absolutely necessary for the well-being of the political soul of Massachusetts. In his eyes the people of the colony were lucky to have him; but, so far as the people were concerned, they could not get rid of him soon enough.[7]

From the opening days of his tenure as acting governor, Boston's patriots attacked Hutchinson for who he was rather than for what he had done. John Adams particularly rebuked his performance as chief justice in a case involving impressment and murder in June 1769.[8] For example, Adams had been the attorney for four sailors accused of murdering a British Lieutenant Panton who had tried to coerce them into the service. Adams prevailed and the seamen were acquitted with a decision of justifiable homicide. The whig lawyer's criticisms of the chief justice were, however, both personal and professional. Adams resented how Hutchinson had rudely cut him off from making an argument on the defendant's behalf. He recalled: "I had scarcely risen and said 'May it please your Excellencies and your Honors,'. . . when Hutchinson again darted up, and moved that the court should adjourn to the council chamber! . . . Alas, for me, my glass bubble was burst! My *boule de savon* was dissolved! All the inflammable gas was escaped from my balloon, and down I dropped like *Pilâtre des Rosiers.*"[9] Elsewhere Adams attributed the chief justice's behavior to fear, announcing that the court could not allow a decision which endorsed impressment as it would have been too unpopular to risk.

Hutchinson's accommodating attitude toward the customs commissioners and his willingness to support the continued use of general writs of assistance further antagonized Boston's popular party. Customs commissioners were disliked as much for their lavish and decidedly unrepublican lifestyle as for their despised legal function. In the *Journal of the Times* these royal officials were referred to as "mushroom gentry" who attempted to "invert the order of nature" by dining late, traversing the town in luxurious carriages, and generally behaving in a haughty and condescending manner. Meanwhile, Boston's opposition press continued to denounce Hutchinson, constantly reminding the readership of his nepotism, fidelity to British policy, and inherited wealth. "It cannot but excite ridicule to perceive, G——n, L. G——r [Hutchinson] S——r etc. toadying up to and encouraging the extravagant commissioners."[10]

In response to this welter of stringent criticism, the jurist and acting governor maintained a deliberately cautious and nonconfrontational ap-

proach toward his enemies. In public he did as little as he could to antago-
nize his detractors. Privately, however, he expected the worst. "We think
every session of Parliament critical but the crisis is not yet come," he wrote
to Richard Jackson, continuing ominously, "I think it cannot be far off."[11]

Most of all Hutchinson hoped for coherent guidance from England. In
late August 1769, he was uncertain as to what was the best approach to
counteract Boston's nonimportation movement and its attendant crowd action. "But let me beseech you not leave us any longer than the next Session
in this uncertain state," he wrote to Jackson in England, since "government
must lose its vigour without external aid." In the same letter he stated presciently: "Repeal as many of the Laws now in force as you please but what
remain take some effectual method to carry them into execution. It is difficult to do it I confess. But it must be done first or last or you lose the
Colonies."[12]

Clearly he felt himself trapped by vacillating and hesitant British policy,
unable to act constructively until he received solid support from England.
In the meantime, as he awaited any kind of organized or systematic approach from London, he resigned himself to a policy of caution and restraint: "I aim at nothing more with an easy sail to keep the Ship in her
course until a better helmsman comes and takes charge of her."[13]

At this point he remained unsure as to whether he would be awarded the
governorship permanently. Until his appointment was confirmed he resolved to act as a caretaker.

As events unfolded an extraordinary degree of Parliamentary ineptitude
and fecklessness contributed immeasurably to Hutchinson's failure to resist
successfully the radical challenge to royal authority. He never received coherent guidance from his British political superiors and was left to fight the
imperial battles in Massachusetts alone.

No matter how much he hoped that Boston's political scene would remain tranquil, the growing momentum of the nonimportation movement,
along with the perpetual irritant of the continued British martial presence,
guaranteed that sooner or later a confrontation would occur. In the meantime, Hutchinson's political fortunes took a mild turn for the better, late in
1769, with the demise of James Otis, Jr.

The intemperate radical lawyer became enraged in August 1769 after
learning that he had been accused in British correspondence of being one
of Boston's leading political troublemakers. By way of revenge for the perceived attack on his reputation, Otis wrote in the *Boston Gazette* that his ac-
cusers were "superlative blockheads," and he promised physical reprisal on

John Robinson in particular. Robinson was a long-time acquaintance of Hutchinson and a loyal customs official.[14] Eventually Otis and Robinson clashed physically in the British Coffee House on Tuesday evening, September 5, 1769. Robinson had the better of the exchange, and Otis sustained a cut on the forehead accompanied by many bruises.

From that unfortunate evening onward, James Otis, Jr., began to suffer from increasingly lengthy periods of mental confusion and verbal incoherence. It is unlikely that this incident alone accounted for Otis's irrationality. By January 1770, his friend John Adams observed that "Otis is in confusion yet; he loses himself; he rambles and wanders like a ship without a helm. . . . I fear he is not in his perfect mind. The nervous, concise, and pithy, were his character till lately; now the verbose, round-about, and rambling and long-winded."[15] We cannot know the extent to which the fight and the subsequent derangement were related. However, Otis's effectiveness as a radical initiator diminished considerably during this time-frame.

While Boston's popular party supporters mourned Otis's demise, Hutchinson certainly did not. When he heard the news of the fight he recorded quite dispassionately and approvingly the "very decent drubbing" that the annoying Otis had received.[16] At first he thought Otis's mental problems were another example of his famous political disingenuousness. To another correspondent he playfully suggested that Otis was capable of committing suicide and then blaming it on someone else.[17] His opinion mellowed, however, with the passage of time. Never one to bear a grudge, and by temperament a humane and decent man, Hutchinson eventually came to sympathize with Otis's plight. A year later he recorded a diary entry which indicated that, given Otis's now deplorable circumstances, the governor bore his erstwhile nemesis no lingering ill-will. He wrote plaintively, "Mr. Otis stopped at my house at Milton . . . in the morning, about 8 or 9, he smelt strong of rum, and carried the disorder of a mind which that had increased in his countenance. He said he was an unhappy man, and had been cruelly persecuted, . . . I made him a very soft reply, assured him of all the protection in my power, and he with ceremony, took leave."[18]

Even with the troublesome Otis removed from the political scene, Hutchinson did not have to wait long for a new crisis to appear. Boston's nonimportation movement, which began after August 1768, provided the context for this latest political furore.[19]

In Hutchinson's opinion, the nonimportation movement represented little more than a convenient means to rationalize business for those "such as have vast quantities of goods on hand."[20] The entire ruse of introducing an economic boycott of British goods seemed to him to be the political triumph of "designing men etc. who take advantage of weak minds," and who, "if the Acts were repealed would complain as much of Acts of Trade."[21] From Hutchinson's viewpoint Boston's whigs would oppose any British trade legislation. Clearly, he regarded the embargo effort as primarily political and unrelated to matters of legal or constitutional principle. From his perspective, a declaration such as the Circular Letter amounted to little more than a political tract. As he stated in a letter to Bernard: "the merchants now hold their meetings in Faneuil Hall and it is difficult to distinguish them from the town meeting for every master of a sloop and broker, shopkeeper or huckster is admitted and has a vote in ordering the property of the first trades in the province."[22] He implied that nonimportation represented the expression of the economic and political interests of the lower economic order. From his establishment point of view, nonimportation contained little by way of moral principle.[23]

Throughout the fall of 1769, Boston's popular party increased the imposition of direct pressure on the merchant community to embrace nonimportation. In the process physical threats and the promise of crowd violence became more frequent and overt. Hutchinson's sons, Thomas, Jr., and Elisha, and his merchant nephew Nathaniel Rogers soon experienced firsthand this growing urgency to conform. In October, Hutchinson recorded, in reference to enforcement of the nonimportation agreement that "My sons were the Butt. They have imported from England near 200 chests of Tea since the agreement which they have been able to sell so low as to discourage the illicit trade." He continued "this has enraged the Smugglers who expected a great harvest from the agreement not to import goods from England and they have bent their whole force against my sons." Additionally he recorded "yesterday one of the principal sellers of Dutch tea was heard to say if 500 men would not do 1000 should and [that] my brother [Foster] and others who were anxious for them, without giving me previous notice of their design, persuaded them to submit."[24]

The Hutchinson family, by virtue of its mercantile and social prominence, occupied the center of political controversy by holding out against nonimportation. He occasionally worried that this conflict would produce violence. When the family finally complied, which Thomas, Jr., and Elisha did without his permission, he wrote that he was glad since "if any tumults should happen, I shall be under less difficulty than if my own children had been the pretended occasion of them."[25] If he needed to use troops to suppress rioting, the acting governor would find objective law enforcement an easier task if he was free of this family connection.

Popular party enforcers of nonimportation also attacked Hutchinson's nephew Nathaniel Rogers in 1769. Rogers was slower to comply with the demands of the crowd and suffered the consequences of the usual radical technique. "Twice my house was besmeared," wrote the unfortunate merchant, "the last time with the Vilest filth of the Vilest Vault, that my poor little wife could not bear to stay in the House."[26] He referred here to the patriot practice of smearing the property of their enemies with a toxic mixture of animal oil, human excrement and urine, known as "Hillsborough Paint" or "Hillsborough Treat" after the despised British secretary for American Affairs. Shortly after this warning Rogers decided to join the Hutchinson brothers and relinquish his trade goods to the Merchants' Committee. Later in August 1770, he died of apoplexy, apparently brought on by the strain of crowd intimidation of him as an importer.

In Hutchinson's view, such incidents of mob intimidation were appalling and unrelated to any serious political principle. They represented outbursts of pure thuggishness. In his correspondence he deplored the collapse of law and order as well as the hypocrisy of the instigators of the rioting. He wrote of the nonimporters: "Tho' they talk a great deal of fundamental natural rights which no power on earth can take from them . . . yet they themselves in the most arbitrary manner . . . deprived others of their fundamental rights."[27] He continued, "the Sons of Liberty are the greatest tyrants which were ever known for they will suffer no man to use his property but just in such a way as they approve of."[28] Even in the midst of the growing breakdown of civility in Boston, the Council, by now dominated by popular party advocates, found the time to harass Hutchinson on seemingly inconsequential matters. The acting governor met with the Council on October 23, 1769, in order to discuss the arrangements for Thanksgiving celebrations. Pro-whig councilors Dexter, Pitts, and Tyler, took the opportunity to object to the presence of two paintings of Charles II and the Duke of York that were hanging in the chamber. They requested that these be removed from the room. Hutchinson disagreed but acquiesced nevertheless.

Although many Bostonians suffered harassment and intimidation from the radicals, no one experienced more direct pressure than John Mein. Scotsman Mein was the printer of the *Boston Chronicle*, a successful bookseller, and a committed importer. Mein's fate illustrated the increasingly brazen and direct methods employed by the Sons of Liberty to disturb those who opposed the radical challenge to royal authority. Hutchinson's political maturity and equanimity were also demonstrated in the Mein affair. Finally, Mein's story reveals the degree to which political discourse in Boston could be reduced to the level of personal antipathy and physical intimidation.

John Mein was the pugnacious proprietor of the "London Bookshop" and lending library. Although a relatively recent arrival in Boston, he had been elected to the minor position of constable. Mein had also established connections with the opposition activists of the town. He ran a thriving business and John Adams was said to frequent his bookshop. His whig acquaintances and affiliations notwithstanding, by 1767, Mein's royalist leanings began to prevail in his political pronouncements. He began publishing the *Boston Chronicle* in late 1767 as a public outlet for his political positions.[29]

Sarcastic, satirical, and amusing, Mein possessed the political pundit's gift of the poison pen. For example, he offered this famous and oft-quoted treatment of John Hancock which caricatured him as the very rich but slightly dim financier of the American Revolution: "Johnny Dupe, Esq., alias the Milch cow . . . a good natured young man with long ears—a silly conceited grin on his countenance—a fool's cap on his head—a bandage tied over his eyes—richly dressed and surrounded by a crowd of people some of whom are stroking his ears, others tickling his nose with straws, while the rest are employed in rifling his pockets." Similarly, Mein skewered the nonimporters, mocking their earnest pretensions and characterizing them as "grave, well-disposed dons." Samuel Adams was "Samuel the Publican," "noted for his Psalm singing" and "sanctified, Hypocritical appearance." James Otis, Jr., was "Counsellor Muddlehead," while the lesser figures of the patriot party generally were referred to as "outlines."[30]

On January 19, 1768, the hot-tempered Mein found himself in an altercation with John Gill. Mein attacked Gill, who was the rival editor of the opposition newspaper the *Boston Gazette*, after the latter refused to reveal the true identity of the author "Americus."[31] Mein's complaint was that Gill had insulted him by publishing a letter that criticized the Scotsman in his newspaper. After exchanging a few heated words Mein summarily thrashed the unfortunate Gill with his walking cane. The courts eventually settled this affair by a criminal fine with civil damages levied against the feisty royalist editor. Nevertheless, the overt, personal animus that existed between the two continued.

For the next two years Mein employed his paper to ridicule and caricature his opponents as freely as they did the same to Boston's royal authorities. This practice of verbal mudslinging and character assassination reached
a critical level of intensity during the nonimportation controversy of 1769.

In August 1769, "the Merchants and Traders" of Boston denounced
Mein as "an enemy of the country," along with the other opponents of nonimportation Theophilus Lillie, Nathaniel Rogers, Thomas and Elisha
Hutchinson, and James and Patrick McMasters. Mein decided to respond
in kind to Boston's whigs. Beginning on August 21, and continuing in subsequent editions of the *Boston Chronicle*, he published cusᴛom house records
that revealed the names of everyone who received imported English goods.
These devastating lists demonstrated that many "well disposed" whig merchants violated their own boycott. One of the most damaging pieces of information to come to light as a result of Mein's expos, was that John Hancock himself had illegally imported one hundred pieces of British linen.[32]

As if these revelations were not enough, Mein deliberately antagonized
and enraged his opponents by employing a vituperative and sarcastic wit.
John Adams, James Otis, Jr., Joseph Greenleaf, and other whigs, enjoyed
seeing their own, often anonymous and pseudonymous, satires appear in
the *Boston Gazette*. They did not, however, relish being the recipients of
similar treatment. Mein quickly became a hated figure among Boston's
whigs.

By October he carried a pistol everywhere he went. The Sons of Liberty
inundated him with threatening letters as the organizers of nonimportation
increased the pressure on their insistent and vociferous antagonist. An unfortunate man who physically resembled Mein was unceremoniously
beaten in the street by patriot thugs. Obviously aware of the danger he was
in, Mein petitioned Hutchinson for protection. The chief justice and acting governor responded with circumspection. He replied that no "previous
steps" could be taken unless Mein could name his assailants so that they
could be bound over to keep the peace.[33]

Eventually the animus between the irascible Scotsman and his opponents came to a head. On October 28, Mein and his partner John Fleming
were crossing King Street. Suddenly, a crowd of about twenty people surrounded them. This threatening group included William Molineux, the
whig merchant Edward Davis, and an opposition trader and mariner Captain Samuel Dashwood. Also on the scene was the well-know radical activist Thomas Marshal who was a lieutenant colonel in the Boston militia
regiment.[34] Angry and determined, especially Dashwood whom Mein had

cruelly referred to in print as "the Grunting Captain, an unclean Beast," the men began, as the *Evening-Post* account later put it, "to catechize Mein."[35] A physical assault soon followed the preliminary verbal exchanges. Mein cocked his pistol and pointed it at Davis who had poked him with a walking stick. The crowd kept its distance as Mein and Fleming moved toward the protection of the main British Guard that was posted at the south end of King Street. Narrowly avoiding serious injury from a blow by a shovel wielded by Marshal, the two printers ducked past the British sentries to safety. Sometime in the confusion of escaping the scene Fleming fired a pistol. The gunshot provoked the crowd, which then proceeded to surround the barracks shouting angrily at the soldiers, demanding that their antagonist reappear.

Shortly after this brush with the radicals, Mein went into hiding. Later, perceiving himself to be at the "mercy of the populace, with law in their mouths, but rapine in their hands," he decided to leave Boston for good. Mein had effectively been martyred as the unjustly persecuted advocate of loyal opposition to nonimportation.

Throughout this affair, Hutchinson's responses and actions reflected his knowledge that crown authority could not adequately protect Mein. When first driven underground the printer wrote to Hutchinson several times, to remind him that the peace had been broken and that some action should ensue. Mein stated: "I luckily got into the guardroom where I now am; I write to know what protection the law can afford . . ."[36] When Hutchinson received these letters he counseled Mein to be careful, knowing that it would be suicidal for the contentious Scotsman to show himself in Boston again under any circumstances.

In Hutchinson's opinion this state of affairs was far from satisfactory but he understood the government's weakness in the face of crowd action. A less reasonable or flexible official could well have exacerbated tensions by precipitately applying martial pressure to ensure justice for Mein. Instead, he wisely chose to "avoid everything which may unnecessarily irritate the minds of the people," and arranged for Mein to leave Boston quietly with a letter of recommendation to Lord Hillsborough.[37] Of course the wisdom of Hutchinson's actions can be second-guessed. Clearly the radicals perceived Mein's exit as a capitulation by the government. Probably Hutchinson did too, but he had to make a decision whether or not to risk more violence and potential bloodshed. To his credit, under the circumstances, he chose peace; he received little thanks for this judicious decision.

*

The above events illustrated that Boston's nonimporters were willing to employ direct physical violence to silence an articulate and persuasive opponent. Hutchinson's first priority seems to have been to re-establish the peace. To achieve this objective, he had to act in such a way as to disavow a legal principle, for Mein was clearly the aggrieved party. On this occasion, Hutchinson subordinated what was right under the law to what was attainable. This action does not indicate an unnecessarily rigid, legalistic, or impractical person. Rather, the Mein affair suggests that Hutchinson well appreciated, especially from personal experience, how powerful the crowd was in Boston, and how capable it was of disrupting the peace. Thus he compromised to maintain authority. This response was that of a mature political leader who was beginning to recognize the fact that public opinion could not be ignored, or profitably subordinated to abstract formal principle, however misguided he considered it to be. This realization represented a significant shift in attitude from Hutchinson's earlier career. Later the governor would actively attempt to employ the print media to influence opinion, thereby following the radical example and ensuring that Mein's fate was not completely without benefit for the royalists.[38]

Hutchinson remained convinced of the rectitude of his position despite the relative success of Boston's whigs in silencing Mein. He declared to John Pownall "the false ideas of America so suddenly started will not have a very long duration." He continued: "I have . . . always been very free in declaring my Sentiments upon the inexpediency [if there was any] of the Revenue Acts. . . . By this Freedom I have made my self Enemies but they have been such principally as have supposed me to be dangerous to their designs of bringing government into confusion which is the only way of making themselves to be of any consequence."[39] In his opinion, the ascendant position of Boston's popular party regarding the success of nonimportation, along with its attendant personal criticism of him, would only be temporary.

To some degree Hutchinson's optimistic assessment of events late in 1769 seemed justified. Notwithstanding the increased violence to encourage compliance, Boston's nonimportation policy was in trouble. Lack of support from other seaport towns, particularly New York and Philadelphia, had weakened local resolve. Furthermore, the deadline for the expiration of the initial agreement approached, and discipline among subscribers seemed to be faltering. Smaller businessmen began to withdraw from the agreement to boycott English goods. As those in possession of large inventories took the opportunity of selling their surplus stock at higher prices, those with few extra goods on hand could no longer reconcile their self-interest with maintenance of the nonimportation embargo. Many smaller traders faced bankruptcy and needed to resume trade with Britain.

Mein, despite his facetious eloquence, had been quite right in identifying dry goods merchants and smugglers as the most prominent whigs. Moreover, his scintillating journalism had done considerable damage to the reputations of the nonimporters by exposing their hypocrisy to the wider community.

In January 1770, Boston's nonimportation movement visibly crumbled. Younger, newly established merchants, many of whom were little more than shopkeepers turned importers, began to abandon the agreement, thus risking reprisal at the hands of the Sons of Liberty. To these smaller-scale businessmen, who were probably unwilling to endure a protracted embargo of highly profitable English manufactured goods, nonimportation increasingly appeared as little more than an economic device, proposed by politically powerful opposition merchants and smugglers, to drive them out of business.

Patriot merchants regrouped and responded to this challenge by establishing a new deliberative organization called "the Body of Trade," or "the Body" for short. The Body organized Boston Town Meetings that usually attracted anywhere between one thousand and fourteen hundred participants. This group represented a purposeful effort by the patriots to involve as many people as possible in the anti-British nonimportation movement. Operating under the chairmanship of William Phillips, the archetypal wealthy merchant prince, the Body attempted to coerce and intimidate opponents of nonimportation. The Boston crowd was freely invoked in this endeavor.[40]

An example of this technique occurred on January 18, 1770, when a crowd of some one thousand people convened at acting Governor Hutchinson's house to question him regarding the refusal of his sons, Thomas and Elisha, to surrender their goods to the nonimporters.[41] His sons had failed to fulfill an earlier promise to relinquish their trade goods to the nonimporters. Hutchinson argued with the crowd from his window, cleverly reminding them that if mob violence ensued, "men of property would answer for it with their lives and estates." The next day, he agreed to allow his sons to turn over their goods to the committee so they could not be sold. His explanation for this apparent *volte-face* was that he would be better able to support the other importers as acting governor after his own family was no longer directly involved in the issue. One suspects, however, that he made the decision after he had been satisfied that observers would not think that he had been intimidated into compliance by the crowd. His life-long approach to leadership demonstrated that he was willing to compromise to keep the peace, but only after his honor had been secured. He never wished to appear coerced in any way. Throughout this period, he demonstrated a stubborn resilience to intimidation by the crowd, unlike many of his less activist conservative friends.[42]

As the Body continued to struggle to maintain nonimportation, the language employed in its pronouncements became increasingly inflammatory. After having identified by name a list of importers, the Body declared in January 1770, "that they have in the most insolent manner too long affronted this people . . . and that they deserve to be driven into that obscurity, from which they originated, and to the Hole of the Pit from whence they were digged."[43] This hostility of language was accompanied, through the month of February 1770, by a commensurate increase in the use of street-level violence to intimidate importers. Precisely what the Body hoped to achieve by mobilizing crowds to coerce importers is unclear. Probably the whigs wished for nothing more than to bring nonsubscribers into line. However, an accident in February 1770, which resulted directly from a routine incident of organized, political crowd action, produced a major propaganda coup for Boston's whig leaders.

On the morning of February 22, 1770, the North End shop of importer Theophilus Lillie became the target of the Boston crowd. Earlier in the year he had written, "it always seemed strange to me that people who contend so much for civil and religious Liberty [Boston's whigs] should be so ready to deprive others of their natural liberty. . . " Lillie continued to critique the whigs by observing that "the men who are guarding against being subject to laws [to] which they never gave their consent, in person or by their representative, should at the same time make laws, and in the most effectual manner execute them upon me and others, to which laws I am sure I never gave my consent either in person or by my representative."[44] Importer or not, this kind of trenchant, forthright exposé of patriot hypocrisy inevitably guaranteed problems for its author. Not surprisingly, the accusatory patriot symbol of the pointing hand, so often used to rally the crowd, appeared affixed to a post in front of Lillie's shop. Before long, a large number of people gathered to heckle him and harass potential customers.

Unfortunately perhaps for everyone, the hot-tempered Ebenezer Richardson lived nearby.[45] Already notorious and despised among opposition circles as a former customs service informer, Richardson took it upon himself to remove the effigy placed in front of Lillie's business. As he did so, the crowd pelted him with a noxious mixture of feces and rotten food-stuff and referred to colloquially at the time as "Hillsborough Treat." Forced to retreat he decided to go home, but on the way encountered and apparently threatened several Sons of Liberty who then followed him with the crowd not far behind. Henry Knox was soon pounding on Richardson's door, shouting, "Come out, you damn son of a bitch, I'll have your heart out, your liver out!"[46]

Responding to this graphic challenge, Richardson re-emerged. As he shouted insults at the crowd, they returned his words in kind as well as showering him with stones, breaking the windows of the house and hitting his wife. Soon an angry, stone-throwing mob had the hapless fellow besieged in his own house.

During this stand-off the ill-fated Richardson fired his musket from the window and seriously wounded eleven-year-old Christopher Sneider. Weight of numbers overwhelmed him before he could fire again. Surprised, horrified, and incensed, the crowd was ready to lynch him on the spot. However, the influential patriot William Molineux persuaded the people to desist and Richardson was instead taken into custody.

Later that same evening, Christopher Sneider died. Boston's radicals had their first martyr to liberty, "willfully and feloniously shot by Ebenezer Richardson."[47] On Monday, February 26, Samuel Adams and the opposition party orchestrated an enormous funeral procession, "the largest perhaps ever known in America."[48] Political symbolism permeated this somber event. The procession began at the Liberty Tree. More than two thousand mourners assembled, most of whom could not possibly have known the victim. Always mindful of the political climate, John Adams recorded, "this shows there are many more lives to spend if wanted in the service of their country."[49]

Notwithstanding the excitement of February and March 1770, by April, confirmation of the partial repeal of the Townshend Duties seriously undermined the efforts of the Boston patriots to enforce their embargo.[50] In addition, the news of the termination of nonimportation agreements by merchant groups in New York and Philadelphia further weakened Boston's boycott. In May 1770, fifty of Boston's more moderate merchants led by Jonathan and John Amory met at the British Coffee House to initiate a public campaign to dissolve the agreement. Further minor riots occurred in June 1770; this time the victims were Patrick McMasters and Jesse Saville, whom Hutchinson later referred to having been "great sufferers."[51]

However, as spring gave way to summer in 1770, Boston's more radical merchants struggled unsuccessfully to find a formula to keep nonimportation alive.

As the temporary merchant consensus on nonimportation gradually fell apart, with its attendant name-calling, occasional rioting, and personal haranguing, Hutchinson observed matters with his customary equanimity. He provided a historic context for the violent events of the early months of his governorship when he observed that, "You certainly think right when you think Boston people are run mad." He explained: "The frenzy was not higher when they banished my great grandmother, when they hanged the Quakers, when they afterwards hanged the poor innocent witches, when they were carried away with a Land Bank, nor when they all turned new Lights, than the political frenzy has been for a Twelve month past."[52]

The Deepening Crisis

Nonimportation was not the only issue to animate the Boston scene following the passage of the Townshend Duties. The continued presence of four regiments of British troops in Boston also caused resentment. This ill-fated and eventually tragic policy had been undertaken at the insistence of Lord Hillsborough in the wake of the rioting in March and June, 1768.[1] Since October 1768, the citizens of Boston had been compelled to tolerate this uninvited contingent of British redcoats. The dissatisfactions generated by the martial presence in Boston served to exacerbate all other political difficulties afflicting Massachusetts throughout 1769 and 1770. Crowd action in support of nonimportation contained the additional dimension of the tangible hatred felt by Boston's populace toward the troops. Political discourse between those in power and the opposition became poisoned and supercharged. It was in this strained climate of opinion that Boston's infamous "massacre" transpired.

The massacre severely tested Hutchinson's political skills. Although he successfully managed to defuse the explosive situation, by the end of March 1770, he admitted to feeling the strain of the governorship. Even before George III had formally approved his commission, he had already sent his letter of resignation to Great Britain.[2] Hutchinson had grown fatigued with his role as the focus of every radical attack on government. He pleaded with the British for a more forceful approach to the Massachusetts rebellion and threatened to resign if this was not forthcoming. Eventually, unfortunately for Hutchinson, his British superiors convinced him to continue in the position of governor while never really developing the policies necessary for his tenure to be successful.

The presence of British troops chafed colonial sensibilities almost from the very day of their arrival in Boston. Unruly behavior by the soldiers coupled with economic competition as both troops and locals chased part-time work, soon led to friction with the civilian population. For example, "Capt. Willson was carried before Justice Dana for drunken behavior and bound over to the sessions." Willson had urged some slaves to: "Go home and cut your Master's Throats; Ill treat your masters and come to me to the parade and I will make you free, and if any person opposeth you I will run my Sword thro' their Hearts." This type of language would, of course, offend Bostonians of all social classes. Hutchinson recorded that, "the two regiments in the Town were a continual eyesore to the inhabitants . . . there appeared a rooted enmity in each side."[3] In early March the friction between soldiers and civilians produced a violent confrontation.

The Boston Massacre originated in a conflict between British troops in search of supplementary employment and local workers at John Grey's ropewalk. British soldiers received meager financial reward for their services. It was common practice to look for additional income. On Friday, March 2, 1770, a British soldier by the name of Patrick Walker requested employment at Grey's business. He was unceremoniously rejected, and he left feeling angry and insulted. One of the workers at Grey's had ordered Walker to "go empty his sh— house" if he wanted work. The next day a "quarrel" occurred between the antagonists "in which one of the soldiers was very dangerously wounded."[4]

On Saturday evening tension mounted when a rumor spread among the troops that one of the 29th regiment's sergeants had been killed. Maurice Carr, lieutenant colonel in command of this regiment, and some other officers undertook to search the ropewalk on Sunday morning to look for the missing sergeant. Predictably, Boston's radicals interpreted this suggestion as needlessly provocative and intolerable. By Sunday evening Bostonians from chambermaids to clergymen knew that trouble was imminent.

On Monday morning, March 5, 1770, Hutchinson attempted to persuade the Council to address the problem of growing tension between the troops and the townspeople. His efforts yielded no progress, since "the Council, however, could not agree in any advice; though it was apprehended the smaller frays would be followed by one more general."[5] Personal and partisan divisions within the Council precluded coherent action to ameliorate a tense and dangerous situation.

The confrontation that Hutchinson feared began around 8:00 P.M. on March 5, in King Street, when a British sentry named Hugh White who was on duty outside the Customs House struck Edward Garrick with his musket. Garrick, a wigmaker's apprentice, had verbally insulted a British officer named Captain Lieutenant John Goldfinch for allegedly not repaying a debt.[6] The young wigmaker was part of a small crowd of club-carrying townspeople, some of whom immediately came to his aid. As this was happening, a church bell began tolling which was universally understood to be the alarm for fire. Soon, as the whig sympathizer and diarist John Rowe trenchantly observed, "a great Number Assembled in King Street."[7]

Meanwhile, Private White endured mounting verbal assaults from the assembled crowd. As the hostile mob pressed in on him, assailing him with ice and snowballs, White loaded his musket. Soon the frightened soldier was hammering on the Customs House door requesting entry and shouting for help, while simultaneously enduring the insults of the assembled crowd.

Nearby, at Murray's Barracks, other British soldiers were being attacked by angry Bostonians. Simultaneously, a crowd gathered in Dock Square, ostensibly responding to the fire alarm. Equipped to battle the alleged fire with sticks and bludgeons, this crowd soon began advancing toward the Customs House.

Captain Thomas Preston was the British officer of the day on that infamous Monday evening. According to his own explanation which was offered later at his trial, the safety of the beleaguered Private White was his primary concern. With this in mind Preston dispatched a rescue party of eight grenadiers, including himself, to help his comrade-in-arms.

After the soldiers had reached and rescued the terrorized White the real trouble occurred. Reluctant to permit the hated redcoats a quiet retreat and, clearly spoiling for a fight, the crowd apparently goaded the grenadiers. "Damn you, you sons of bitches, fire. You cannot kill us all," they cried. Shortly after having received this challenge, the soldiers obliged the eager crowd and began to shoot. Five men were killed. "Three men were killed outright, two mortally wounded, who died soon after." John Rowe wrote: "they killed five—wounded several others, particularly Mr. Edward Payne in his right arm."[8]

Before long, Hutchinson appeared on the scene, hoping to "satisfy the people."[9] He inherited an extremely tense situation in which neither soldiers nor civilians were willing to withdraw first. In stabilizing this volatile confrontation he demonstrated considerable political ability, and personal courage. Less experienced leaders might have panicked and overreacted which would probably have resulted in more bloodshed.

Careful to avoid issuing a direct order to the troops, an action which could have had adverse future legal ramifications, Hutchinson tactfully suggested to the commander of the regiment, Lieutenant Colonel Maurice Carr, that the troops should disperse. Carr took the hint with equal tact, and the troops withdrew to the barracks. Next, Hutchinson addressed the crowd verbally from the second-floor balcony of the adjacent town house. He "expressed his deep concern, at the unhappy event, assured them that he would do everything in his power in order to [ensure] a full and impartial inquiry, that the law might have its course, and advised them to go to their several homes."[10] As the crowd drifted home, warrants were immediately issued for the arrest of Captain Preston and Lieutenant James Basset. Preston was imprisoned for allegedly issuing the illegal order to fire, while Basset was interviewed and released. The next day, all eight soldiers involved in this pivotal event surrendered and were incarcerated to await a separate trial.

Hutchinson clearly realized from March 6, 1770, onward, that he would have an enormous uphill battle persuading Bostonians of the benign nature of British authority. If Boston's opposition could mobilize two thousand people for the funeral of a child who had been inadvertently killed by an excitable civilian, as they had in the Sneider incident, they would certainly be able to mobilize the populace following the deaths of five martyrs at the hands of the agents of organized state power. The Boston massacre enhanced immeasurably the potential of the radicals to organize ritualistic and festival-like crowd events. From the radical perspective, the "Boston Massacre" yielded the first adult victims of the American struggle for liberty. Nothing would now be able to prevent Boston's radicals from immediately inducting the dead into the folklore of "the cause" of freedom.

Nevertheless, Hutchinson seemed outwardly confident that most Bostonians could be convinced that British government should be respected and that his administration could survive. With these objectives in mind, in the period immediately following the "massacre," he worked to engineer a public policy designed "to preserve the form, or the appearance, of government until Parliamentary measures shall restore the spirit and vigor of it."[11]

Privately, however, he doubted whether he should continue as acting governor. Although coherent and logical in his public actions and pronouncements, he personally related to Lord Hillsborough, on March 27, 1770, that he wanted to resign.[12] He cited a number a reasons for his decision to tender his resignation, including "the prospect of increasing difficulties, and a desire to apply myself to the most agreeable office I ever sustained—that of Chief Justice, in which I thought I had done good, and had been very little abused for it." Later he provided more specific detail. As he wrote in the third person, "he found his health affected by the difficulties and vexations of a short administration of six or eight months, and was diffident whether he should have firmness of body or mind, equal to the violent opposition with which he was threatened." He wrote later: "The designs of particular persons to bring about a revolution, and to attain independence were apparent . . . and he hoped to pass the remainder of his days, without molestation, in the character of chief justice. He therefore determined to be excused from the honor intended for him."[13]

Hutchinson anticipated difficult times ahead if he remained as the governor of Massachusetts. He was convinced that a conspiracy to declare independence was well under way. He knew that he would experience popular party opposition on every issue. However, it was not in character for him to offer to resign so readily. Above all, he viewed himself as a man of honor, duty-bound to fulfill all the class and dynastic expectations that he had been raised to personify. Furthermore, he had the utmost confidence in his political skills. Personal embarrassments or even physical danger mattered very little when off-set against discharging his duty and maintaining an honorable reputation. Moreover, he was too easily reassured for his offer of resignation to have been completely serious.

Hutchinson, along with his family, had suffered considerably, but he had devoted to British authority in Massachusetts too much of his life to turn back now. He needed recognition from his British colleagues in March 1770. He demanded some tangible sign that he was their first choice to occupy the position that he had assiduously worked for all his political life. In keeping with the code of the gentleman-politician, his resignation offer represented an opportunity for the Crown to replace him. If he was not Britain's first choice for the post then he could withdraw without either party losing face. In suggesting his own resignation Hutchinson clarified his ambition as the gentleman-in-politics. His obligation was to serve or step-down according to the requirements, demands, and expectations of his British superiors. Fully aware that the days ahead would be extraordinarily difficult for any governor, he offered to resign as a method of testing British resolve and continued commitment to royal government for Massachusetts.

By June 1770, he had been sufficiently reassured by Lord Hillsborough. With remarkable speed Hutchinson changed his mind, withdrew his offer to resign, and agreed to serve as governor after all. In Hutchinson's words, "my Lord Hillsborough advised me that he would keep the place of Governor untill my further answer. This mark of confidence with so much condescension, put it out of my power to hesitate."[14] Again he presented himself as the willing servant of Great Britain, his momentary doubts as to British faith in his leadership apparently resolved.

Despite his private reservations with regard to the governorship, Hutchinson's public actions in the wake of the Boston Massacre remained confident and sure-footed. He consistently lobbied, requested, beseeched, and cajoled his superiors in London for firmer leadership and guidance. He was certain that sooner or later his imperial colleagues in England would arouse themselves. For example, in reference to nonimportation he wrote: "To what length may they go before Lord ——— Mr.——— and the other Members of the two Houses of Parliament will allow these confederacies to be illegal? I think the Nation has lost all spirit or they could not bear the Insult and high Contempt."[15]

In a long letter to the influential ex-governor, Francis Bernard, Hutchinson detailed at length three distinct courses of action for the British to consider. He suggested that the British government could either reduce the radicals by force, impose stringent trade restrictions, or endeavor to divide the radicals among themselves. Hutchinson predicated his reasoning in this communication explicitly on the belief that if the British Parliament demonstrated unity and "resolved at all Events to maintain its Authority over the Colonies we should be as tame as Lambs and I have still but very little doubt of it."[16] Following the Boston Massacre, Hutchinson endeavored to apply common sense in the conduct of public affairs, to placate and assuage public opinion and engender peace and orderliness. He engineered the removal of the remaining troops from Boston to Castle William. He delayed Captain Preston's trial until tempers had cooled. He attempted to build a consensus among potential loyalists to uphold the government's position. He insisted on moving the General Court across the Charles river to Cambridge in the hope that its meetings would not be adversely affected by the tense political climate that prevailed in Boston proper.[17] In these substantive ways, Hutchinson offered coherent, mature, and effective political leadership for the government party immediately after the Boston Massacre. In response to this performance, Boston's whigs increasingly targeted him as the enemy.

On March 6, 1770, Hutchinson, the Council, and Lieutenant Colonel William Dalrymple, made the decision collectively to remove the 29th and 14th regiments to Castle William.[18] Samuel Adams, speaking as the representative of the Boston Town Meeting, warned Hutchinson that "nothing can rationally be expected to restore the peace of the town and prevent blood and carnage but the immediate removal of the troops."[19] Although understandably reluctant to give in to such intimidation, he concurred with the decision. Dalrymple issued the order to evacuate the troops.

The patriots and the people of Boston regarded removing the troops to the castle to be a significant victory. To the extent that the presence of British troops after March 6, 1770, inflamed and antagonized public opinion, Hutchinson and the Council assuaged everybody's worries by evacuating them. This particular decision did not seem to cost the acting governor very much politically or emotionally. Certainly a more stubborn person could have insisted on keeping the troops within the confines of the town, thereby engaging the wrath of Boston's radicals. Hutchinson, however, appeared quite willing to face the reality that the unpopular troops would probably face more violence if they were not relocated.

In his letters from the period immediately following the Boston Massacre, Hutchinson lamented the weakness of British Parliamentary authority and the growing power of the merchants and the Sons of Liberty. In April 1770, he confided to the newly knighted Sir Francis Bernard that "to see Molineux, Young, Hancock, Phillips, Cooper, Adams and half a dozen more determining upon measures and then assembling the populace by ringing of Bells to carry them into execution, threatening all who oppose them with ruin in their trade and estates and intimating even something worse . . . gives me infinite uneasiness and anxiety of mind."[20] Nevertheless, even in the wake of the Boston Massacre, he remained convinced that British authority could somehow be maintained and legitimized. Certainly he appeared committed to achieve this objective. He was fully aware of how the Boston Massacre and its immediate consequences were being put to partisan use by Boston's radicals, especially in the newspapers. However, in his view, "the designs of particular persons to bring about a revolution and to attain to independency, were apparent; but he [Hutchinson] did not think it possible for them and bring the people, in general, to declare for it."[21]

Hutchinson displayed an impressive degree of flexibility and political maturity when he supervised the delay of the trial of Captain Preston and the other soldiers. Ostensibly the acting governor wanted to ensure that the soldiers involved in this unfortunate incident received a fair trial. He appeared concerned that if the trial occurred too soon, the jury would convict Preston and his comrades in a hasty, emotional manner, without giving due consideration to the facts of the situation. Alongside this admirable desire to see justice served, probably equally important to him were the political considerations of avoiding additional rioting, denying his popular party adversaries any cause for celebration, and pleasing his British superiors.

Operating primarily here as chief justice, he engineered a "continuance" of the trial. He reflected later: "The people of the Town and Province were inflamed and prepossessed with a full persuasion, that a horrid massacre has been wantonly, or with little or no provocation, committed upon the innocent inhabitants." He continued, "in the midst of this heat, very irregular steps were take to induce the Judges of the Superior Court to bring on the trials of the officers and soldiers, contrary to the judgment of the Court, to continue them to another term." Therefore, he explained: "The trials, however, were continued, and came on when the temper of the people was moderated, and by a fair and impartial jury, both the Officers and Soldiers were acquitted of the murder, and the Court gave their opinion that some of the inhabitants of the town were the aggressors. . . ."[22]

By delaying the trial until October 1770, Hutchinson was indubitably instrumental in securing justice for the beleaguered Preston. Defended by the prominent radicals John Adams and Josiah Quincy, Jr., the soldiers were acquitted.[23] In his terse summary he noted that, "these acquittals did not discourage the friends of liberty, but then deprived them of the great advantage which convictions would have given them for promoting the cause."[24]

No popular rioting occurred following the trial although, in Boston's newspapers, the virtue of the people was vociferously reaffirmed in equal measure to the venality of the soldiers. Through the fall of 1770, the controversy of the Boston Massacre gradually drifted into the background. In November 1770, Hutchinson with his characteristic optimism, and obviously proud of his performance, wrote to his political confidant in England, Sir Francis Bernard: "Affairs certainly wear a better face than they have done since you left the province." In December, Hutchinson reassured Lord Hillsborough that, in the wake of the acquittal of Preston and the other soldiers "the present face of affairs is much more favorable than it has been at any time for eighteen months past." "There certainly is a store of virtue in the country," Hutchinson happily wrote to Thomas Pownall from his country home in Milton.[25]

Hutchinson's skillful handling of the removal of the redcoats in conjunction with his management of Captain Preston's trial temporarily assuaged his critics in Boston. In February 1771, he recorded that "we have been surprisingly quiet and peaceable for several months and we should not know that there was any remains of the Faction, if it was not for the malicious strokes in the News papers, which will not cease until the publisher finds that they lessen his custom." By the time he had officially received his commission as governor on March 14, 1771, his correspondence reflected a sincere belief that "a very great majority of the people in the country Towns rejoice at the appointment." He remained optimistic that royal government could be maintained under his stewardship despite his belief in the popular party's conspiracy to gain independence.[26]

Given this generally calm atmosphere, largely due to the absence of crown initiatives, Hutchinson suggested that the court party mobilize to consolidate its apparently favorable position. To the Earl of Hillsborough he recommended that an appointed or mandamus Council be introduced as a key reform of the constitutional mechanism in order to weaken the power of the radicals in the House of Representatives. He also proposed militarizing Fort Hill, which was normally used "by the inhabitants for walking."[27] In his opinion, since Boston's political problems were generated by an unhappy handful of dissidents, if Britain demonstrated a consistently firm hand most of the challenges to authority would soon disappear. As he confided to a superior in London: "A firm persuasion that Parliament is determined, at all events, to maintain its supreme authority is all we want. If Acts were passed more or less to controll us, every session, we should soon be familiarized to them and our erroneous opinions would die away and peace and order would revive." He wrote: "If it was not for 2 or 3 Adamses we should do well eno'."[28]

Economic matters also figured in the politics of the day. In addition to the above reforms, Hutchinson recommended a Parliamentary Act to separate valuable timber lands located in Maine, adjacent to Massachusetts, thereby ensuring that the Crown monopolize this resource and exclude whig businessmen from the region.[29] Both of these suggestions enraged the popular party. From the perspective of the gentleman-politician Boston's whig merchants should accustom themselves to imperial edicts generated, as such measures were, by a privileged class whose munificence and benevolence were beyond dispute. Elisha Cooke's heirs did not readily accept this point of view.

Despite everything that had gone before, early in 1771, Hutchinson appeared prepared to carry out his duty and endeavor to negotiate with the popular party. If the radicals would not compromise he seemed willing to lead the charge to crush Boston's troublesome lower-class challengers in the name of continued government by the gentlemen-politicians. He believed this to be nothing less than his duty. It was a matter of honor to Hutchinson to enforce British policy, even though he was not aggressive in forming any specific program of action. For Hutchinson, remaining in government was not particularly a matter of money or personal aggrandizement. It was a matter of living up to his conception of his obligations and of fulfilling the expectations of his name. He wrote to Richard Jackson that "the utmost prudence is necessary to maintain and encourage the present spirit, but all will be insufficient if Parliament should give us any room to suppose they will ever give up their authority. How to avoid it is not for one to suggest."[30] Hutchinson, who conceived of the world in rigidly hierarchical and regimented terms, accepted that his superiors would set policy. It was his duty to carry out these orders. Others had a similar duty to accept the imperial will.

Similarly, for Hutchinson, outward displays of opulence to demonstrate class were unimportant. When writing to Bernard in reference to purchasing a new coach, he stated that "everybody urges me to provide one more in fashion" now that he was governor. However, his own frugal inclination was to continue to use his father's vehicle and to have it "serve as long as I shall use a coach."[31] He resisted having a fashionable portico added to his country residence at Milton until he felt that there was some more justifiable reason than merely a rich man's vanity.[32] Outward demonstrations of wealth and status were unnecessarily gaudy and déclassé to the aristocratic Hutchinson. He eschewed conspicuous consumption and needed no display of wealth to justify the expectation of obedience. When he was not automatically obeyed, he was surprised, angered, and eventually profoundly disappointed. Early in 1771 the gentleman-politician stood ready to do his duty, awaiting the word from Britain. Another indication of his security with his established social status was his refusal to allow his daughter Peggy to marry the English aristocrat William Fitzwilliam.[33]

Governor Hutchinson met the General Court at Cambridge on April 3, 1771, with what he considered to be conciliatory words: "I have no particular interior business of the province now to lay before you."[34] The lower house immediately presented two combative messages requesting that the court be moved back to Boston. When he refused, a committee from the House responded testily that "it would have given us no uneasiness, if an end had been put to the present Assembly, rather than to have been again called to this place."[35]

Following this initial sparring, Hutchinson and the General Court locked horns with regard to the more fundamental issues of the governor's salary and who would be acceptable as Councilors. The lower house demanded to know if Hutchinson had another source of income for his salary since he had vetoed their appropriation measure. The governor replied with the terse statement: "I will not enter into a dispute with you" regarding the origins of the money. Privately he wrote "nothing can be more criminal than the message of the House. If this does not incense Parliament I don't know what will."[36]

The controversy regarding who would pay the governor's salary was an ancient, perennial dispute in Massachusetts politics dating back to the days of Sir William Phips in 1692.[37] Governors requested a permanent salary to be granted to them automatically by the General Court. On the other hand, the Massachusetts legislature preferred a system of annual or semi-annual grants, supplemented by occasional "gifts," to be awarded according to the governor's political performance. For example, Governor Samuel Shute received £1200 for the years 1717 to 1719 "in consideration of the dearness of all necessaries of housekeeping."[38] Later, however, in 1720 the legislature reduced Shute's allowance to £500 following a quarrel concerning the governor's right to approve the choice of speaker. Furthermore, the General Court withheld the money until Shute had signed all the bills that the legislature had requested. Traditionally, the General Court regarded control over the governor's salary as an important right, and jealously defended this privilege over the years. Gradually royal governors accommodated themselves to the General Court's insistence on limiting salary disbursements to annual grants and gifts. By the time of Francis Bernard's administration, royal governors had given up requesting a permanent grant or threatening to solicit a Parliamentary inquiry into the matter.

When Hutchinson acceded to the governorship, however, royal officials had discovered a new way to challenge the General Court's control of the salary. This was the use of revenue legislation to provide a salary fund for crown officials. As a consequence, in 1771, the problem of who paid the governor flared up again. Hutchinson received instructions to draw his salary money from the tea tax collected by the American Board of Customs Commissioners, and to take nothing from the General Court. The legislature predictably insisted on its right to control all taxes and disbursements for the support of the government. Hutchinson equally predictably argued for the right of the king to compensate his governor as he saw fit. He ignored the grants offered by the General Court, thereby arousing the antagonism of the legislature and re-opening this traditional area of conflict.[39] The salary dispute demonstrated an important historic inability by the royal government to force an unacceptable policy on the Massachusetts General Court. Furthermore, this issue illustrated the futility on the part of royal officials in dictating to the provincial legislature. The General Court enjoyed a long history of independent deliberative action in this particular area and continued to resist royal encroachment vigorously.

Meanwhile, governor and legislators wrangled over the Council elections. This dispute reflected the mounting tensions of partisan politics. In spring 1771, Boston's popular party experienced considerable disarray owing to the rift that had developed between John Hancock and Samuel Adams. The disagreement between these two leading patriots resulted from Hancock's belief that Adams's radicalism, particularly regarding the nonimportation movement, damaged the opposition cause in the eyes of some of Boston's whig merchants whose financial support was badly needed. Hutchinson vetoed John Hancock's election to the Council despite pressure from within the court group to alienate Adams by concurring with the choice. "I was much pressed by persons well affected in general to consent to the election of Mr. Hancock" he recorded, "his connections being large which are strongly prejudiced against me for the frequent refusal to accept him in office." He continued: "They assured me [that] he [Hancock] wished to be separated from Mr. Adams, another representative of the Town and an Incendiary equal to any at present in London and, if I would admit him [Hancock] to the Council, they had no doubt there would be an end to the Influence he now has by means of his property in the town of Boston." He later revealed that he "was bound to refuse" Hancock since he had "a principal share in the meeting of the people in Boston."[40]

These two matters of partisan dispute dominated the legislative meeting of 1771. Hutchinson later wrote of the term, "the laws that have passed this session are of no great moment."[41] The House of Representatives rejected a bill to pay for the renovation of the governor's official residence. The governor took his revenge by vetoing a bill to prohibit the importation of slaves on the grounds that the King's instructions to ex-governor Bernard prevented gubernatorial assent to any innovative legislation. There remains little wonder that Hutchinson lamented to his erstwhile mentor Bernard, "I am not able to perfect a plan for accomplishing what I know to be the *one thing needful.* I mean the punishment or prevention of the denial of the authority of parliament over the colonies."[42] The combination of chronic partisan political wrangling, personal dislike of Hutchinson on the part of many of Boston's whigs, and the absence of any clear policy instructions from Britain, ensured that his governorship amounted to little that was positive in the summer of 1771.

While executive and legislature remained deadlocked at Cambridge, a particularly vituperative assault on the governor developed in the radical press. "In Boston," wrote Hutchinson, "they lay nothing to my charge but my bad principles in Government. It would be to no more purpose to reason with them than with an Enthusiast who holds an absurd tenet in Religion."[43] Usually these by now familiar attacks on his character went unanswered, but, by 1771, he acknowledged that public opinion had become far more of a factor in Boston's politics then before. He began to fight back in the newspapers. As he indicated to Bernard, "I have taken much pains to procure writers to answer the pieces in the newspapers. . . . I hope for some good effect."[44] By 1771 he realized that he must attempt to articulate the government's point of view in public if he was to prevail in the struggle for power. This realization, however late in coming, constituted an important departure in Hutchinson's overall political style. However contemptuous of public opinion he remained, he joined the newspaper wars. Moreover, this decision indicated his growing awareness of the necessity to fight the whigs and answer their attacks if he was to survive. Far from being confused or mystified by the radical challenge to royal authority, as Bernard Bailyn has asserted, in 1771 he emerged as an accomplished political force willing to stand up as best he could for his position and convictions.[45]

Boston's radical media inflicted withering personal criticism on Hutchinson throughout the fall and winter of 1771 and into 1772. Usually with specific reference to the seemingly innocuous issues of the governor's and judges' salaries, "Junius Americus," "Candidus," and "Valerius Poplicola" pilloried Hutchinson in particular and the court party generally. Radical writers seized every available opportunity to question his motivations, trustworthiness, and patriotism. Drawing attention to plural office-holding, "Junius Americus" warned that, "your very obsequious Governor Mr.

Hutchinson, . . . He indeed has betrayed their liberties, which he has taught us were so dearly purchased, for the pitiful ambition of being a governor. He has betrayed his country and ruined his character forever." Other members of the Hutchinson-Oliver oligarchy also came in for stringent criticism of their plural office-holding. Arthur Lee who wrote as "Junius Americus" continued, ostensibly for the benefit of Lord Hillsborough, "The perfidy too, of Mr. Oliver, has its reward. . . . The account of Mr. Oliver's promotion [to the lieutenant governorship] is worthy of the attention of the public. It will show to what a consummate degree corruption has arrived under Your Lordship's American Administration."[46]

Samuel Adams, writing as "Candidus," summarized the alleged central concerns of Boston's opposition most succinctly. He wrote, "Kings and Governors may be guilty of treason and rebellion. . . . Nay, what have been commonly called rebellions in one country by the people has been nothing but a manly and glorious struggle in opposition to the lawless power of rebellious Kings and Princes." He continued, "who, being elevated above the rest of mankind, and paid by them only to be their protectors, have been taught by enthusiasts to believe they were authoris'd by God to enslave and butcher them."[47] Here in typically exaggerated and highly personal language Adams warned against the dangers of what he perceived to be the emergence of an unaccountable and uncontrollable governing class.

Perhaps Hutchinson could not quite believe what he read. Demonstrating a capacity for humor which parodied the whig preference for Roman pen names, he wrote in reference to a whig journalist who employed the pseudonym "Vindex," "The name of Vindex . . . is characteristic. I could wish he would add Malignus and Invidius to make his names a little more significant."[48]

The Hutchinson-Oliver plural office-holding oligarchy had monopolized political power in Massachusetts for a long time.[49] By 1771 many critics of royal government were firmly convinced that Hutchinson, along with his friends and family, constituted a real threat to self-government and to traditional forms of political expression that Bostonians especially had long enjoyed in the form of their revered town meeting. Just as Hutchinson was convinced of a radical conspiracy to declare independence from royal government, so Boston's popular party spokespersons believed that court party plural office-holding constituted an omnipresent threat to traditional liberties. Plural office-holding and responsibility for the governor's salary constituted key issues in the ongoing debate between royal government and its popular party opponents concerning the distribution of political power. However, the importance of these whig attacks on Hutchinson reside not in the types of issues that were raised but in the nature of the rhetoric of the assault. Boston's whigs smeared and demonized him to ensure that he would become unacceptable to a critical number of politically active individuals. The merchant-smuggler alliance had resolved to replace him; the creation of a tyrannical symbolic threat to liberty was their method.

In Isaiah Thomas's radical broadsheet *Massachusetts Spy*, as well as in the more established *Boston Gazette*, Boston's literary whigs denounced Hutchinson as "a smoothe and subtle tyrant."[50] Here we see the employment of the highly emotional and symbolic language of slavery and corruption. According to Boston's radicals, he was capable of leading his people "gently into slavery" since he was endowed with the powers of Caesar.[51] "Mucius Scaevola" declared that he was "a ruler independent of the people," by virtue of his crown salary. And that he was a "monster in government; and such a one is Mr. Hutchinson." "I cannot but view him as a usurper," Mucius continued, "and absolutely deny his jurisdiction over his people."[52] All these criticisms claimed far too much for Hutchinson. But the form of the claim, not the content, was what mattered most. For the whig claim to liberty and the maintenance of free institutions to be credible, someone must be presented to threaten these cherished qualities of government. In the important formative era of revolution, when Boston's polemicists were still not ready to attack George III directly, Hutchinson occupied that position.

With the purpose of answering these attacks, Hutchinson and Andrew Oliver established the *Censor* in November 1771 as a newspaper presenting the government view of public affairs in Massachusetts. In the governor's words: "The strange notion of independence was so generally favored that I thought it necessary that people should have a just view of the constitution."[53] Between November 1771, and May 2, 1772, in twenty-five separate issues, the court party published the *Censor* in an attempt to counter the whig interpretation of recent events in the Bay Colony.[54] Although Hutchinson's willingness to present his views for public consideration demonstrated considerable political growth on his part, the *Censor* failed miserably as a propaganda tool. While this organ attempted to debate the whigs within the framework of the well-established country versus court party dialogue, the radical press pursued an entirely different agenda of personal demonization.

The *Censor* contained exclusively political arguments and divorced itself from the concerns of the broader commercial community. As such, the newspaper faced insuperable obstacles in attaining and retaining readers. Since it contained no news or advertisements, there was no point in buying the *Censor* unless one particularly wished to follow the pros and cons of the constitutional debate. Only those predisposed to the court party point of view would purchase the publication. This remains the best explanation for why the tories closed the newspaper down in May 1772, after having had no discernible impact on the enthusiasm of the whig press to continue to advance their cause.[55]

Nevertheless, the *Censor* contained some lively writing usually from Andrew Oliver's pen and constituted a determined, if ultimately unsuccessful, effort by Hutchinson and the court party oligarchy to persuade the public of their solicitude for the best interests of the province and the rectitude of their interpretation of the constitution. In reference to the whig opposition a writer in the *Censor* declared "there are others, may shame mar their cheeks, who for the vain purpose of creating *a temporary importance* to themselves, or from the viler *motive of personal malice and revenge*, take pleasure in producing disorder in the machine of government, and wickedly seek occasion to endanger the shipwreck of the commonwealth."[56]

Overall, however, the constitutional arguments advanced in the *Censor* must have appeared recondite and arcane to the average reader. Furthermore, unlike the whig polemicists, the writers for the *Censor* faced the uphill task of defending Boston's privileged few. Although Boston's whigs overtly catered to the wishes and aspirations of "the people" to participate in politics, the *Censor* predicated many of its legal positions on the assumption that the public was being misled, "intoxicated with the dazzling idea of patriotism and unhappily seduced" by "demagogues" and "mountebanks."[57] According to Hutchinson's royalist newspaper, "murmurs and discontents however groundless, fears and jealousies however ill founded, are still the successful weapons of turbulent demagogues, the honest and illiterate unwarily catch the enthusiasm." The *Censor* continued, "distrust industriously disseminated among the inconsiderate multitude, naturally awakens their [the people's] attention; and when thoroughly alarmed with apprehensions of danger, they submit to the guidance of any Massaniello to shun their imaginary evils." Such a distrustful view of the public, so clearly enunciated, would only have been attractive to those who already subscribed to that position and would win the court party few new working-class supporters.[58]

Similarly, the *Censor* employed the unmistakable tone of the gentleman-politician. "Person, character, and station were the select prey of this matchless political vulture," declared the *Censor*, in reference to the whig scribes "Leonidas" and "Candidus."[59] To fear God and honor the King were accordingly incompatible with the objectives of Boston's whigs; candor and a respect for justice similarly irrelevant to the agenda of the "state desperadoes." In an obvious piece of advice on politics The *Censor* stated, "it is absolutely necessary for the advantage of this Community that men of fortune, probity, and religion, should be elected to office."[60] The writing of the *Censor* implicitly contained respect for class deference and the code of social hierarchy, which was deeply embedded within the worldview of the gentleman-politician. This attitude was a hard sell to the restive, egalitarian, and nationalistic inhabitants of Boston's counting houses, taverns, markets, and waterfronts. Especially when compared with the simplistic moralistic raving of the radical competition.

By the end of 1771, despite the war raging in the newspapers, Hutchinson still had some reason for optimism. Radical political unity seemed to have been temporarily disturbed by the rift between Adams and Hancock. Captain Preston's trial had passed without incident, and the threat of rioting had, for the time being, abated. What was needed now more than ever from the royalist perspective was unequivocal and sensible leadership from Great Britain. "There must be firmness on the part of the Kingdom," asserted Hutchinson to Richard Jackson. "Like all other Countries," he continued, "the body of the people are easily influenced by those who make the greatest regard to their interest and they are carried away with the sounds of Tyranny and Liberty and other big words whereof they do not comprehend."[61] If Britain had designed a coherent plan to re-establish political control over Massachusetts, Hutchinson later recalled, "there was a high degree of probability that such measures would have restored peace to America." Instead, however, "irresolution on the part of government in England tended to strengthen and encourage opposition to it in America."[62]

CHAPTER SEVEN

Hutchinson's Final Humiliation

Thomas Hutchinson began 1772 in high spirits. "Our affairs are not yet in a right state," he observed, "but they are in a better state than they were 2 years ago."[1] As he awaited instructions from England, he appeared particularly delighted at the difficulties of Boston's popular party. "Mr. Hancock, I have reason to think, is upon such terms with his colleagues the Town Representatives that they will not easily be reconciled. When divided we may hope they will be less capable of mischief."[2] He wrote to Lord Hillsborough, again in reference to Hancock: "A gentleman who has assisted them [Boston's radical group] much by his money and by his reputation which his fortune gives him among the people seems to weary of them and I have reason to think is determined to leave them." Elsewhere he recorded that the popular party "is evidently much weakened." He predicted that they would challenge him at the next assembly meeting, but declared that he was "prepared for them" and hoped "to defeat their designs."[3] After proroguing the General Court owing to the absence of instructions from England, Hutchinson wrote with reference to the opposition party, "they mutter," but "all confidence is at an end."[4] By April, he appeared so positive that the influence of Boston's radicals was in decline that he announced confidently, "I have so little to ask of them that no great mischief can arise from their being out of humor."[5] While Samuel Adams and the patriots argued among themselves, Governor Hutchinson communicated with his friends for sponsorship for his undistinguished youngest son Billy, and he patiently awaited further instructions from Britain.

Insight regarding his staid, unimaginative, and fastidious personality can be gathered from brief consideration of the type of advice that he offered to his son following his decision to allow Billy to go to England. The elder man urged his ne'er-do-well youngest to "improve in knowledge and virtue as a way to get himself a benefactor." He wrote to Hillsborough in fawning terms: "My greatest prospect for my son is that he may so accomplish himself as to be worthy of your Lordship's favorable notice." He urged Billy to rely on his father as his only true friend in the world and "to be continually on your guard and to consider the distress it will give me if I should receive any unfavorable account of your conduct." Hutchinson counseled his son to practice "modest inoffensive obliging behaviour" and "to avoid any breach with your fellow traveler." Finally, his paternal advice included the time-honored clichés that many a father has impressed upon unheeding sons: "If you neglect improving the Spring you'll find no fruit in summer nor at harvest time"; and "without labor and application you will acquire nothing valuable." The record reveals that Billy ignored his father's advice and he apparently wasted his time at the University of Edinburgh.[6]

The General Court reconvened, from April 8, to July 14, 1772. After the House and governor had disputed at some length the legality of meeting in Cambridge, the balance of the legislative session revolved around disagreement concerning the origin of the governor's salary.[7] This dispute represented a reprise of the gubernatorial salary debate of 1771.

On June 13, 1772, Hutchinson informed the General Court "that his Majesty has been graciously pleased to make provision for my support, in the station, in which he has thought fit to place me." Furthermore, he explained "as this is judged to be an adequate support, I must conclude it cannot be his Majesty's pleasure, that, without his special permission, which has not yet been signified to me, I should accept of any grant from the province, in consideration of the ordinary government services done, or to be done, by me."[8] In this simple statement the governor infuriated the legislators by indicating that not only would he accept a crown salary but that he would also reject payment from the province. He then adjourned the proceedings for three days until the General Court could reconvene in Boston, a move that he had approved earlier.

In the opinion of Boston's radicals, the acceptance of a crown salary by the governor was dangerous in principle, insulting to the people of

Massachusetts, and completely illegal. On July 10, 1772, a House committee dominated by whigs enthusiastically registered their point of view.[9] In the preamble of the report the House of Representatives unequivocally stated that "the making provision for the support of the Governor of the province, independent of the grants and acts of the General Assembly, is, in the opinion of the committee, an infraction upon the rights granted to the inhabitants, by the royal charter, and in derogation of the constitution."[10] Once again Hutchinson found himself involved in the center of an important political controversy with the opposition party. On this occasion, the ensuing debate produced radical consequences that he did not anticipate.

Hutchinson's attitude toward the House of Representatives' position was to write to Britain for clarification and await further instructions. Meanwhile, as he reported to Thomas Pownall, "government is in a languid state."[11] The problem was the administrative deadlock caused by the disagreement between the governor and the legislature. The disinclination of the customs commissioners to enforce the trade laws exacerbated this atmosphere, along with the noisy silence emanating from the corridors of power in Whitehall.

While the governor awaited his orders from Britain, smuggling continued apace in Massachusetts. "All seem determined to pay as little regard to all the Laws of Trade as possible," Hutchinson observed, "and if let alone will pay none at all. The Officers of the Customs everywhere pretty near alike had rather take their Fees and be quiet than increase the profits of their office by troublesome seizures."[12] In reference to the recent *Gaspée* incident, Hutchinson observed to Lord Hillsborough that the government of Rhode Island could not enforce the law and "must be subservient to the designs of the illicit traders."[13]

The burning of the *Gaspée* came as the culmination of a series of confrontations between Rhode Island businessmen and the customs service. On June 9, 1772, the *Gaspée*, under the command of Lieutenant William Dudingston, ran aground in Narraganset Bay while in pursuit of a suspected smuggler. When word of this misfortune spread, that same evening, a contingent of citizens from Providence found the ship and proceeded to burn it. Two days later Dudingston stood trial in Rhode Island for the illegal seizure of casks of sugar and rum. He was found guilty, and soon dispatched to England to face further charges for losing the ship.

In January 1773, British authorities in Rhode Island appointed a royal commission to inquire into these events. The commission constituted chief justices from New York, New Jersey, and Massachusetts, the judge of the Vice-Admiralty Court in Boston, and Governor Joseph Wanton of Rhode Island. Opponents of British policy railed against the tyrannical implications of this "court of inquisition," and committees of correspondence throughout America warned of the dangers of allowing British authorities to examine the activities of liberty-loving colonists. The commission's report, however, concluded that there was no advance intention of destroying the *Gaspée* and that Rhode Island officials had behaved properly regarding the entire affair. To Hutchinson the failure of the commission constituted more evidence of the inherent weakness of British control in America.

Hutchinson's hope was for explicit and committed leadership from Britain. Instead he received no guidance whatsoever. Even after the *Gaspée* had been destroyed, an incident that he expected would "certainly arouse the British lion which has been asleep these four or five years," Parliament did not respond to colonial acts of provocation.[14]

He attempted to warn his colleagues in government of the dangers of vacillation. "A gentleman who dined with me today" he wrote, "and who is fully acquainted with all the designs and expectations of the Sons of Liberty assures me that they look upon that affair [the *Gaspée* incident] as a test. If Great Britain does nothing, they can go on to measures of independence." His suggestion was that the authorities should "carry a few of those who burned the *Gaspée* to the executioners dock in London."[15] He again complained of press attacks, recording that the whig commentators were "now going to the utmost length . . . in order to raise fresh riots and other disorders."[16] Here resided one of his central concerns regarding the decline of royal government in Massachusetts. He was convinced that an organized conspiracy to declare independence existed and that this must be addressed immediately and forcefully if the dissolution of the empire was to be averted.

Great Britain did not provide the strict and purposeful leadership that Hutchinson hoped for in 1772. Rather, Lord Hillsborough resigned, to be replaced by Lord Dartmouth, and a prolonged period of vacillation and silence ensued. While Hutchinson and the British appeared hamstrung, Boston's whigs were revivified in the fall of 1772. Even as he began the tedious process of educating the incoming Lord Dartmouth about affairs in Massachusetts, the Boston Town Meeting seized the political initiative on November 30, 1772, by publishing a comprehensive statement of colonial rights from the opposition perspective, in a pamphlet entitled *Votes and Proceedings of the Freeholders of Boston*. Hutchinson wrote to Dartmouth that: "The source, My Lord, of all this irregularity is a false opinion broached at the time of the Stamp Act that the people of the colonies are subject to no authority but their own legislatures and that the Acts of Parliament of Great Britain, which is every day in print termed a foreign state, are not obligatory." He continued: "All attempts to punish the publick assertors of this doctrine and other seditious and treasonable tenets deduced from it have failed." Expecting leadership from Dartmouth, he concluded: "Reason and argument have proved insufficient. I know the cause of the distress but am at a loss for a proper remedy."[17]

The Boston Committee of Correspondence prepared the pamphlet entitled *Votes and Proceedings*. This innovative political organization was engineered into existence by Boston's leading whigs both to counter the efforts of the court party and to ensure that the noisy struggle for liberty continued. In Samuel Adams's self-righteous words, the committee was formed "to state the rights of the colonists and of this Province in particular, as Men, as Christians, and as Subjects; to communicate and publish the same to the several Towns in this Province and to the World as the sense of this Town, with the Infringements and Violations thereof that have been, or from time to time may be made—also requesting of each Town a free communication of their Sentiments on the Subject."[18] Eventually the network of Committees of Correspondence crisscrossed the province and constituted an indispensable organizational mechanism devoted to advance the challenge to royal government.

Hutchinson disdained the people comprising Boston's committee. He observed that "some of the worst of them one would not chose to meet in the dark and three or four at least of their correspondence committee are as black hearted fellows as any upon the Globe."[19] However, following publication of the *Votes and Proceedings*, he found himself compelled to address the Committee's concerns and arguments.

In his view, the *Votes and Proceedings*, incorporating as it did a clarion call to the towns throughout Massachusetts to meet and declare their opposition to the policies of his administration, should not go unanswered. The Boston Committee of Correspondence produced the pamphlet ostensibly as a response to the news that Massachusetts judges were to receive crown salaries. This news, combined with the ongoing struggle over the governor's salary, provided a convenient catalyst for renewed whig criticism of Hutchinson and the British.

The most controversial proposal of the *Votes and Proceedings*, however, and the aspect of the pamphlet that most upset Hutchinson, resided in its tendency to radicalize Town Meetings.[20] In his opinion, the *Votes and Proceedings* encouraged the local town meetings to overstep their constitutional authority by assembling to consider matters beyond their jurisdiction. In Hutchinson's view, the purpose of the pamphlet was entirely political, "to bring the several towns and districts into an avowal of independency, and then to bring this avowal . . . into the Assembly." He observed: "The inhabitants of the Town of Boston were the first convened, and certain Resolves [the *Votes and Proceedings*] were prepared, one of which expressly excluded the authority of Parliament in all matters civil or ecclesiastical, another . . . declared against the admission of this authority in all cases whatsoever." Referring to the encouragement of independence which he regarded as the central danger of the pamphlet he continued: "These Resolves were sent to every Town and District in the Province, accompanied with a letter recommending them to consideration. About one third part of the towns and Districts had convened and adopted the Resolves when the General Assembly met, upon a prorogation, at Boston, and the rest, in general, would have followed the example."[21]

Hutchinson correctly perceived the workings of a political revolution in motion. In his view nothing short of independence from British authority appeared to be the objective of Boston's radical activists. He wrote to Lord Dartmouth, who had still not sent any explicit policy instructions from London, "the dispute between the Kingdom and the colonies I have kept as clear of as I could. I have not been forward in proposing measures for restoring us to a state of order . . . the way and manner in which Parliament was to proceed it did not become me to suggest." However, he explained, "a right to independence . . . is more and more asserted every day and the longer such an opinion is tolerated the deeper the root it takes in men's minds and becomes more difficult to eradicate but it must be done or we shall never return to good government and good order."[22] Employing his characteristic tone of self-deprecation and understated modesty, he warned the ministry of the dangers of indecision.

From Hutchinson's perspective Boston's political problems emanated from the activities of a small group of evil people who were determined to lead America to independence at any price. The opponents of royal government corrupted the people, misrepresented the motives of others, and maliciously denigrated English law. Adams, Hancock, Cushing, and the rest threatened Massachusetts with mob rule and denied individuals the right to dispose of their private property as they saw fit.[23] Complete political independence appeared to be the radicals' objective. In the governor's opinion only a firm stand by his superiors in England could prevent this from happening.

Notwithstanding all of his warnings, however, it was still far from clear whether anyone in England attributed any serious weight to his correspondence. From the point of view of the beleaguered governor, Massachusetts appeared to be declaring independence from royal government while Britain temporized. With these thoughts in mind Hutchinson left Boston to spend the Christmas period with his family at his country home in Milton. During this break from public business he prepared a critically important speech that he planned to deliver to an emergency session of the General Court when politics resumed in January 1773.

On January 6, 1773, Hutchinson addressed the Massachusetts General Court. This speech provoked an unprecedented amount of attention being paid to the fundamental political and constitutional problems that plagued Britain's North American empire. The ensuing debate lasted until the end of the legislative session on March 6, and its consequences reverberated throughout the British-American colonies. In the end the divisions between the government and its opponents only deepened; no one appeared convinced of the validity of his opponent's point of view, and in the wake of the confrontation the unfortunate Hutchinson reflected that he would not mind a trip to England if only to escape "the most perverse set of men upon earth."[24]

To some degree the governor was a victim of his own ability to view with clarity the basic political conflicts that were being explored in the Anglo-American world. One reason why this particular speech attracted the interest of observers from Massachusetts to Georgia, and beyond the Atlantic, was his facility in advancing his cautionary philosophy. Whig theorists of the highest caliber, including John Adams, Samuel Adams, Joseph Warren, Joseph Hawley, James Bowdoin, were provoked by Hutchinson to produce their most well-conceived responses.

By directly challenging Boston's whigs to explain themselves, the governor brought almost forty years of traditional political thought to bear. He was unquestionably America's leading royalist public servant and thinker. By engaging Boston's whigs intellectually, he, albeit inadvertently, secured for himself a permanent niche in the narrative of the unfurling American Revolution. However, despite the centrality of his position as America's most articulate loyalist, his stand was not popular with his friends or his enemies. John Adams was correct when he observed in reference to the speech:

> He will not be thanked for this, his ruin and destruction must spring out of it, either from the ministry and Parliament on one hand, or from his countrymen on the other. . . . The Governor's reasoning, instead of convincing the people that Parliament had sovereign authority over them in all cases whatsoever, seemed to convince all the world that Parliament had no authority over them in any case whatsoever. Mr. Hutchinson really made a meager figure in that dispute. He had waded beyond his depth.[25]

Notwithstanding this harsh judgment, Hutchinson demonstrated an impressive understanding of the decline of royal authority in Massachusetts. The explanation as to why he was unable single-handedly to prevent this demise and thereby survive politically clearly resides beyond any weakness of character on his part.

He delivered the speech on January 6, 1773, before the combined houses of the Massachusetts General Court. His reasoning for the address was that the time was ripe for a clear enunciation of the government's position to counter the damage incurred by the court party owing to the success of the *Votes and Proceedings*. As he wrote later with reference to the illegality of the Town Meetings, "The Governor, therefore, was laid under the necessity of calling upon the Assembly to join with him in checking these illegal and unconstitutional proceedings."[26] By the beginning of 1773 Hutchinson concluded that his policy of avoiding "disputing with the assembly upon points which I wished to see the Government in England undertake . . . to determine and settle" had failed.[27] Now he was ready to dispute and argue with Boston's radicals, and his speech constituted the first salvo in this important conflict.

His arguments were simple and familiar. He began by asserting that, according to the 1692 charter which facilitated the establishment of Massachusetts as a royal colony, the settlers "were to remain subject to the supreme authority of Parliament." This admission had not been, according to him, seriously challenged until the Stamp Act. He acknowledged that since "the spirit of liberty breathes through all parts of the English Constitution," local institutions and agencies could legally undertake some decision making which in England would undoubtedly fall under Parliamentary purview. Nevertheless, he maintained, despite some provincial latitude, Parliamentary authority remained unquestioned. "Under this constitution, for more than one hundred years," in the governor's view, "peace and order have been maintained."[28]

He continued by drawing attention to the fact that in the town meetings of 1772 this constitutional model had now been fundamentally challenged. Especially significant were the direct denials of Parliamentary authority which had been placed in town records and published in pamphlets and newspapers. His response to these announcements was to declare that "I know of no arguments, founded in reason, which will be sufficient to support these principles, or to justify the measures taken in consequence of them."[29] He then amplified his reasoning.

The heart of the analysis resided in his interpretation of the nature of the Massachusetts charter. The charter allowed the General Court power to enact any law so long as Parliament concurred. If the latter body disagreed, then the General Court's power ended. Next, Massachusetts citizens were not exempted from Parliamentary authority on the grounds that they were not represented in that body. Rather, since the colonies had historically remained annexes of crown territory, in the governor's view, people in Massachusetts were simply distant subjects virtually represented enjoying essentially the same legal status *vis-à-vis* London as did other similarly distant subjects of English provincial towns such as Leeds, Newcastle, Plymouth, or Manchester.[30]

Furthermore, not all Englishmen enjoyed the same legal rights. In plain language, he stated: "They who claim exemption from acts of Parliament by virtue of their rights as Englishmen, should consider it impossible the rights of English subjects should be the same, in every respect, in all parts of the dominions." By voluntarily leaving England, as their ancestors had, a degree of English political liberty previously enjoyed by virtue of representation had been forfeited. In the governor's words, by "their voluntary removal, they have relinquished for a time at least, one of the rights of an English subject, which they might, if they pleased, have continued to enjoy, and may again enjoy, whensoever they will return to the place where it can be exercised." Hutchinson had little patience for natural rights philosophy, arguing that all governments represent some infringement of natural rights. For the practical gentleman-politician of the school of patronage, ideas such as natural law appeared to be meaningless abstractions.[31]

His final argument was to reiterate a position that he had held privately at least since 1768. He declared in January 1773, "I know of no line that can be drawn between the supreme authority of Parliament and the total independence of the colonies: it is impossible there should be two independent Legislatures in one and the same state." If the colonies were independent, he claimed, they would inevitably fall victim to "one or the other powers of Europe," thereby suffering badly from the rejection of English military protection.[32] For Hutchinson nothing could be worse for America than independence, since whatever authority ensued from rejecting British government would be ephemeral, followed by much worse government at the hands of the Spanish, French, or Dutch.

The governor ended with a note of optimism. His argument was not that British decision making should never be challenged, only that the basis of that authority should not be questioned. All governments occasionally made mistakes, he suggested, and the British Parliament was no exception. "The Acts and doings of authority, will not always be thought just and equitable by all parts of which it consists." However, "the manner of obtaining redress, must be by representations and endeavors, in such ways and forms, as the established rules of the constitution prescribe or allow," and certainly not by denying or renouncing authority, or by refusing to submit to it.[33] Parliamentary decision making had occasionally been misguided. However, Parliament was always benign, ultimately concerned with colonial well-being, and never malevolent. Moreover, the extant system of royal government was perfectly capable of rectifying errors if the people did not tear the fabric of the social contract to pieces with their professions of exemption from Parliamentary authority. He lamented the lawlessness of his day and complained that "the law in some important cases cannot have its course; offenders ordered, by advice of His Majesty's Council, to be prosecuted, escape with impunity, and are supported and encouraged to go on offending; the authority of the government is brought into contempt, and there are but small remains of that subordination, which was once very conspicuous in this colony, and which is essential to a well-regulated state."[34] He concluded by urging the General Court to consider his position with care. He promised to listen to counterproposals with an open mind and indicated that he remained willing to be convinced of another point of view.

By making this speech, and thereby catapulting the Anglo-American constitutional debate once again to the forefront of Massachusetts politics, he hoped he could shock British policy makers from their torpor and force them to justify vigorously their continued authority. To John Pownall Hutchinson confided that "you know I have been begging for measures to maintain the supremacy of Parliament."[35] Now, by taking this aggressive step, even though in the short run the address "has engaged the Faction," he believed he had discharged his duty and acted in such a way as to force the British to support him.[36]

He was wildly mistaken and his objective in making the speech was never realized. In February he informed Lord Dartmouth that he had received a reply to his address that predictably denied Parliamentary authority, however, "upon such principles and such reasoning as must bring great dishonour upon them." He planned a rebuttal that was to be "in so full a manner as would leave them without any room for a rejoinder."[37] At the same time he instructed all justices of the Superior Court not to claim money from the province in salaries since the crown salary would begin in July. In Hutchinson's opinion, although "200 in the House of Representatives voted unanimously the answer to my speech not ten could give any account of what they had done."[38] So long as he remained convinced that Parliamentary authority was only being denied due to the actions of a troublesome opposition minority, he continued to be enthusiastic that he could prevail in the debate that he had invited.[39]

It must have come as a considerable surprise to Hutchinson to receive the news that the government in Britain was not particularly pleased with his new assault on the opposition party in Massachusetts. Apparently, unbeknown to him, Lord Dartmouth's overall strategy in dealing with Massachusetts had been to leave well enough alone. This was the reason for his deliberate policy of silence since he took over in August 1772. It was Dartmouth's conviction that Anglo-American disagreement would abate so long as the basic causes remained unexplored. Now Hutchinson had stirred things up again, and Dartmouth was upset. As Benjamin Franklin recorded in a letter from Britain to Thomas Cushing, "If he [Hutchinson] intended, by reviving that Dispute, to recommend himself here, he has greatly missed his Aim; for the Administration are chagrin'd with his Officiousness, their Intention having been to let all Contention subside . . . They are now embarras'd by his Proceedings." Franklin continued, "Yesterday I had a conversation with Lord D[artmouth] . . . what Difficulties says he, that Gentlemen [Hutchinson] has brought us all by his Imprudence!—tho' I suppose he meant well."[40] By the end of March, Hutchinson's enthusiasm of the previous month had evaporated. "I am utterly at a loss what would be most expedient," he wrote to an unknown correspondent. By April, 1773, he again recorded that "the newspapers are as abusive and seditious as ever" and that "reason and argument have no weight."[41]

Hutchinson explored his own frame of mind following his unsuccessful attempt to vanquish the popular party. He did so in a long letter which he decided not to send to Lord Dartmouth, his governmental superior in Britain. After reiterating his opposition to the Stamp Act, he traced the development of what he saw as an independence movement, and eventually concluded that he now doubted that Parliament could do anything to reverse the trend. He concluded, "I must humbly pray that His Majesty will be pleased to appoint such person to the command of the Province in my stead." "I must beg your Lordship's favour and interest," the now thoroughly discouraged Hutchinson continued, "that I may quit the Government without dishonour and that provision may be made for me equal to what I parted with to take the trust upon me." This letter concluded with the sentence, "I humbly pray His Majesty's leave of absence and directions that I may have a passage on board one of the Ships under Admiral Montagu's command which may be ordered home."[42]

Privately then, by the beginning of June 1773, he was ready to admit defeat. He thought he had done his duty to the home government and discharged his gubernatorial responsibility. He had attempted to find a reasonable solution to the ongoing problems of the Anglo-American empire. His efforts had met only with a renewed avalanche of radical criticism. By the end of June 1773, this defeat had become a matter of public record, owing to the procurement and publication by Boston's whig press of a number of letters that Hutchinson had written to Thomas Whately several years earlier.

In June 1773, more bad news descended on Hutchinson's hapless administration. On June 14, he wrote, "The clerk [of the House] informed me that there had been put into his hands a number of letters wrote by persons of rank in America . . . and they were read." "They have been represented as highly criminal," he concluded lugubriously.[43] In an incident that almost exactly replicated the fate of Francis Bernard in 1769, Boston's whigs procured and publicized several of Hutchinson's private letters. Six letters were published in 1773, all written by him to Thomas Whately between June 1768, and January 1769.[44]

The General Court probably received these letters sometime in May 1773. A closed session of the legislature read them on June 2. The pamphlet containing the first edited version of the letters for public consumption appeared approximately two weeks later. This publication contained six letters from Hutchinson to Whately, four from Oliver, and one each from Charles Paxton and Nathaniel Rogers. One additional letter from Hutchinson to the royalist judge Robert Auchmuty was also enclosed.

Although he did not know it at the time, the letters had been sent to Thomas Cushing by Benjamin Franklin who, in June 1773, acted as an unofficial agent from Massachusetts in London. Franklin wrote to Cushing: "As to the letters I communicated to you, tho' I have not been able to obtain Leave to take copies or publish them, I have permission to let the Originals remain with you, as long as you may think it of any use to have them in your Possession."[45]

Later, the Reverend Samuel Cooper, who was pastor of the pro-whig Brattle Street Church and whose brother William was the clerk of the lower house, informed Franklin of Boston's reaction to the letters. Cooper wrote, "upon the first appearance of the letters in the House, they voted by a majority of one hundred and one to five, that the design and tendency of them were to subvert the constitution, and introduce arbitrary power. Their committee upon this matter reported this day a number of resolutions, which are to be printed by tomorrow morning." Cooper further reflected with obvious approval:

> Nothing could have been more seasonable than the arrival of these letters. They have had great effect; they make deep impressions wherever they are known; they strip the mask from the writers, who, under the professions of friendship to their country, now plainly appear to have been endeavoring to build themselves and their families upon its ruins . . . the confidence reposed in them by many is annihilated; and the administration must soon see the necessity of putting the provincial power of the crown into other hands.[46]

Hutchinson's pro-British politics were of course well known to the Boston political class long before the publication of his correspondence with Whately. Nevertheless, the public impact of this demonstration, in direct terms and for all the world to see, of the inner workings of imperial administration clearly left a deep and lasting impression on the Boston political scene. Gentlemen in opposition to royal authority who were directly involved in politics, and ordinary people alike, must have been electrified as they read "keep secret everything I write until we are in a more settled state." Publication of the letters seemed to verify and vindicate long-standing whig arguments accusing Hutchinson of duplicity, self-aggrandizement, and excessive secrecy. The letter dated January 20, 1769, particularly damaged his reputation and credibility as a trustworthy spokesperson for American interests since it contained the inflammatory sentence: "There must be an abridgement of what are called English liberties."[47]

"These cool projectors and speculators in politics will ruin this country," John Adams ruefully declared in reference to Hutchinson and his court party oligarchy. Adams, on the verge of acquiring public office for the first time, partly in response to the furor created by the letters, lamented; "Bone of our bone; born and educated among us? Mr. Hancock is deeply affected; is determined, in conjunction with major Hawley, to watch the vile serpent."[48] The event of the publication of Hutchinson's letters brought the whigs together, galvanized opposition activists, and mobilized public opinion against the governor. Here at last was the smoking gun that Boston's radicals had searched for in their long struggle to depose Hutchinson. In a matter of days the General Court passed a resolution requesting the governor's removal from office along with his lieutenant governor Andrew Oliver.

Hutchinson, understandably, was outraged by what he considered to be the audacity of the legislature in demanding his removal. With genuine remorse he wrote to his erstwhile governmental superior Sir Francis Bernard, "it mortifies me to think the propriety of what I have done is questioned." He denied that his letters indicated evidence of a conspiracy. For example, he stated, " . . . by every maladversion which the talents of the party in each house could produce they have raised the prejudices of the people against me and it is generally supported all the writers [Hutchinson, Oliver, Rogers, and Auchmuty] were concerned in one plan tho' I suppose no one of them ever saw or knew the contents of the letters of any of the other unless by accident."[49] Bernard probably read these words with a familiar feeling since he had been similarly traduced and exposed by Boston's wily radicals.

Hutchinson mistakenly blamed the disaster on the influence of supporters of the radical American cause in England. "The party here say they do nothing without directions" he indicated on one occasion, while on another he stated, "This plot, I have no doubt originated in England. The leaders here give out that they take no step without advice or direction from England." He blamed the disaster with some justification on a lack of guidance from Parliament, lamenting that, "could I have known what was expected from me I certainly would have conformed to it." Finally, predictably, he attributed the collapse of his ability to govern to the malevolent ambitions and constant scheming of his popular party opponents. "They sometimes own that they have no objection to me except that I stop them in their career," suggested the disgruntled Hutchinson, "and the only chance they have is by worrying me out of Government." To another close correspondent he confided, "they have certainly managed this affair with very great art as well as by sticking at no falsehoods ever so glaring. . . any attempt by me to support government will meet with much greater opposition than it ever has done." He continued gloomily "I have withstood them as long as I could but I am now left without any support in the Province. It was not in the power of human wisdom to guard against this last villainy." On another occasion he noted, "I pity the poor people who suffer themselves to be duped by a few men who seem to drive things to the utmost extremity against all connexion with the kingdom and never to be easy til they have a Governor who will join with them."[50] For Hutchinson here was proof of his long-standing contention that independence from royal authority constituted the ultimate objective of a politically ambitious minority.

By the mid-summer of 1773 he was ready to retire, convinced that he could do no more to resist the conspiracy for independence. Although he remained convinced that his letters demonstrated no maleficence on his part, he recognized that he could not significantly influence either public opinion or, perhaps more importantly, opinion within the General Court to that effect. While refusing to admit to having done anything wrong, by mid-July he eagerly anticipated being replaced, "more than a war horse feels when his heavy Accoutrements are to be taken off and he sees a quiet Stable or Pasture just by him."[51] The publication of his letters, and the attendant public denunciation, disgusted the private and proper gentleman-politician. In August 1773, Hutchinson wrote to Lord Hillsborough, no longer in office but still an influential figure, for help, requesting that "before my removal I humbly hope, however, I shall be honorably acquitted and that I shall not be left wholly without imployment and support in advanced life, for my private fortune is not sufficient unless I sink below the moderate living I had always been used to before I came to the chair." He also wrote: "If by the arts of my enemies or from any other cause my interest is lessened with the Administration I would not wish to continue in so difficult a service much longer and I would endeavour to obtain some provision for my future support."[52] Up to the very end of his career he manipulated the patronage system as best he could.

Dismal as things appeared for Hutchinson and the court party in August, however, one more great political confrontation remained to be endured. Despite some minor indications through the early fall of 1773 that the power of Boston's opposition group was waning, by November the storm clouds of political conflict were again organizing above Hutchinson's ill-fated administration.

In early November 1773, Thomas Hutchinson's merchant sons, Thomas, Jr., and Elisha, received an ominous invitation from, "the freemen of the province."[53] The younger Hutchinsons had been identified as consignees of the tea belonging to the East India Company and earmarked to be sold in Boston. Popular party politicians, however, had decided that this was an issue upon which British legislation could again be directly challenged. Crowd action and intimidation of the consignees constituted a central element of the radical challenge, as the threatening note to the Hutchinson family clearly indicated. Boston's radical popular party employed a politicized crowd to invite the Hutchinson brothers to appear publicly to formally resign their responsibilities as tea consignees. "Fail not at your peril" were the mysterious words concluding the anonymous missive to the Hutchinson brothers.

When Parliament adopted the Tea Act in May 1773, it inadvertently threatened the illicit business of a significant group of Boston merchants who routinely smuggled Dutch tea into the Boston marketplace. Hutchinson wrote extensively in his correspondence about this issue, clearly identifying that Britain's failure to withdraw the tea duty, when the other Townshend Duties were retracted in 1770, helped to make smuggling economically viable. His unequivocal position on this issue was that Britain should withdraw the tea duty. "I know not what reason may make it necessary to continue the Duty on Tea," he wrote, "but I think the repeal of it . . . is necessary to prevent disorders in the colonies."[54]

Patriot smugglers, a politically radical element among Boston's merchants, were behind this challenge to the Tea Act. Other structural economic difficulties drove this direct conflict with British political authority. During the period following the collapse of nonimportation, there were still too many merchants in Boston for the town's commerce to support. Competition was tight and prices were falling. Moreover, debts to British suppliers weighed heavily on the books in many Boston counting houses. These important and persistent economic factors informed and shaped the radical political assault on British legislative authority constituted by Boston's response to the Tea Act.

Newspaper propaganda and organized political crowd action played vital roles in tea crisis politics. Hutchinson was probably correct when he wrote that when news of the Tea Act first arrived in Boston, "the body of the people were pleased with the prospect of drinking tea at less expense than ever."[55] Nevertheless, by framing the act as a dangerous precedent for government-sanctioned monopolies, the *Massachusetts Spy* and the *Boston Gazette* began a campaign to convince their readership that the Tea Act represented far more than innocuous and legitimate economic management.[56] Soon the familiar radical contention arose that the Tea Act and, by implication, any Bostonians associated with its enforcement constituted part of a dire conspiracy to subvert colonial commerce and choke colonial liberties. Behind these catastrophic predictions for the future lay the economic self-interest of the smugglers, combined with the political demands of Boston's radicals, who were always on the lookout for an issue upon which to challenge Hutchinson's claim to political pre-eminence.[57]

Mobilization of the Boston crowd proved to be the radicals' trump card as the confrontation over the Tea Act moved from the pages of the newspapers to the streets and warehouses of Boston's waterfront. Citing the authority of the North End Caucus, an important collection of popular party activists including Samuel Adams, Joseph Warren, John Adams, erstwhile Loyal Nine members (see Chapter 3) and Dutch smugglers William Molineux and William Dennie, a crowd visited consignee Richard Clarke's warehouse to intimidate this potential seller of British tea into submission. On November 3, a crowd of one to two hundred people collected outside Hutchinson's house, later moving on to Clarke's residence where they broke windows and doors in an effort to persuade the unfortunate consignees to resign.[58]

The first ship containing the controversial East India Company tea arrived in Boston on Sunday, November 28, 1773. The *Dartmouth*, owned by Joseph Rotch and Son, docked in Boston's inner harbor while the captain filed a cargo report with the customs house. Hutchinson now faced the central legal dilemma of the entire controversy. The Massachusetts Council quickly declared its opposition to landing the tea, so the governor could expect no assistance from this now whig-dominated body. His choices were either to order the return of the tea to England, illegal under existing regulations and potentially financially disastrous for the consignees; or, to order the tea to be landed, thereby risking the anger of the popular party and the certain violence of their thousands of frenzied supporters. Hutchinson could have defused the crisis by overriding the Council and the customs service by issuing a permit to allow the ship to return to England. However, by this time he was in intransigent mood since he believed that unless the British authorities took a firm stand they would be forced to look on helplessly as the empire crumbled. While he contemplated these unenviable alternatives, John Hancock supervised an armed guard on Griffin's Wharf to prevent a clandestine landing of the *Dartmouth's* cargo.

As if the situation were not dramatic enough, and Hutchinson's dilemma not sufficiently complex, British law imposed a twenty-day limit on cargoes filed with the customs house before they became liable for seizure by His Majesty's authorities and sold at public auction to recover potentially lost trade duties. Boston's warring political factions had until December 18 to resolve their quandary.

Little progress toward a moderate resolution of the tea crisis ensued during the twenty-day grace period. The tea consignees retreated to the confines of Castle William, fearful for their personal safety in Boston. Boston's radical patriots, advancing the agenda of the smugglers, held raucous meetings of the Body, denounced the Tea Act, and resolved that no duted tea would ever be landed in Boston. Governor Hutchinson remained at his country home in Milton and contemplated his conviction that "there is no tyranny so great as that which is exercised by the people when they take the government from the hands of those who are entrusted with it by the constitution."[59]

On December 16, Hutchinson refused a last-ditch appeal made by Joseph Rotch for permission to allow the *Dartmouth* to leave Boston harbor. When Rotch returned to Boston, the news quickly spread of his failure to convince the governor to send the tea back to London. According to Hutchinson, the people awaiting the news at Boston's Old South Meeting House, "gave a loud huzza and many of them cried out a mob, a mob, and broke up in great numbers and ran to the wharf where three of the vessels having on board 340 chests of tea lay and in about two hours the whole of it was hoisted out and thrown into the dock."[60]

"It appears to have been a concerted plan" was Hutchinson's laconic observation upon the evening's events.[61] The next morning an ecstatic John Adams recorded in his diary:

> Last night three cargoes of Bohea tea were emptied into the seas. . . . This is the most magnificent movement of all. There is a dignity, a majesty, a sublimity, in this last effort of the patriots, that I greatly admire. The people should never rise without doing something to be remembered, something notable and striking. This distruction of the tea is so bold, so charming, so firm, intrepid and inflexible, and it must have so important consequences, and so lasting, that I cannot but consider it as an epocha in history.[62]

*

Following the tea party the beleaguered governor convened an emergency Council meeting at Cambridge. His objective was to begin an official investigation of what had happened but the Council disagreed over what strategy to follow. He recorded pessimistically that four members wanted the attorney general to launch an inquiry while three councilors preferred to issue a proclamation to reward informers. The governor and the Council could not arrive at any agreement, since they were unable to find anyone willing to give an account of the evening's actions. Hutchinson informed Lord Dartmouth that he doubted any prosecution would ever be possible.[63]

Hutchinson refused to accept any personal responsibility for the destruction of the tea. In his view he had done nothing to provoke the tea party and declared, "I shall have nothing to charge myself with on account of this mad action of the people seeing I could not by any justifiable means have prevented it." In his opinion he was legally prohibited from having the *Dartmouth* removed from the dock and placed "in the stream" against the wishes of the owner. For the governor to take this action required the Council's approval and "this I endeavoured to obtain but could not."[64] He could have unilaterally issued a permit to allow the tea ships to return to England. His frame of mind at the time however prevented him from taking such an action. Since in Hutchinson's view this crisis represented another clear challenge to the fundamental right of the royal authorities to govern Massachusetts, he resolved to allow the confrontation to run its course. As he later communicated to Francis Bernard: "It would have given me much more painful reflection if I had saved it [the tea] by any concession to a lawless and highly criminal assembly of men to whose proceedings the loss must be consequentially attributed and the probability is that it was a part of their plan from the beginning."[65] By the time of the tea crisis, Hutchinson believed that the British government should take a stand or concede independence to Boston's radicals. Obviously he had tired of assuming all the personal responsibility for the flaws and weaknesses of royal government in England's most troublesome colony.

He had lost faith in the ability of the British to govern Massachusetts by the end of 1773. In the opinion of this aging gentleman-politician, the Boston Tea Party constituted one more example of the orchestrated assault upon the natural governors of the colony by a power-hungry faction that had been in operation since before the Stamp Act. He had done everything in his power to resist the radical forces pushing toward independence. As he waited for official permission to take a leave of absence in order to go to

England to defend his record and secure his future, he concluded that he was now powerless. "The Governor himself," he wrote in the third person, "and his situation is so unfortunate that by discovering his disposition he exposes himself to the most illiberal abuse of the most abandoned part of the people and has nothing more in his power than to refuse his assent to any acts which they think proper for their purpose."[66] When he heard of the unfortunate experience of the customs official John Malcolm, who was tarred and feathered by an angry crowd, Hutchinson observed pessimistically: "There is no spirit left in those who used to be friends of the government to support them or any others who oppose the prevailing power."[67] For the discouraged and disconsolate governor, there now seemed little alternative except to prepare for his departure.

In February 1774, Hutchinson wrote to Lord Dartmouth, "Despairing of success in any further attempts for His Majesty's service, I had determined to avail myself of the leave given me to go to England, and was preparing for my passage with a view of being there before the middle of April."[68] He continued, with reference to the health of his royalist associate and brother-in-law, Andrew Oliver, "but, before it would have been possible for me to embark, the Lieutenant Governor had declined so much in health, that I was obliged to put a stop to the provision which was making for my accommodation on board a large merchant ship at Casco Bay bound to Bristol; the physicians pronouncing his case very hazardous from a bilious disorder."[69] It is convincing testimony to Hutchinson's extreme sense of duty to office and loyalty to his family that he was willing to postpone his departure because of Andrew Oliver's illness. Oliver had, like Hutchinson, experienced harassment and personal vilification at the hands of Boston's popular party. He would not abandon him or his brother Peter, now that Andrew was dying.

Andrew Oliver was a few years older than Hutchinson, and he had spent most of his early life in business with his younger brother Peter. Representative of the gentleman-politician ethos, embodying as it did an aristocratic obligation to serve the public, Oliver occupied a wide range of offices. From 1737 until 1764, he concerned himself primarily with town affairs, although he also found time to serve as a temporary justice on the Superior Court, provincial secretary, and member of the Council.

John Adams wrote that Oliver was one of "the original conspirators against the public liberty, since the conspiracy was first regularly formed and began to be executed in 1763 or 1764."[70] This point of view helps explain why he was so ill-treated during the Stamp Act period. Following a highly unpopular public association with the hated Jared Ingersoll, Connecticut's stamp agent, Oliver suffered public humiliation and some property damage in August and December of 1765.

As the Stamp Act rioting receded into memory, Oliver developed very similar beliefs to those of Hutchinson regarding the affairs of Massachusetts. He believed Bostonians were being deluded by the sons of violence. He welcomed troops to Boston, and he favored crown salaries for the executive branch. He disapproved of smuggling and of crowd intimidation. According to one newspaper, Oliver was an informer to the hated customs service. Above all Oliver believed that "an order of Patricians and Esquires" comprising "all men of good fortune or good landed estates" should govern Massachusetts.[71]

Throughout the 1760s and early 1770s Oliver stood accused by Boston's popular party of transmitting "secret" information to Britain as well as supporting and endorsing the growing tyranny that threatened patriotic Americans.[72] Oliver became lieutenant governor when Hutchinson assumed the governorship in March 1771, and he held that post until his death on March 3, 1774.

After Andrew Oliver's funeral on March 8, 1774, which was a rowdy affair owing to the disruptive behavior of certain radical elements in the crowd observing the proceedings, Hutchinson again applied himself to the task of preparing for his departure. While he waited for the arrival of his replacement who turned out to be General Thomas Gage, he made his plans from Milton, and rarely ventured into Boston. General Gage was the commanding general of the British army in North America in 1774. His appointment as governor was supposed to be temporary while his predecessor traveled to England.[73]

Hutchinson officially relinquished his authority to Gage on May 13, 1774. By the end of that month, he was ready to sail to England along with his daughter Peggy and his son Elisha. The deposed governor and his family boarded the *Minerva* on June 1, 1774. He would never again set foot in Massachusetts. He later recalled wistfully that, "any marks of respect from the council and house of representatives, or from the inhabitants of Boston collectively, were not to be expected upon the governor's leaving the province. They would have been the contrast of all the treatment, which the controversy he had been engaged in had occasioned from his first taking the chair."[74]

CHAPTER EIGHT

Exile

"Old trees do not thrive when transplanted," wrote Thomas Hutchinson to an old friend on December 31, 1765. Those words were written during the months of the Stamp Act crisis when his political position seemed in dire jeopardy. Hutchinson weathered that particular storm without needing to leave Massachusetts, and he managed to retain his authority until the disastrous events of 1773 forced him into exile. Now, from June 1774 onward, he was able to test this belief as he began his period of residence in Great Britain. His observation from the year of the Stamp Act crisis proved correct. He was always uncomfortable with life in England. What began as a temporary leave of absence became a period of permanent political isolation and personal tragedy. He died in 1780 and was buried in Croydon near London.[1]

Hutchinson's last six years of life, his period of exile in Britain, was a time of continued partisan persecution and political struggle. In Parliament, in Boston's newspapers, and in the person of Josiah Quincy, Jr., his actions and reputation continued to be assailed by political opponents, despite his physical removal from Boston. In practical terms, his public life in Massachusetts terminated as soon as he set foot on the *Minerva* to sail for England. Peace and reconciliation between the royal authorities and Boston's radicals had proven elusive objectives while Hutchinson was resident governor of Massachusetts. These worthy goals would be all the more difficult to achieve as an absentee governor in London. The revolutionary government formally prohibited Hutchinson from returning in July 1779. Long before this date, however, it was clear that he would never again wield significant political influence in Massachusetts. His status as a major public servant dwindled and diminished with every passing month of residence in London.

Upon arrival in England, Hutchinson almost immediately received the opportunity to represent himself and his actions personally before George III.[2] On July 1, 1774, the King, accompanied by Lord Dartmouth, asked the weary Bostonian a variety of incisive and broad-minded questions about Massachusetts politics, personalities, and colonial American culture. This interview constituted the high-water mark of Hutchinson's potential for political influence in Britain. Despite the hundreds of letters he wrote subsequently, all the royal *levées* he attended in the next six years, and the innumerable efforts he made to influence American affairs, he never came so close to the center of British political decision making again.

In 1774 Hutchinson wrote optimistically: "My reception here exceeded everything I could imagine." Similarly, in July 1774, he stated that "a great number of persons of the first rank are continually calling upon me."[3] This attention did not last, however, and by April 1776, he realized that: "We Americans are plenty here and very cheap. Some of us at first coming, are apt to think of ourselves of importance, but other people do not think so, and few of us if any are much consulted, or enquired after."[4] He even encouraged his friends no longer to address him as "His Excellency," since in Britain such a salutation only incurred ridicule. Despite his honorary degree from Oxford, received in July 1776, and the offer of a baronetcy which he refused, Hutchinson's political influence was minimal by early 1776.[5]

He missed his great opportunity to influence British policy making by appearing too reticent during his critical interview with George III. King George asked Hutchinson for his opinion of how Americans received the Boston Port Act which the monarch had signed into law on March 31, 1774. The measure completely closed the post of Boston, prohibiting all shipping except those vessels carrying food and firewood. Even these ships were liable to search by customs officials of the Salem district, and had to be accompanied by Boston customs officials and armed force. Finally, under the terms of this act Boston was not to be re-established as a port until it paid for the tea, and until the governor certified that it had compensated the customs officers who had suffered damages during the riots.[6]

Along with this inquiry the king solicited Hutchinson's opinion about the Virginia resolution that had been issued in response to the Boston Port Act. The exiled governor's opportunity to register unambiguously his disapproval of both the Port Act and the negative response it provoked resided in these two questions. Whether because of fatigue, as Britain's graceless monarch kept the elderly Bostonian standing throughout the interview which lasted for more than two hours, or an excess of deference, he answered vaguely, and King George somehow misconstrued his response to be one of approval. Later in the day, George wrote to Lord North, "I have seen Mr. Hutchinson, late Governor of Massachusetts, and am well now convinced they will soon submit. He owns the Boston Port Bill has been the only wise and effectual method."[7]

In fact, Hutchinson firmly opposed the Boston Port Bill as well as the New England Restraining Act which followed in March, 1775. According to his recollection of the conversation, he gave no such positive endorsement of either the Boston Port Bill or Virginia's response to it. Later, throughout his diary entries and letters, he consistently registered his opposition to the Boston Port Act and to subsequent Coercive Acts. He wrote to General Thomas Gage in July 1774, regarding Boston's maritime businesses, "that it would make me happy, if in any way consistent with His Majesty's honour, I might be instrumental, whilst I remained in England, to obtaining their relief." To his friend Thomas Flucker, a future loyalist who still resided in Boston, he stated that: "I made it my chief object to represent matters so as to obtain relief for the Town of Boston on the easiest terms."[8]

During his critical interview with George III, Hutchinson failed to communicate his negative assessment of the Boston Port Act. His degree of influence diminished in the months and years following this critical interview. As the Anglo-American crisis became more intense, he became increasingly marginalized in the areas of both policy assessment and formulation.

Besides the important missed opportunity in the interview with George III, more obviously partisan factors contributed further to Hutchinson's political isolation throughout his period of exile. His opponents discovered more personal letters at Milton in 1775 and published them in various organs of the whig press throughout the following year. Cleverly and tendentiously edited by William Gordon, these new letters allegedly demonstrated how he had plotted against the liberties of Massachusetts citizens while governor. In Hutchinson's estimation these articles were guilty of "torturing his words to an unnatural sense and meaning totally different from what they were intended to convey."[9] It must have been extremely painful for him to be forced to witness his reputation being further besmirched without any chance of representing his version of events. By the middle of 1775, when Boston's public consumed this new material, he enjoyed almost no political power. Dissemination of the material was obviously a partisan political action designed to discredit what was left of his memory. By thoroughly dishonoring his career as a public servant, those who replaced him in positions of political leadership gained increased legitimacy in the eyes of the Massachusetts populace.

The decision to dispatch Josiah Quincy, Jr., to London represented an additional partisan political measure to neutralize and marginalize the exiled governor. Quincy arrived in London in November 1774, and spent most of his stay undermining Hutchinson's position on the British political scene.[10] He concurred with the disgruntled customs inspector Jonathan Williams that the British Ministry followed Hutchinson's advice. Thomas Pownall confided in an interview with Quincy that "America has not a more determined and inveterate enemy than Governor Hutchinson." Quincy visited whomever he could in Britain to outweigh and offset whatever influence he believed Hutchinson exerted. He suggested to Lord North that the last civilian governor's influence constituted "gross misrepresentation and falsehood."[11] When North intimated that perhaps Britain's advisers had made honest mistakes, Quincy responded, "it would be happy if none of those who had given accounts relative to America had varied from known truth, from worse motives." In an interview with Lord Dartmouth Quincy asserted: "I was convinced that the British and American controversy would be much sooner and much more equitably settled if it was not for the malevolent influence of a certain Northern personage now in Great Britain."[12] This was a clear reference to Hutchinson whom Quincy obviously sought to make the solitary scapegoat for the crisis that his whig colleagues had engineered.

Opposition and criticism from British whigs in Parliament constituted another debilitating source of pressure exerted upon Hutchinson throughout his period of exile. His tenure and performance while governor of Massachusetts soon became an issue of partisan political conflict in the House of Commons. As the imperial crisis grew, and both American and British resolve stiffened, he observed that it was "strange to what length party spirit carries men." In a debate late in 1774, Lords Richmond, Camden, and Shelburne all made speeches critical of Hutchinson's gubernatorial performance. Later, in response to criticism of him offered in another Parliamentary session, he published a nineteen-page reply to a hostile speech made by George Johnstone.[13] Even in exile Hutchinson continued to struggle with the vicissitudes of party politics and personal attacks.

On a more personal level Hutchinson's years of exile in Britain were not happy ones. Although accompanied by numerous family members and never short of money, he was homesick.[14] He moved residences frequently and often appeared unsettled and ill at ease in his new surroundings. "My thoughts day and night are upon New England," he wrote on October 1774, and "with all our Gaiety we live as much in the New England way as ever we can, and I have not missed either Church or Meeting any Sunday since I have been in England except one, when bad weather and a cold kept me at home . . . and I can with good truth assure you that I had rather live at Milton than at Kew." Elsewhere Hutchinson stated: "New England is wrote upon my heart in as strong characters as Calais was upon Q. Mary's." After visiting Lord Hardwicke's sumptuous residence at Wimpole Hall in Cambridgeshire, Hutchinson recorded: "This is the high life; but I would not have parted with my humble cottage at Milton for the sake of it."[15]

Occasionally he registered his disgust at what appeared to him to be the corruption endemic to English politics and the callousness of everyday life. He seemed shocked at the uncaring behavior of the rich when he witnessed an accident as a carriage ran over a child.[16] In the political sphere he noted that Lord Barrington, secretary of state for the colonies in November 1774, justified his political survival by comparing "the state to a great plum-pudding which he was so fond of that he would never quarrel with it, but should be for taking a slice as long as there was any left."[17]

On another occasion he observed: "I am astonished at seeing so little concern upon the minds of so great a part of the people—I might almost say all, when it appears to me that the nation is in such imminent hazard of some grand convulsion." After having been angered by a speech by Lord Camden that was critical of his stewardship of affairs in Massachusetts, Hutchinson stated that "attending two or three debates in the House of Lords has lessened the high opinion I had formed of the dignity of it when I was in London before."[18]

Overall, he appeared disillusioned with English life, and his reflections became increasingly nostalgic or emotionally introverted. On August 16, 1777, he wrote: "In this kind of life the days and nights pass incredibly swift, and I am six months older and nearer to my own death . . . and it appears like the dream of a night." Concerning nostalgia for New England, he recorded: "I assure you that I had rather die in a little country farm house in N. England, than in the best nobleman's seat in Old England."[19] These reflections directly contradict the portrait painted of him by the whigs as a luxury-loving placeman, eager to emulate his English superiors.

His unhappiness increased considerably following the death of his youngest daughter Peggy in September 1777. In his diary he confessed: "No distress since the death of her dear mother has equalled this." Later, in February 1780, he again bore the painful loss of a child when twenty-seven-year-old Billy died. He stated "I could not help taking a look at his dead countenance, which I wished I had not." Before his own demise, Hutchinson endured considerable personal tragedy in matters quite removed from his public career. It was not surprising that by March 1780, as his own health was failing and his days reduced to testing his strength and "hoping my distemper was going off," that he noticed "My imagination always takes the dark side."[20]

"Governor Hutchinson is dead," announced the Boston *Independent Chronicle* in January 1781, in an obituary composed by John Adams, who was then the American representative to the Netherlands.[21] According to Adams, avarice and ambition, combined with blindness to anything opposed to his point of view were the culprits in explaining Hutchinson's demise. Elsewhere Adams wrote of him: "Fled, in his old age, from the detestation of a country, where he had been beloved, esteemed, and admired, and applauded with exaggeration—in short where he had been everything from his infancy—to a country where he was nothing . . . . I know he was ridiculed by the courtiers. They laughed at his manners at the *levée*, at his perpetual quotation of his brother Foster, searching his pockets for letters to read to the king, and the king turning away from him with his head up etc."[22]

At the end of his life Hutchinson's descent was complete. In the eyes of his contemporaries he had become a pathetic caricature of his former self, compelled to make a fool of himself in England, "abhorred by the greatest men, and soundest part of the nation, and rejected, if not despised by the rest."[23] By the time of his death he was almost completely dispossessed. George Washington owned Hutchinson's green coach, James and Mercy Otis Warren were about to move into the house that he had built at Milton, and his American property was soon to be auctioned to the highest bidder. Few in America disputed Arthur Lee's point of view which he expressed in a letter that congratulated the Warrens on acquiring Hutchinson's comfortable house at Milton: "It has not always happened that the forfeited seats of the wicked have been filled with men of virtue. But in this corrupt world it is sufficient that we have some examples of it for our consolation."[24]

As Hutchinson endured his final years in England, he observed many of the political certainties he had accepted for his entire adult life melt into air. One principle remained, however. Hutchinson knew instinctively, as all politicians must, that personal ambition and self-interest, the drive to exercise power by one group over another, would always remain a constant and critical factor in public life. As the aging ex-governor recorded wistfully in his diary, "it is sometimes a matter of painful admiration to see how much trouble clever people will take to make black look white and white look black."[25]

Notes

NOTES TO THE PREFACE AND ACKNOWLEDGMENTS

1. Bernard Bailyn, *The Ordeal of Thomas Hutchinson* (Cambridge: Belknap Press, 1974). Other major treatments of Hutchinson are: James K. Hosmer, *The Life of Thomas Hutchinson* (Cambridge: Riverside Press, 1896); James H. Stark, *The Loyalists of Massachusetts and the Other Side of the American Revolution* (Boston: James H. Stark, 1907); Malcolm Freiberg, *Prelude to Purgatory: Thomas Hutchinson in Provincial Massachusetts Politics, 1760 to 1770* (New York: Garland, 1990); Clifford K. Shipton, ed., *Sibley's Harvard Graduates*, vol. 8 (Boston: Massachusetts Historical Society, 1951); William Pencak, *America's Burke: The Mind of Thomas Hutchinson* (Washington, D.C.: UP of America, 1982).

2. Peter Shaw, *American Patriots and the Rituals of Revolution* (Cambridge: Harvard UP, 1981).

3. Theodore Draper, *A Struggle for Power: The American Revolution* (New York: Random House, 1996).

NOTES TO THE PROLOGUE

1. Mercy Warren to Sally Sever, December 1781, Mercy Otis Warren Letterbooks, Massachusetts Historical Society.

2. John C. Miller, *Samuel Adams: Pioneer in Propaganda* (Stanford: Stanford UP, 1936).

NOTES TO CHAPTER ONE

1. Emery Battis, *Saints and Sectaries: Anne Hutchinson and the Antinomian Controversy in the Massachusetts Bay Colony* (Chapel Hill: U of North Carolina P, 1962), 248; David D. Hall, ed., *The Antinomian Controversy, 1636–1638: A Documentary History* (Middletown: U of Connecticut P, 1968); Lyle Koehler, "The Case of the American Jezebels: Anne Hutchinson and Female Agitation during the Years of Antinomian Turmoil," *William and Mary Quarterly* 31 (January 1974): 55–78.

2. Thomas Hutchinson, "Hutchinson in America," Hutchinson Papers, Massachusetts Historical Society. Thomas Hutchinson wrote this document in England between 1777 and 1778. He never intended this essay for publication and it is the only detailed primary source available concerning Hutchinson's lineage and early family life.

3. Ibid., 27–28; Peter O. Hutchinson, ed., *The Diary and Letters of His Excellency Thomas Hutchinson* 2 vols. (Boston: Houghton, Mifflin, 1884–86), 2, 466–67.

4. Hutchinson, "Hutchinson in America," 39.

5. Ibid., 41.

6. Ibid., 39 and 43.

7. Frank J. Sulloway, *Born to Rebel: Birth Order, Family Dynamics, and Creative Lives* (New York: Pantheon, 1996).

8. Hutchinson, "Hutchinson in America," 43–46; Peter O. Hutchinson, *Diary and Letters*, 1, 47.

9. "Hutchinson in America," 44; *Diary and Letters*, 1, 46.

10. "Hutchinson in America," 49; *Diary and Letters*, 1, 48.

11. "Hutchinson in America," 46.

12. Peter O. Hutchinson, *Diary and Letters*, 1, 33–46.

13. Charles Francis Adams, ed., *The Works of John Adams, Second President of the United States: With a Life of the Author, Notes and Illustrations*, 10 vols. (Boston: Little, Brown, 1856), 10: 231; Lawrence Shaw Mayo, "Governor Hutchinson's Own Copies of His History of Massachusetts," Colonial Society of Massachusetts, *Publications*, 28 (Boston, 1935): 438–446; Lawrence Shaw Mayo, "Thomas Hutchinson and His History of Massachusetts-Bay," American Antiquarian Society Proceedings, 41 (Worcester, 1932), 321–339.

14. William Pencak, *America's Burke: The Mind of Thomas Hutchinson* (Washington, D.C.: UP of America, 1982).

15. William Palfrey to John Wilkes, October 30, 1770; John Gorham Palfrey, "Life of William Palfrey," in Jared Sparks, ed., *The Library of American Biography*, 25 vols. (New York: Harper, 1848–64), 17, 368–369.

16. John W. Raimo, *Biographical Dictionary of American Colonial and Revolutionary Governors, 1607–1789* (Westport: Meckler Books, 1980); Michael Clement Batinski, "Jonathan Belcher of Massachusetts, 1682 to 1741" (unpublished Ph.D. dissertation, Northwestern University, 1970).

17. "Hutchinson in America," 50.

18. Bailyn, *Ordeal*, 30–32.

19. "Hutchinson in America," 50.

20. Ibid., 51.

21. The Hutchinson children were: Thomas, Jr., b. 1740 d. 1811 (m. Sarah Oliver); Elisha, b. 1743 d. 1824 (m. Mary Watson); Sarah, b. 1744 d. 1780 (m. Peter Oliver); William (Billy), b. 1752 d. 1780 (unmarried); Margaret (Peggy), b. 1754 d. 1777 (unmarried).

22. "Hutchinson in America," 76.

23. Ibid., 76.

24. Ibid., 51.

25. Jonathan Belcher to Francis Harrison, June 27, 1734, Belcher Papers, Massachusetts Historical Society, *Collections*, 2 vols. (Boston, 1893), 2, 77.

26. The Massachusetts legislature was referred to collectively as the General Court. This body comprised two houses. The lower house was referred to as the House of Representatives. The upper house was referred to as the Council. The Council was elected by the House of Representatives and then subjected to the governor for approval or rejection. Boston was governed by the Town Meeting. This body elected selectmen to conduct town business as well as representatives to the General Court.

27. *A Report of the Records Commissioners of the City of Boston Containing the Boston Records from 1729 to 1742* (Boston: Rockwell and Churchill, 1885), 197–201.

28. Malcolm Freiberg, "Thomas Hutchinson and the Province Currency," *New England Quarterly* 30 (June 1957): 190–208; Gary Nash, *The Urban Crucible: Social Change, Political Consciousness, and the Origins of the American Revolution* (Cambridge: Harvard UP, 1979), 112–118; William Douglass, *A Discourse Concerning the Currencies of the British Plantations in America* (Boston: Kneeland and Green, 1740); Theodore Thayer, "The Land Bank System in the American Colonies," *Journal of Economic History* 13 (June 1953): 145–159.

29. *Boston Town Records, 1729–1741*, 197.

30. Peter O. Hutchinson, *Diary and Letters*, 1, 50.

31. Lawrence Shaw Mayo, ed., *Thomas Hutchinson's History of the Province of Massachusetts Bay*, 3 vols. (Cambridge: Harvard UP, 1936), 2, 297.

32. Peter O. Hutchinson, *Diary and Letters*, 1, 50.

33. "Hutchinson in America," 43; Peter O. Hutchinson, *Diary and Letters*, 1, 50.

34. Ibid., Jonathan Belcher to Thomas Hutchinson, October 30, 1740, May 11, 1741, Belcher Papers, 2, 341, 343, 389, and 523: Belcher to Richard Partridge, no date, Belcher Papers, 2, 342.

35. Ibid., 340.

36. Ibid., 341.

37. Thomas Hutchinson to Josiah Willard, July 31, 1741, Hutchinson Papers, Massachusetts Historical Society, box number 25, 1; *The National Cyclopaedia of American Biography*, 63 vols. (New York: James T. White, 1898), 4, 431.

38. Mayo, *Hutchinson's History*, 2, 298–304; Nash, *Urban Crucible*, 212–219; Andrew MacFarland Davis, "Papers Relating to the Land Bank of 1740," Massachusetts Historical Society, *Publications*, 4 (Boston, 1910): 1–199; idem, "Currency and Banking in the Province of Massachusetts Bay," Colonial Society of Massachusetts, *Collections*, 2 (New York, 1901): 293–632; George Billias, "The Massachusetts Land Bankers of 1740," *University of Maine Studies* 74 (April 1959): 5–35.

39. Mayo, *Hutchinson's History*, 2, 299.

40. Ibid., 299.

41. Ibid., 301.

42. Miller, *Samuel Adams*, 9; William M. Fowler, Jr., *Samuel Adams: Radical Puritan* (New York: Longman, 1997).

43. Belcher Papers, 2, 388.

44. Ibid.; Jonathan Belcher to Thomas Hutchinson, May 11, 1741. Belcher wrote, "You say it would be much better if some other way than by application to Parliament could be found to suppress it."

45. Mayo, *Hutchinson's History*, 2, 301; Belcher Papers, 2, 388.

46. Mayo, *Hutchinson's History*, 2, 301.

47. Andrew MacFarland Davis, "A Calendar of the Land Bank Papers," Colonial Society of Massachusetts, *Publications*, 4 (Boston, 1910): 19.

48. Adams, *Works*, 4, 39; Davis, "Currency and Banking," 2, 256.

49. Edward J. Young, "Subjects for Masters' Degrees in Harvard College from 1655 to 1741," Massachusetts Historical Society, *Proceedings*, 18 (Boston, 1880–1881): 119–151.

50. G. B. Warden, *Boston, 1689–1776* (Boston: Little, Brown, 1970), 34–60.

51. Clifford K. Shipton, *Sibley's Harvard Graduates*, (Boston: Massachusetts Historical Society, 1951), 8, 349–356; M. Halsey Thomas, ed., *The Diary of Samuel Sewall*, 2 vols. (New York: Farrar, Strauss, Giroux, 1973), 2, 367–369; Everett Kimball, *The Public Life of Joseph Dudley: A Study of the Colonial Policy of the Stuarts in New England, 1660 to 1715* (New York: Longmans, Green, 1911), 81–89, 178–187.

52. Warden, *Boston*, 94; Douglass Adair and John A. Schutz, eds., *Peter Oliver's Origin and Progress of the American Rebellion: A Tory View* (Stanford: Stanford UP, 1961), 25; William Pencak, *War, Politics, and Revolution in Provincial Massachusetts* (Boston: Northeastern UP, 1981).

53. The Boston Town Meeting remained until 1822. Borough incorporation administered by a mayor and aldermen was the usual English form of municipal government at this time.

54. Nash, *Urban Crucible*, 33–99.

55. Mayo, *Hutchinson's History*, 2, 334–335, 337.

56. Thomas Hutchinson, "Account and Defense of Conduct," Hutchinson Papers, Massachusetts Historical Society. The original manuscript of this document is in the Chapin Library, Williams College, Williamstown, Massachusetts.

57. George A. Ward, ed., *Journal and Letters of the Late Samuel Curwen* (New York: Leavitt, Trow, 1845), 456.

58. Thomas Hutchinson to William Bollan, December 14, 1761, Hutchinson Papers, 26, 3; Mayo, *Hutchinson's History*, 2, 334–337.

59. Eliot, *Biographical Dictionary*, 272.

60. "Hutchinson in America," 52.

61. Davis, "Currency and Banking," 295–313; Warden, *Boston*, 139; "Hutchinson in America," 52; *Boston Post-Boy*, November 5, 1745.

62. "Hutchinson in America," 52.

63. "The Journal of the Commissioners Appointed by the Province of Massachusetts Bay to Treat with the Indians of the Six Nations and with the Commis-

sioners of the Other Governments at the City of Albany in the Province of New York," Massachusetts Historical Society, 29, 388–415; *Boston News-Letter,* October 24, 1745.

64. Mayo, *Hutchinson's History,* 3, 3–4; James Otis, Sr. and Jr., were both commissioners and Hutchinson's colleagues on this occasion.

65. Shaw, *Rituals,* 78–101.

66. Mayo, *Hutchinson's History,* 3, 4.

67. Thomas Hutchinson to unknown, July 25, 1769, Hutchinson Papers, 25, 322.

68. C. H. Lincoln, ed., *The Correspondence of William Shirley, 1731–1760,* 2 vols. (New York: Macmillan, 1912); John A. Schutz, *William Shirley: The King's Governor of Massachusetts* (Chapel Hill: U of North Carolina P, 1961).

69. Peter O. Hutchinson, *Diary and Letters,* 1, 55.

70. Carl Van Doren, ed., *The Letters of Benjamin Franklin and Jane Mecom* (Princeton: American Philosophical Society, 1950), 87; Carl Van Doren, *Jane Mecom: The Favorite Sister of Benjamin Franklin* (New York: Viking Press, 1968), 77.

71. Thomas Hutchinson to Robert Wilson, June 15, 1765, Hutchinson Papers, 25, 24.

72. Mayo, *Hutchinson's History,* 3, 30; Adair and Schutz, *Peter Oliver's Origins,* 34; John Grant to Thomas Hutchinson, May 1, 1767, Hutchinson Papers, 25, 161. Here Grant wrote that Hutchinson was a man of "enlarged views with a feeling heart, when he sees a fellow creature in distress, will not enquire whether he be a protestant, papist or musselman."

73. John A. Schutz, *Thomas Pownall: British Defender of American Liberty: A Study of Anglo-American Relations in the Eighteenth Century* (Glendale: A. H. Clarke 1951), 64–65.

74. Thomas Hutchinson to Lord Dartmouth, April 23, 1773, Hutchinson Papers, 27, 483.

75. Ibid., 483.

76. Loudoun Papers, Henry E. Huntington Library, San Marino, California.

77. Peter O. Hutchinson, *Diary and Letters,* 1, 55–56.

78. Thomas Hutchinson to Lord Loudoun, April 6, 1757, Loudoun Papers.

79. Ibid., January 1757.

80. Loudoun Speech to the New England War Commissioners, January 30, 1757, Loudoun Papers.

81. Ibid., January 20, 1757, Loudoun Papers.

82. Peter O. Hutchinson, *Diary and Letters,* 1, 56.

83. Thomas Hutchinson to Lord Loudoun, February 5, 1757, Loudoun Papers.

84. Ibid., February 5, 1757.

85. Thomas Hutchinson to Lord Loudoun, March 16, 1757, Loudoun Papers.

86. A snow was "a small sailing vessel resembling a brig, carrying a main and a foremast and a supplementary trysail mast close behind the mainmast; formerly employed as a warship." *Oxford English Dictionary,* vol. 15 (Oxford: Clarendon Press, 1989), 873.

87. Loudoun Papers, March 16, 1757.

88. Thomas Hutchinson to Lord Loudoun, February 21, 1757, Loudoun Papers.

89. Thomas Hutchinson to Lord Loudoun, July 6, 1757, Loudoun Papers.

90. Thomas Hutchinson's new military commander was Major General James Abercrombie, with whom he began corresponding in January 1759. Three letters remain in the Loudoun Papers.

91. Thomas Hutchinson to Lord Hillsborough, April 10, 1772, Hutchinson Papers, 27, 559.

92. Thomas Hutchinson to Lord Loudoun, March 7, March 16, April 23, and June 7, 1757, Loudoun Papers. Hutchinson wrote in April 1757, "there is a universal complaint of the weight of the taxes and the entire cessation of all trade."

93. Thomas Hutchinson to Lord Loudoun, March 7, 1757, Loudoun Papers.

94. *Boston Evening-Post*, September 23, 1751.

95. William O. Sawtelle, "Thomas Pownall, Colonial Governor and Some of His Activities in the American Colonies," Massachusetts Historical Society, *Proceedings*, 63 (June 1930): 233–284.

96. Thomas Hutchinson to Israel Williams, July 17, 1758, Williams Papers, 2, 131, Massachusetts Historical Society; Thomas Hutchinson to Israel Williams, August 11, 1758, Caleb Davis Papers, 3, 24, Massachusetts Historical Society.

97. Thomas Hutchinson to Major General James Abercrombie, August 8, 1758, Loudoun Papers.

98. Ibid.; Schutz, *Pownall*, 67–159; Mayo, *Hutchinson's History*, 2, 41–42; Bailyn, *Ordeal*, 42–43; John Adams to William Tudor, February 4, 1817, in Adams, *Works*, 10, 241–242.

NOTES TO CHAPTER TWO

1. Thomas Hutchinson to William Bollan, July 14, 1760, Hutchinson Papers, 25, 16–17.

2. Francis Bernard to Lord Barrington, April 19, 1760, in Edward Channing and Archibald C. Cooldige, eds., *The Barrington-Bernard Correspondence and Illustrative Matter, 1760–1770* (Cambridge: Harvard UP, 1912), 12.

3. Ibid., 15.

4. Ibid., 12, 15; Francis G. Walett, "Governor Bernard's Undoing: An Earlier Hutchinson Letters Affair," *New England Quarterly* 38 (June 1965): 217–226; John D. Fiore, "Francis Bernard, Colonial Governor" (unpublished Ph.D. dissertation, Boston University, 1950).

5. Mayo, *Hutchinson's History*, 3, 60.

6. Ibid., 62–63.

7. Shaw, *Rituals*, 83.

8. Otis authored several influential pamphlets including: *A Vindication of the Conduct of the House* (1762); *The Rights of the Colonies Considered* (1764); and, *Considerations on Behalf of the Colonists* (1765). Hugh Bell, "'A Personal Challenge': The Otis-Hutchinson Controversy, 1761–1762," *Essex Institute Historical Collections* 106

(January 1970): 297–323; John J. Waters, *The Otis Family in Provincial and Revolutionary Massachusetts* (Chapel Hill: U of North Carolina P, 1968).

9. *Boston News-Letter*, April 7, 1763; *Boston Gazette*, April 4, 11, 1763; Peter O. Hutchinson, ed., *Diary and Letters*, 1, 65; Francis Bernard to the Earl of Shelburne, December 22, 1766, Bernard Papers, 4, 275–276, Massachusetts Historical Society.

10. Mayo, *Hutchinson's History*, 3, 64; *Boston Gazette*, April 4, 1763; William Palfrey to John Wilkes in George M. Elsey, ed., "John Wilkes and William Palfrey," Colonial Society of Massachusetts, *Publications*, 34 (1943).

11. Shaw, *Rituals*, 91.

12. Adams, *Works*, 2, 100.

13. Ibid., 10, 233.

14. Ibid., 233; William E. Nelson, *Americanization of the Common Law: The Impact of Legal Change on Massachusetts Society, 1760–1830* (Cambridge: Harvard UP, 1975).

15. John Adams to Dr. J. Morse, November 29, 1815, and John Adams to William Tudor, March 11, 1818, in Adams, *Works*, 10, 183 and 298.

16. James Otis, Jr., observed, "His Excellency [Bernard] has more than once intimated that the Lieutenant-Governor's connections were too formidable to be disobliged." *Boston Gazette*, April 4, 1763.

17. Adams, *Works*, 4, 17–19, 63. Here, as "Novanglus," John Adams wrote that Hutchinson's offices were "too many offices for the greatest and best man in the world to hold, too much business for any man to do; besides that, these offices were frequently clashing and interfering with each other." "Bernard, Hutchinson, and Oliver, whom I call the 'junto' had, by degrees, and before the people were aware of it, erected a tyranny in the province." Richard D. Brown, *Revolutionary Politics in Massachusetts: The Boston Committee of Correspondence and the Towns, 1772 to 1774* (Cambridge: Harvard UP, 1970); Robert Zemsky, *Merchants, Farmers, and River Gods: An Essay on Eighteenth-Century American Politics* (Boston: Gambit, 1971); G. B. Warden, *Boston, 1689–1776* (Boston: Little, Brown, 1970); Stephen Patterson, *Political Parties in Revolutionary Massachusetts* (Madison: U of Wisconsin P, 1973); Ellen E. Brennan, *Plural Office-Holding in Massachusetts, 1760 to 1780: Its Relation to the "Separation" of Departments of Government* (Chapel Hill: U of North Carolina P, 1945).

18. William H. Whitmore, *The Massachusetts Civil List for the Colonial and Provincial Periods, 1630–1770*, (Albany, Munsell, 1870); Harry Alonzo Cushing, ed., *The Writings of Samuel Adams*, 4 vols. (New York: Putnam, 1904; reprint, New York: Octagon, 1968); According to Bernard Bailyn, "in the early 1770s, the extent of endogamy . . . had become a public phenomenon." Bailyn, *Ordeal*, 30–31.

19. *Boston Gazette*, April 18 and May 16, 23, 1763. Thacher wrote under the pseudonym "T. Q."; Adams, *Works*, 10, 285–287.

20. Adams, *Works*, 10, 241–244; Mayo, *Hutchinson's History*, 3, 65; John J. Waters and John A. Schutz, "Patterns of Massachusetts Colonial Politics: The Writs of Assistance and the Rivalry between the Otis and Hutchinson Families," *William and Mary Quarterly* 24 (Winter 1967): 543–567.

21. Mayo, *Hutchinson's History*, 3, 65.

22. *Boston Gazette*, December 6, 1761, article by "Fair Trader."

23. Memorandum in the Joseph Hawley Papers, February 1761, Massachusetts Historical Society.

24. Thomas Hutchinson to Henry Seymour Conway, October 1, 1765, Hutchinson Papers, 25, 18–19.

25. George G. Wolkins, "Writs of Assistance in England," Massachusetts Historical Society Proceedings, 66 (1941): 362–363; Horace Grey, Jr., *Josiah Quincy, Jr.; Reports of Cases Argued and Adjudged in the Superior Court of Judicature of the Province of Massachusetts Bay, Between 1761 and 1772, With and Appendix upon the Writs of Assistance* (Boston: 1865); George G. Wolkins, "Daniel Malcolm and the Writs of Assistance," Massachusetts Historical Society, *Proceedings*, 58 (October 1924): 5–87; John W. Tyler, *Smugglers and Patriots: Boston Merchants and the Advent of the American Revolution* (Boston: Northeastern UP, 1986), 53–57.

26. Mayo, *Hutchinson's History*, 3, 94–95; *Boston Evening-Post*, April 28, 1760; G. B. Warden, "The Caucus and Democracy in Colonial Boston," *New England Quarterly* 43 (March 1970): 28. In Warden's view, a "Merchant's Club" had been co-operating with the Boston Caucus since 1751, "to protest the oppressive tactics of royal customs officials." These merchants were "a select group of shipowners and wholesalers."

27. John Adams to William Tudor, March 29, 1817, Adams, *Works*, 10, 248.

28. Thomas Hutchinson to unknown, December 14, 1761, Hutchinson Papers, 26, 4–5.

29. *Boston Evening-Post*, December 14 and 21, 1761, January 4 and 11, 1762; Bell, "A Personal Challenge," 297–332.

30. *Boston Gazette*, December 21 and 28, 1761.

31. Brennan, *Plural Office-Holding*, 46.

32. *Boston Gazette*, January 11, 1762.

33. Oxenbridge Thacher, *Considerations on Lowering the Value of Gold Coins Within the Province of Massachusetts Bay* (Boston: Edes and Gill, 1762), 27.

34. Ibid., Adair and Schutz, eds., Peter Oliver's *Origins*, 40.

35. James Otis, Jr., to Jasper Mauduit, October 28, 1762, Collections of the Massachusetts Historical Society 74 (Boston 1918): 76–77; Adams, *Works*, 4, 18–19.

36. Thomas Hutchinson to William Bollan, October 4, 1764, Collections of the Massachusetts Historical Society 74 (Boston 1918): 165.

37. Thomas Hutchinson to William Bollan, March 6, 1762, Hutchinson Papers, 26, 15.

38. Thomas Hutchinson to Richard Jackson, November 15, 1762, Hutchinson Papers, 26, 55–57.

39. Thomas Hutchinson to unknown, April 1762, Hutchinson Papers, 26, 28.

40. Pencak, *America's Burke*.

41. Thomas Hutchinson to William Bollan, November 15, 1767, Hutchinson Papers, 26, 59.

42. Thomas Hutchinson to Richard Jackson, November 15, 1762, Hutchinson Papers, 26, 29.

43. Jonathan Mayhew to Jasper Mauduit, April 26, 1762, and Jonathan Mayhew to Thomas Hollis, April 6, 1762, Collections of the Massachusetts Historical Society 74 (Boston 1918): 30, 37–38.

44. Ibid., James Otis, Jr., to Jasper Mauduit, October 28, 1762, 76–77.

45. Boston Town Meeting, *Sixteenth Report of the Records Commissioners of the City of Boston Containing the Boston Town Records, 1758 through 1769* (Boston, 1886), 36–37; *Boston Gazette*, July 14, 1760; Malcolm Freiberg, "William Bollan, Agent of Massachusetts," *More Books* 23 (May 1957): 169–170.

46. Ibid., James Otis, Jr., to Jasper Mauduit, October 28, 1762, Collections, 80.

47. Thomas Hutchinson to Richard Jackson, August 3, 1763, Collections, 127.

48. Benedict Anderson, *Imagined Communities: Reflections on the Origin and Spread of Nationalism* (London: Verso, 1983).

49. Thomas Hutchinson to unknown, February 14, 1763, Hutchinson Papers, 26, 89; *Boston Gazette*, January 31, 1763. In this edition Otis wrote of Hutchinson, "The Arts of Hypocrisy and Chicanery he [Hutchinson] has cultivated and improved to Perfection. The principles of arbitrary Power descended to him from his Ancestors; the Nourishment of a perpetual Dictator flowed from his Mother's Breasts, and the Maxim *aut Caesar aut Nullus*, was inscribed upon his swaddling Bands."

50. *Boston Gazette*, February 21, 1763.

51. Thomas Hutchinson to Richard Jackson, August 3, 1763, Hutchinson Papers, 26, 126.

52. Thomas Hutchinson to Richard Jackson, June 14, 1763, Hutchinson Papers, 26, 117.

53. Thomas Hutchinson to David Cheseborough, September 16, 1763, Hutchinson Papers, 26, 130.

54. Thomas Hutchinson to Ezra Stiles, July 4, 1764, Hutchinson Papers, 26, 174.

55. Thomas Hutchinson to Nathaniel Rogers, July 5, 1762, Hutchinson Papers, 26, 17.

56. Thomas Hutchinson to Edward Lloyd, December 3–8, 1762, Hutchinson Papers, 26, 68–69.

57. Thomas Hutchinson to Peter Leitch, January 17, 1763, Hutchinson Papers, 26, 42–43.

58. Thomas Hutchinson to Peter Leitch, July 13, 1764, Hutchinson Papers, 26, 427. "I always liked a frog trimming for a surtout but not to be singular."

59. Thomas Hutchinson to David Cheseborough, March 9, 1763, Hutchinson Papers, 26, 47.

60. Adams, *Works*, 2, 134–135.

61. Thomas Hutchinson to Israel Williams, April 15, 1763, Israel Williams Papers, Massachusetts Historical Society. Williams, farmer, soldier, land speculator and judge of the Hampshire County Court, was a leading tory and old Harvard friend to Hutchinson. The chief political challenge to Williams and his supporters came from his radical whig cousin Joseph Hawley. Williams was eventually attacked in 1774 and placed in his smokehouse overnight as a penalty for his

loyalist sympathies. This event is alleged to have provided the basis for John Trumbull's tory squire in the popular poem *M'Fingal* which dates from the revolutionary era. *The Concise Dictionary of American Biography* (New York: Scribner's, 1964), 1212.

62. Thomas Hutchinson to Richard Jackson, September 17, 1763, Hutchinson Papers, 26, 133.

63. Cited in Tyler, *Smugglers and Patriots*, 131.

64. Thomas Hutchinson to Edward Lloyd, January 11, 1763, Hutchinson Papers, 26, 40.

65. Thomas Hutchinson to Edward Lloyd, November 10, and December 7, 1762, Hutchinson Papers, 26, 35, 53. The actual wording of this quotation is "there does not appear to have been any special cause of dissatisfaction with the administration of government."

66. Mayo, *Hutchinson's History*, 3, 73–74.

67. Ibid., 74.

68. Ibid., 74.

NOTES TO CHAPTER THREE

1. Thomas Barnard, *A Sermon Preached Before His Excellency Francis Bernard . . . May 25th., 1763* (Boston: Richard Draper, 1763), 44.

2. Danby Pickering, ed., *The Statutes at Large*, 26 vols. (Cambridge, England, 1764), 33.

3. William James Smith, ed., *The Grenville Papers*, 4 vols. (London, 1852; reprint, New York: A.M.S. Press, 1970). For a more complete discussion of the legislation, see Oliver M. Dickerson, *The Navigation Acts and the American Revolution* (Philadelphia: U of Pennsylvania P, 1951).

4. Province of Massachusetts Bay, *Reasons Against the Renewal of the Sugar Act, As It Will Be Prejudicial To The Trade, Not Only Of The Northern Colonies, But To That Of Great Britain Also* (Boston: Thomas Leverett, 1764), 12.

5. Oxenbridge Thacher, *The Sentiments of a British American* (Boston: Edes and Gill, 1764), 14. For an alternative interpretation of the motivation of the Grenville administration for passing the Sugar Act, see John W. Tyler, *Smugglers and Patriots: Boston Merchants and the Advent of the American Revolution* (Boston: Northeastern UP, 1986), 35, 92.

6. Thomas Hutchinson to ?, July 11, 1764, Hutchinson Papers, 26, 180–181.

7. Mayo, *Hutchinson's History*, 3, 78.

8. Francis Bernard to The Lords of Trade, December 1763, Bernard Papers, vol. 2, 89.

9. Thomas Hutchinson to ?, July 11, 1764, Hutchinson Papers, 26, 180–181.

10. Ibid., 181.

11. James Otis, Jr., *The Rights of the British Colonies Asserted and Proved* (Boston; Edes and Gill, 1764); Thacher, *Sentiments*.

12. Thomas Hutchinson to Richard Jackson, July 23, 1764, Hutchinson Papers, 26, 192–193.

13. Writers in the *Boston Gazette* hoped he would go to London thereby temporarily vacating his numerous offices, "consequently they [the offices] must be divided among a number. And in this case there will be little or no danger of any ONE man's arriving to such a degree of *power* and *influence* as to become the object of either *dread* or *envy*." *Boston Gazette*, February 6, 1764.

14. Thomas Hutchinson to John Cushing, January 28, 1764, Cushing Papers, Massachusetts Historical Society.

15. Sir Lewis Namier and John Brooke, *The House of Commons, 1754–1790*, 2 vols. (New York: Oxford UP, 1964), 1, 668–671.

16. Thomas Whately to John Temple, June 8, 1764, Bowdoin and Temple Papers, *Collections* (Boston: Massachusetts Historical Society, 1897), 59, 20.

17. Otis, Jr., *Rights*, 42–43.

18. Thomas Hutchinson to Richard Jackson, July 23, 1765, Hutchinson Papers, 26, 90–100.

19. Edmund S. Morgan, "Thomas Hutchinson and the Stamp Act," *New England Quarterly* 21 (1948): 459–492.

20. Richard Jackson to Thomas Hutchinson, March 3, 1766, Hutchinson Papers, 26, 65; *The Parliament History of England*, vol. 16 (London: T. C. Hansard, 1813), 134–135.

21. Alden Bradford, ed., *Speeches of the Governors of Massachusetts, 1765 to 1775* (New York: Da Capo Press, 1971), 21–23; Thomas Hutchinson to ?, November 5, 1764, Hutchinson Papers, 26, 110; Francis Bernard to Richard Jackson, November 17, 1764, Bernard Papers, 3, 262; *Journal of the Massachusetts House of Representatives*, November 2, 4, 1764, 134, 137.

22. Thomas Hutchinson to ?, November 6, 1766, Hutchinson Papers, 26, 202; Mayo, *Hutchinson's History*, 3, 115.

23. James Otis, Jr., *A Vindication of the Conduct of the House of Representatives of the Province of Massachusetts Bay, more particularly in the Last Session of the General Assembly* (Boston: Edes and Gill, 1762), preface.

24. The secondary literature which informs these observations is found below in note 47.

25. *Boston Gazette*, September 2, 1765; Peter O. Hutchinson, *Diary and Letters*; *Boston Evening-Post*, March to December, 1765; *Boston Town Records*, vol. 16, 1764 to 1766; Mayo, *Hutchinson's History*, 3, *passim*.

26. *Boston Evening-Post*, March to December, 1765.

27. Ibid., August 26, 1765.

28. Thomas Hutchinson to ?, August 15, 1765, Hutchinson Papers, 145.

29. Ibid., 145a.

30. Francis Bernard to Thomas Pownall, August 18, 1765, Bernard Papers, 3, 11–15.

31. Francis Bernard to Lord Halifax, August 15, 1765, Bernard Papers, 3, 141.

32. Thomas Hutchinson to Israel Williams, April 26, 1765, Hutchinson Papers, 265–267. Hutchinson continued, "As soon as I heard of it I declared everywhere that I knew nothing more than was known publicly, but I find this report has spread behind my back."

33. Thomas Hutchinson to ?, August 16, 1765, Hutchinson Papers, 145–146.

34. Ibid., 146.

35. Justin Winsor, ed., *Memorial History of Boston*, 4 vols. (Boston: J. R. Osgood, 1880–1881), 3, 134.

36. *Boston Gazette*, September 2, 1765.

37. "Diary of Joshua Quincy, August 27, 1765," *Proceedings*, Massachusetts Historical Society, April 1858, 41–44.

38. *Boston Gazette*, September 2, 1765.

39. "Diary of Joshua Quincy," 43.

40. Thomas Hutchinson to Richard Jackson, August 30, 1765, Hutchinson Papers, 26, 146; Thomas Hutchinson to Thomas Pownall, August 31, 1765, 26, Hutchinson Papers, 149.

41. *Boston Gazette*, September 2, 1765.

42. Miller, *Samuel Adams*, 51, 53, 61, 63; G. B. Warden, *Boston, 1689–1776* (Boston: Little, Brown, 1970).

43. George P. Anderson, "Ebenezer Mackintosh: Stamp Act Rioter and Patriot," *Publications*, Colonial Society of Massachusetts 26 (March 1924): 15–65.

44. Peter O. Hutchinson, *Diary and Letters*, 1, 70.

45. Ibid., 71; *Boston Evening-Post*, October 7, 1765.

46. Peter O. Hutchinson, *Diary and Letters*, 1, 123; Thomas Hutchinson, "Address to the Massachusetts General Court," August 27, 1765, Houghton Library, Harvard.

47. John Osborne to Thomas Hutchinson, August 28, 1765, Hutchinson Papers, 25, 27; Gordon S. Wood, "A Note on Mobs in the American Revolution," *William and Mary Quarterly* 3rd ser. 23 (1966): 635–642; Jesse Lemisch, "Jack Tar in the Streets: Merchant Seamen in the Politics of Revolutionary America," *William and Mary Quarterly* 3rd ser. 25 (1968): 371–407; Pauline Maier, *From Resistance to Revolution: Colonial Radicals and the Development of American Opposition to Britain, 1765–1776* (New York: Knopf, 1972); Dirk Hoerder, *Crowd Action in Revolutionary Massachusetts, 1765–1780* (New York: Academic Press, 1977).

48. *Boston Town Records*, vol. 16, 152; *Boston Gazette*, September 2, 1765; Samuel Adams to John Smith, December 20, 1765, in Harry A. Cushing, ed., *The Writings of Samuel Adams*, 4 vols. (New York: Octagon, 1968), 1, 60.

49. Mayo, *Hutchinson's History*, 3, 125; Anderson, "Ebenezer Mackintosh," 26–27.

50. Thomas Hutchinson to Henry Seymour Conway, October 1, 1765, Hutchinson Papers, 26, 154–156; William Gordon, *The History of the Rise, Progress, and Establishment of the Independence of the United States of America*, 4 vols. (New York: Hodge, Allen & Campbell, 1789); Malcolm Freiberg, *Prelude to Purgatory: Thomas Hutchinson in Provincial Massachusetts Politics, 1760 to 1770* (New York: Garland, 1990); Edmund S. and Helen Morgan, *The Stamp Act Crisis; Prologue to Revolution* (Chapel Hill: U of North Carolina P, 1953); Robert E. Brown. *Middle-Class Democracy and the Revolution in Massachusetts, 1691 to 1780* (Ithaca: Cornell UP, 1955); G. B. Warden, *Boston, 1689–1776* (Boston: Little, Brown, 1970); Bernard Bailyn, *The Ordeal of Thomas Hutchinson* (Cambridge: Belknap Press, 1974); Gary Nash, *The Urban Crucible: Social Change, Political Consciousness and Origins of the American Revolution* (Cambridge: Harvard UP, 1979).

51. Francis Bernard to the Earl of Shelburne, January 24, 1767, Bernard Papers, 4, 299–300.

52. Nash, *Urban Crucible*, 155; *Boston Post-Boy*, June 3, 1765; Arthur M. Schlesinger, *Colonial Merchants and the American Revolution, 1763–1776* (New York: Columbia UP, 1968), 57; Carl Bridenbaugh, *Cities in Revolt* (New York: Knopf, 1955), 281.

53. *Boston Evening-Post*, December 14, 1761; *Boston Gazette*, December 28, 1761; Cushing, *Samuel Adams*, 4, 67.

54. Charles Francis Adams, ed., *The Works of John Adams*, 10 vols. (Boston: Little, Brown, 1850–1856), 2, 165–166.

55. Benedict Anderson, *Imagined Communities: Reflections on the Origin and Spread of Nationalism* (London: Verso, 1983).

NOTES TO CHAPTER FOUR

1. William Bollan to Thomas Hutchinson, October 12 and October 14, 1765, Hutchinson Papers, 25, 34–37.

2. Ibid., 37 and 44.

3. Thomas Hutchinson to ?, January 2, 1766, Hutchinson Papers, 26, 193; *Boston News-Letter*, January 2, 1766; *Boston Post-Boy*, January 6, 1766.

4. William Bollan to Thomas Hutchinson, January 18, 1766, Hutchinson Papers, 25, 45.

5. Francis Bernard to the Earl of Shelburne, January 24, 1767, Bernard Papers, 4, 297–298.

6. Thomas Hutchinson to Thomas Pownall, August 31, 1765, Hutchinson Papers, 26, 301.

7. *Boston Town Records, 1758 to 1769* (Boston: Rockwell and Churchill, 1886), 159.

8. *Boston Gazette*, January 27, 1766.

9. Adams, *Works*, 2, 189; Mayo, *Hutchinson's History*, 3, 106.

10. Thomas Hutchinson to ?, April 27, 1766, Hutchinson Papers, 26, 229.

11. Ellen E. Brennan, *Plural Office-Holding in Massachusetts, 1760 to 1780* (Chapel Hill: U of North Carolina P, 1945), 15–21; Francis G. Walett, "The Massachusetts Council, 1766–1774: The Transformation of a Conservative Institution," *William and Mary Quarterly* 3rd ser. 6 (Winter 1949), 605–627: Mayo, *Hutchinson's History*, 3, 210–211.

12. Francis G. Walett, "James Bowdoin: Patriot Propagandist," *New England Quarterly* 27 (September 1950): 320–338.

13. Thomas Hutchinson to Israel Mauduit, June 6, 1767, Hutchinson Papers, 25, 164.

14. William Bollan to Thomas Hutchinson, October 12, 1765, Hutchinson Papers, 25, 34–37.

15. John Cushing to Thomas Hutchinson, December 15, 1766, Hutchinson Papers, 25, 119.

16. Thomas Hutchinson to ?, May 28, 1766, Hutchinson Papers, 26, 233; *Jour-*

nal of the Massachusetts House of Representatives, 1766 (Boston: Green and Kneeland, 1766), 7.

17. *Boston Evening-Post*, April 28, 1766; *Boston Gazette*, March 31 and April 14, 1766.

18. *Boston Gazette*, April 14, 1766 (emphasis in original).

19. Thomas Hutchinson to Lord Halifax, August 30, 1765, Hutchinson Papers, 26, 299.

20. "An Address to the True-Born Sons of Liberty," by "A Countryman," *Boston Gazette*, March 31, 1766.

21. Thomas Hutchinson to ?, February 26, 1766, Hutchinson Papers, 26, 196; Thomas Hutchinson to ?, March 25, 1766, Hutchinson Papers, 26, 219; Thomas Hutchinson to ?, July 18, 1767, Hutchinson Papers, 26, 275.

22. Thomas Hutchinson to Thomas (Tommy) Hutchinson, Jr., no date (probably March 1766), Hutchinson Papers, 26, 429.

23. Ibid.

24. E. Francis Brown, "The Law Career of Major Joseph Hawley," *New England Quarterly* 4 (July 1931): 482–504; Thomas Hutchinson to ?, November 7, 1766, Hutchinson Papers, 26, 249; *Boston Evening-Post*, July 6 and July 13, 1767; Mayo, *Hutchinson's History*, 3, 127, 212–213; Franklin Bowditch Dexter, *Biographical Sketches of the Graduates of Yale with Annals of the College History* (New York: Holt, 1885–1919), 1, 709–712.

25. Thomas Hutchinson to ?, November 7, 1766, Hutchinson Papers, 26, 469; Thomas Hutchinson to William Bollan, November 22, 1766, Hutchinson Papers, 26, 468.

26. Israel Williams to Thomas Hutchinson, December 28, 1767, Hutchinson Papers, 25, 228.

27. Thomas Hutchinson to ?, November 7, 1766, Hutchinson Papers, 26, 495.

28. Thomas Hutchinson to Francis Bernard, February 20, 1767, Hutchinson Papers, 25, 164.

29. *Journal of the Massachusetts House of Representatives*, January 28, 1767, 224; Bradford, *Speeches*, 102–103.

30. Bradford, *Speeches*, 104–105.

31. Ibid., 105.

32. Francis Bernard to Richard Jackson, November 17, 1766, Bernard Papers, 5, 166–167; Francis Bernard to the Earl of Shelburne, November 14, 1766, Bernard Papers, 4, 265–267; Francis Bernard to the Earl of Shelburne, January 24, 1767, Bernard Papers, 4, 302–303.

33. Mayo, *Hutchinson's History*, 3, 126.

34. Ibid., 127.

35. Thomas Hutchinson to ?, December 14, 1767, Hutchinson Papers, 26, 225.

36. Francis Bernard to Sir Henry Moore, July 11, 1767, Bernard Papers, 5, 235–237; *A Conference Between the Commissaries of Massachusetts-Bay and the Commissaries of New York at New Haven in the Colony of Connecticut, 1767*, October 21, 1767; *Boston Evening-Post*, February 1, 8, and 15, 1768.

37. *Boston News-Letter*, July 9, 1767; Thomas Hutchinson to Richard Jackson,

July 18, 1767, Hutchinson Papers, 26, 281; Israel Williams to Thomas Hutchinson, December 28, 1767, Hutchinson Papers, 25, 228; Israel Mauduit to Thomas Hutchinson, December 10, 1767, Hutchinson Papers, 25, 231–232; Pencak, *America's Burke.*

38. Thomas Hutchinson to ?, December 14, 1767, Hutchinson Papers, 26, 225.

39. Thomas Hutchinson to Richard Jackson, October 20, 1767, Hutchinson Papers, 25, 183.

40. Thomas Hutchinson to Peter Leitch, December 8, 1767, Hutchinson Papers, 25, 221 and 229; Thomas Hutchinson to Thomas (Tommy) Hutchinson, Jr., July 6, 1766, Hutchinson Papers, 26, 480.

41. Thomas Hutchinson to ?, June 4, 1767, Hutchinson Papers, 25, 174.

42. Sir Lewis Namier and John Brooke, *Charles Townshend* (London: Macmillan, 1964), 1 and 41.

43. *Boston Gazette*, November 9, 1767.

44. *Boston Evening-Post*, October 26, 1767.

45. "A Circulatory Letter Directed to the Speakers of the Houses of Representatives and Burgesses on this Continent," *Journal of the House of Representatives of the Commonwealth of Massachusetts*, February 11, 1768, 20–22.

46. Thomas Hutchinson to Richard Jackson, January 17, 1767, Hutchinson Papers, 26, 524.

47. Ibid., 525; Thomas Hutchinson, "A Dialogue Between an American and a European Englishman," reprinted in *Perspectives in American History* 9 (1975): 343–410.

48. Cushing, *Samuel Adams*, 1, 187.

49. *Boston Gazette*, April 11, 1768.

50. Thomas Hutchinson to ?, July 18, 1767, Hutchinson Papers, 26, 281.

51. Thomas Hutchinson to Richard Jackson, November 19, 1767, Hutchinson Papers, 25, 217.

52. Lord Hillsborough to Francis Bernard, April 22, 1768, Bernard Papers, 11, 172–173; Sir Lewis Namier and John Brooke, *The House of Commons, 1754 to 1790* (New York: Oxford UP, 1964), 627; Edmond Fitzmaurice, *The Life of William, Earl of Shelburne* (London: Macmillan, 1875).

53. The Earl of Shelburne to Francis Bernard, September 17, 1767, in *Journal of the House of Representatives*, March 4, 1768; *Boston Gazette*, August 10, 1767, September 38, 1767, March 7, 1768; Thomas Hutchinson to ?, July 18, 1767, Hutchinson Papers, 26, 277; Thomas Hutchinson to Richard Jackson, October 20, 1767, Hutchinson Papers, 26, 205–206; Francis Bernard to the Earl of Shelburne, September 21, 1767, Bernard Papers, 6, 243–244.

54. *Journal of the House of Representatives, 1768*, 88–96.

55. *Boston Gazette*, March 7, 1768.

56. Thomas Hutchinson to Nathaniel Rogers, May 31, 1768, Hutchinson Papers, 25, 257.

57. Ibid.

58. Ibid., 258.

59. Ibid.

60. Nathaniel Rogers to Thomas Hutchinson, July 2, 1768, Hutchinson Papers, 25, 264; Nathaniel Rogers to Thomas Hutchinson, February 17, 1768, Hutchinson Papers, 25, 245; Nathaniel Rogers to Thomas Hutchinson, December 30, 1767, Hutchinson Papers, 25, 108.

61. Nathaniel Rogers to Thomas Hutchinson, February 17, 1768, 245.

62. Ibid.

63. George G. Wolkins, "The Seizure of John Hancock's Sloop *Liberty*," Massachusetts Historical Society, *Proceedings*, 60 (1923): 239–284; Oliver M. Dickerson, *The Navigation Acts and the American Revolution* (Philadelphia: U of Pennsylvania P, 1951); Hoerder, *Crowd Action*.

64. Nash, *The Urban Crucible*, 155.

65. Francis Bernard to Lord Barrington, July 23, 1768, in, Channing and Coolidge, *Barrington-Bernard Correspondence*, 168; Clarence E. Carter, ed., *The Correspondence of General Thomas Gage*, 2 vols. (New Haven: Yale UP, 1933), 2, 69 and 72–73.

66. Bradford, *Speeches*, 203.

67. Thomas Hutchinson to Thomas Whately, October 17, 1768, Hutchinson Papers, 25, 564; Francis Bernard to the Earl of Shelburne, March 19, 1768, Bernard Papers, 11, 191–193.

68. Thomas Hutchinson to Thomas Whately, October 5, 1768, Hutchinson Papers, 25, 250.

69. Thomas Hutchinson to Richard Jackson, June 16, 1768, Hutchinson Papers, 26, 311.

70. Thomas Hutchinson to ? (probably Lord Hillsborough), December 8, 1768, Hutchinson Papers, 26, 693.

71. Oliver M. Dickerson, ed., *Boston under Military Rule, 1768 to 1769 as Revealed in a Journal of the Times* (Boston: Chapman and Grimes, 1936); Carter, *Correspondence of General Gage*; R. C. Simmons and P. D. G. Thomas, eds., *Proceedings and Debates of the British Parliaments Respecting North America*, 6 vols. (Millwood, NY: Kraus International, 1982–1987).

72. Thomas Hutchinson to ?, December 8, 1768, Hutchinson Papers, 26, 694.

73. Francis Bernard to Captain Corner, July 4, 1768, Bernard Papers, 5, 272–273; Ann Hulton, *Letters of a Loyalist Lady: Being the Letters of Ann Hulton, Sister of Henry Hulton, Commissioner of Customs at Boston, 1767–1776* (Cambridge: Harvard UP, 1927); Thomas Hutchinson to ?, August 9, 1768, Hutchinson Papers, 26, 319.

74. Thomas Hutchinson to ?, December 8, 1768, Hutchinson Papers, 26, 694.

75. Ibid., 695.

76. Thomas Hutchinson to Israel Mauduit, December 5, 1768, Hutchinson Papers, 26, 691.

77. Thomas Hutchinson to Thomas Whately, December 10, 1768, Hutchinson Papers, 26, 696. Hutchinson probably meant that the document was published in New York.

78. Thomas Hutchinson to ?, August 8, 1768, Hutchinson Papers, 26, 321; Hutchinson Essay, in Hutchinson Papers, 25, 123–129; Hutchinson, "A Dialogue Between an American and a European Englishman."

79. Hutchinson to ?, August 8, 1768, Hutchinson Papers, 26, 321; Thomas Hutchinson to John Hely Hutchinson (no relative), January 18, 1769, Hutchinson Papers, 26, 703–704.

80. Thomas Hutchinson to Richard Jackson, no date, Hutchinson Papers, 26, 337.

81. Thomas Hutchinson to John Hely Hutchinson, January 18, 1769, Hutchinson Papers, 26, 708.

82. Thomas Hutchinson to Richard Jackson, January 24, 1769, Hutchinson Papers, 26, 710–713.

83. Ibid., 713.

84. Channing and Coolidge, *Barrington-Bernard Correspondence, 197–198; Merrill Jensen, The Founding of a Nation: A History of the American Revolution, 1763–1776* (New York: Oxford UP, 1968), 189.

85. *Boston Gazette*, February 27, 1769; Sir Francis Bernard to John Pownall, March 5, 1769, Bernard Papers, 7, 262–263.

86. John Irving to William Bollan, August 19, 1769, "The Bowdoin-Temple Papers," *Collections*, Massachusetts Historical Society, 6 ser. 9 (1897): 153; Thomas Hutchinson to Francis Bernard, August 11, 1769, Hutchinson Papers, 26, 363; *Boston Gazette*, December 11, 1769; Francis Bernard to John Pownall, April 12, 1769, Bernard Papers, 7, 282; Thomas Hutchinson to Richard Jackson, April 16, 1769, and to Thomas Pownall, April 17, 1769, Hutchinson Papers, 26, 348–351.

87. Mayo, *Hutchinson's History*, 3, 164.

88. Thomas Hutchinson to Richard Jackson, August 18, 1769, Hutchinson Papers, 26, 774.

89. Channing and Coolidge, *Barrington-Bernard Correspondence*, 218–219; Mayo, *Hutchinson's History*, 3, 182–183.

NOTES TO CHAPTER FIVE

1. Mayo, *Hutchinson's History*, 3, 184; *Boston Gazette*, July 17, 1769; Thomas Hutchinson to Francis Bernard, August 26, 1769, Hutchinson Papers, 26, 783–785.

2. Mayo, *Hutchinson's History*, 3, 184.

3. Ibid.

4. Thomas Hutchinson to William Bollan, June 13, 1769, Hutchinson Papers, 26, 354.

5. Jensen, *Founding*, 303.

6. British policy remained incoherent throughout 1769. Thomas Pownall wrote "I might as well write you the shapes of the clouds that have passed over this island during summer," as attempt to explain Parliamentary policy toward Massachusetts in 1769. Thomas Pownall to Thomas Hutchinson, December 5, 1769, Hutchinson Papers, 25, 339.

7. Pencak, *America's Burke*, 1–22; Peter O. Hutchinson, *Diary and Letters*, 1, 263; Bailyn, *Ordeal*, 150–154.

8. Adams, *Works*, 2, 224–226; Mayo, *Hutchinson's History*, 3, 167.

9. Adams, *Works*, 2, 225.

10. Dickerson, *Boston under Military Rule*, 57 and 92.

11. Thomas Hutchinson to Richard Jackson, August 18, 1769, Hutchinson Papers, 26, 774–777. In September Hutchinson wrote "I tremble for my Country." Thomas Hutchinson to Charles Paxton, September 1, 1769, Hutchinson Papers, 26, 787.

12. Thomas Hutchinson to Richard Jackson, August 18, 1769, Hutchinson Papers, 26, 776.

13. Thomas Hutchinson to Charles Paxton, September 1, 1769, Hutchinson Papers, 26, 240.

14. "Letter of Doctor Thomas Young," September, 1769, Colonial Society of Massachusetts, *Publications*, 11 (Boston, 1906–1907), 5–6; Adams, *Works*, 2, 219; Anne Cunningham, ed., *The Letters and Diary of John Rowe* (Boston: W. B. Clark, 1903), 192; William Tudor, *The Life of James Otis, Jr.* (New York: Da Capo Press, 1970), 345–366; Jensen, *Founding*, 348–349.

15. Adams, *Works*, 2, 226–227.

16. Thomas Hutchinson to General Mackay, September 11, 1769, Hutchinson Papers, 26, 375.

17. Thomas Hutchinson to ?, September 11, 1769, Hutchinson Papers, 26, 376.

18. Peter O. Hutchinson, *Diary and Letters*, 1, 65–66.

19. Tyler, *Smugglers and Patriots;* "Massachusettensis," *Massachusetts Gazette and Boston Post-Boy*, January 2, 1775; Charles M. Andrews, "The Boston Merchants and the Non-Importation Movement," Colonial Society of Massachusetts, *Transactions*, 19 (1916–1917): 159–259; Leslie J. Thomas, "Partisan Politics in Massachusetts during Governor Bernard's Administration, 1760–1770" (unpublished Ph.D. dissertation, University of Wisconsin, 1960); Arthur M. Schlesinger, *Colonial Merchants and the American Revolution, 1763–1776* (New York: Columbia UP, 1968).

20. Thomas Hutchinson to ?, June 10, 1769, Hutchinson Papers, 26, 745.

21. Thomas Hutchinson to ?, July 28, 1769, Hutchinson Papers, 26, 747.

22. Thomas Hutchinson to Francis Bernard, August 8, 1769, Hutchinson Papers, 26, 781.

23. Cunningham, *Letters and Diary*, 177.

24. Thomas Hutchinson to Sir Francis Bernard, October 4, 1769, Hutchinson Papers, 26, 818–820.

25. Ibid., 820.

26. Nathaniel Rogers to ?, October 25, 1769, Sparks Papers Relating to New England, 3, 44; *Boston Gazette*, May 21, 1770; Thomas Hutchinson to ?, August 12, 1770, Hutchinson Papers, 26, 534–536; Thomas Hutchinson to Lord Hillsborough, August 14 and 19, 1770, Hutchinson Papers, 26, 537–538. Rogers had just been appointed to the position of provincial secretary before he died of an apoplectic fit allegedly induced by his experience at the hands of the New York mob.

27. Thomas Hutchinson to Thomas Pownall, September 26, 1769, Hutchinson Papers, 26, 379.

28. Thomas Hutchinson to John Pownall, October 23, 1769, Hutchinson Papers, 26, 387; Thomas Hutchinson to Francis Bernard, October 23, 1769, Hutchinson Papers, 26, 845.

29. Hutchinson may have extended financial assistance to John Mein.

30. *Boston Chronicle*, August and October, 1769.

31. John E. Alden, "John Mein: Scourge of Patriots," Colonial Society of Massachusetts, *Publications*, 26 (1937–1942): 571–599; Mein later wrote a series of anti-American commentaries under the title *Sagittarius's Letters and Political Speculations*, which appeared in Boston in 1775. They were originally published in London in the *Public Ledger* in 1774. Isaiah Thomas, *The History of Printing in America, with a Biography of Printers and an Account of Newspapers* (Worcester: Isaiah Thomas, 1810; repr. Barré, Mass. Imprint Society, 1970), vol. 1, 154.

32. Lyman Butterfield, ed., *John Adams's Diary and Autobiography* (Cambridge: Belknap Press, 1961), vol. 1, 225 and 343; *Boston Evening-Post*, August 28, 1769.

33. John Mein to Thomas Hutchinson, no date, Hutchinson Papers, 25, 455.

34. Adams, *Works*, 10, 252–253; Nash, *Urban Crucible*, 355.

35. *Boston Evening-Post*, October 30, 1769.

36. John Mein to Thomas Hutchinson, no date, Hutchinson Papers, 26, 455–456.

37. Thomas Hutchinson to Lord Hillsborough, November 11, 1769, Hutchinson Papers, 26, 219; Peter O. Hutchinson, *Diary and Letters*, 1, 22.

38. Hutchinson and Oliver participated in the publication of the avowedly "tory" newspaper in 1771 entitled *The Censor*. The newspaper remained in business from November, 1771 until May 1772.

39. Thomas Hutchinson to John Pownall, December 6, 1769, Hutchinson Papers, 26, 901–902.

40. *Boston Chronicle*, January 29 to February 1, 1770.

41. Mayo, *Hutchinson's History*, 3, 91.

42. Ibid., 2, 192.

43. Thomas Hutchinson to ?, November 1768, Hutchinson Papers, 26, 324–325; *Resolves of the Meeting of Merchants and Traders*, January 23, 1770, Massachusetts Historical Society.

44. *Boston News-Letter*, January 11, 1770.

45. Lord Hillsborough to Thomas Hutchinson, February 12, 1771, Hutchinson Papers, Houghton Library, Harvard; James H. Stark, *The Loyalists of Massachusetts and the Other Side of the American Revolution* (Boston: James H. Stark, 1907; reprint, Clifton, NJ: Augustus M. Kelly, 1972), 422–423.

46. L. Kinvin Wroth and Hiller B. Zobel, eds., *The Legal Papers of John Adams*, 3 vols. (Cambridge: Belknap Press, 1965), 2, 416–421.

47. *Boston News-Letter*, March 1, 1770.

48. Thomas Hutchinson to Francis Bernard, February 28, 1770, Hutchinson Papers, 26, 450; Cunningham, *Letters and Diary*, 197. Rowe wrote on "February 26. This afternoon the boy that was killed by Richardson was buried. I am very sure two thousand people attended the funeral."

49. Butterfield, *John Adams's Diary*, 1, 349–350.

50. Thomas Hutchinson to Thomas Whately, October 30, 1770, Hutchinson Papers, 27, 11–12.

51. Thomas Hutchinson to Francis Bernard, September 28, 1770, Hutchinson

Papers, 27, 8; Thomas Hutchinson to Francis Bernard, November 30, 1770, Hutchinson Papers, 27, 102–106.

52. Thomas Hutchinson to William Parker, August 26, 1770, Hutchinson Papers, 26, 540.

NOTES TO CHAPTER SIX

1. Jensen, *Founding*, 289.

2. Thomas Hutchinson to Lord Hillsborough, March 27, 1770, Hutchinson Papers, 26, 460–461. George III approved Hutchinson's commission in April, 1770. Hutchinson officially became the governor of Massachusetts on March 14, 1771. *Boston Gazette*, October 14, 1771; Cushing, *Samuel Adams*, 2, 250–254; Mayo, *Hutchinson's History*, 3, 208.

3. Mayo, *Hutchinson's History*, 3, 194; Cunningham, *Letters and Diary*, 178; Hiller B. Zobel, *The Boston Massacre*, (New York: Norton, 1970), 109; Oliver M. Dickerson, ed., *Boston under Military Rule* (Boston: Chapman and Grimes, 1936).

4. *Boston Evening-Post*, March 5, 1770.

5. Mayo, *Hutchinson's History*, 3, 195.

6. *A Short Narrative of the Horrid Massacre in Boston etc.* (Boston: Edes and Gill and T. J. Fleet, 1770); Frederic Kidder, *The History of the Boston Massacre* (Albany, N. Y.: J. Munsell, 1870); Richard Hale, *The Bloody Massacre Perpetrated in King Street etc.* (Barré, Mass.: Imprint Society, 1970); Zobel, *Boston Massacre*, 180–206; Warden, *Boston*, chapter 9; John Shy, *Toward Lexington: The Role of the British Army in the Coming of the American Revolution* (Princeton: Princeton UP, 1965), 318–319.

7. Cunningham, *Letters and Diary*, 197.

8. Warden, *Boston*, 231; Wroth and Zobel, *Legal Papers*, 3, 75, 76 and 196; Mayo, *Hutchinson's History*, 3, 196.

9. Mayo, *Hutchinson's History*, 3, 196.

10. Ibid.

11. Thomas Hutchinson to Thomas Gage, April 30, 1770, Hutchinson Papers, 25, 465.

12. Thomas Hutchinson to Lord Hillsborough, March 27, 1770, Hutchinson Papers, 26, 460–461.

13. Peter O. Hutchinson, *Diary and Letters*, 2, 192; Mayo, *Hutchinson's History*, 3, 208.

14. Peter O. Hutchinson, *Diary and Letters*, 2, 79; Thomas Hutchinson, "Account and Defense of Conduct", Massachusetts Historical Society; Thomas Hutchinson to Lord Hillsborough, June 29, 1770, Hutchinson Papers, 26, 1113–1116.

15. Thomas Hutchinson to Francis Bernard, April 28, 1770, Hutchinson Papers, 25, 405.

16. Thomas Hutchinson to Francis Bernard, no date, Hutchinson Papers, 26, 42–50.

17. Thomas Hutchinson to Francis Bernard, April 28, 1770, Hutchinson Papers, 25, 405; Thomas Hutchinson to Lord Hillsborough, June 29, 1770, Hutchinson Papers, 26, 1113–1115.

18. Shy, *Lexington*, 318.

19. Mayo, *Hutchinson's History*, 3, 197.

20. Thomas Hutchinson to Francis Bernard, April 28, 1770, Hutchinson Papers, 25, 407.

21. Mayo, *Hutchinson's History*, 3, 198.

22. Thomas Hutchinson. "Account and Defense of Conduct," Massachusetts Historical Society, 3–4.

23. Peter Shaw, *American Patriots and the Rituals of Revolution* (Cambridge: Harvard UP, 1981); Richard D. Brown, *Knowledge Is Power: The Diffusion of Information in Early America, 1700 to 1865* (New York: Oxford UP, 1989); Clifford K. Shipton, *Sibley's Harvard Graduates* (Boston: Massachusetts Historical Society, 1953), 10, 420–465.

24. Mayo, *Hutchinson's History*, 3, 237.

25. Thomas Hutchinson to Francis Bernard, November 30, 1770, Lord Hillsborough, December 5, 1770, and Thomas Pownall, December 5, 1770, Hutchinson Papers, 26, 103, 110 and 113.

26. Thomas Hutchinson to Richard Jackson, February 3, 1771, Thomas Whately, January 25, 1771, Lord Hillsborough, March 9, 1771 and Thomas Pownall, January 7, 1771, Hutchinson Papers, 27, 191, 181, 223 and 156.

27. Thomas Hutchinson to Lord Hillsborough, January 22, 1771, Hutchinson Papers, 27, 169.

28. Ibid., 171; Thomas Hutchinson to John Worthington, January 31, 1771 and Francis Bernard, January 23, 1771, Hutchinson Papers, 27, 175 and 177.

29. Shipton, "Elisha Cooke, Jr.," in *Sibley's;* Thomas Hutchinson to ? (probably Lord Hillsborough) September 30, 1771, Hutchinson Papers, 27, 399.

30. Thomas Hutchinson to Richard Jackson, February 3, 1771, Hutchinson Papers, 27, 191.

31. Thomas Hutchinson to Francis Bernard, February 7, 1771, Hutchinson Papers, 27, 212.

32. Malcolm Freiberg, *Thomas Hutchinson of Milton* (Boston: Massachusetts Historical Society, 1971).

33. William Fitzwilliam to Thomas Hutchinson, April 6, 1771, Hutchinson Papers, 25, 509; Thomas Hutchinson to William Fitzwilliam, April 6, 1771, Hutchinson Papers, 25, 511.

34. Alden Bradford, ed., *Speeches of the Governors of Massachusetts, 1765 to 1775* (Boston: Russell and Brown, 1818; reprint, New York: Da Capo Press, 1971), 295.

35. Ibid., 297.

36. Ibid., 299: Thomas Hutchinson to Francis Bernard, July 8, 1771, Hutchinson Papers, 27, 322.

37. Warden, *Boston*, 37–55; Leonard Woods Labaree, *Royal Government in America: A Study of the British Colonial System before 1783* (New Haven; Yale UP, 1933), 352–372.

38. Albert Cheney Goodell, A. S. Wheeler, and W. C. Williamson, eds., *The Acts and Resolves, Public and Private, of the Province of Massachusetts Bay*, 20 vols. (Boston: Wright and Potter, 1869–1922), 9, 581, 611, 636, 674, 689; Mayo, *Hutchinson's History; A Collection of the Proceedings of the Great and General Court etc.* (Boston: Thomas Fleet, 1729).

39. Mayo, *Hutchinson's History*, 3, 357–361.

40. Thomas Hutchinson to ?, June 5, 1771, Hutchinson Papers, 27, 303; Adams, ed., *Works*, 2, 259.

41. Thomas Hutchinson to Lord Hillsborough, April 29, 1771, Hutchinson Papers, 27, 274.

42. Thomas Hutchinson to Francis Bernard, April 23, 1771, Hutchinson Papers, 27, 267–268.

43. Thomas Hutchinson to Lord Hillsborough, March 9, 1771, Hutchinson Papers, 27, 224.

44. Thomas Hutchinson to Francis Bernard, October 3, 1771, Hutchinson Papers, 27, 455.

45. Bailyn, *Ordeal*.

46. *Boston Gazette*, October 14, 21, and November 4, 1771.

47. Ibid., November 11, 1771.

48. Thomas Hutchinson to John Worthington, January 31, 1771, Hutchinson Papers, 27, 175; "Junius Americus" was Arthur Lee; "Candidus," "Vindex," and "Valerius Poplicola" were all Samuel Adams. *Boston Gazette*, October 7, 14, and 28, 1771. "Mucius Scaevola" was Joseph Greenleaf. *Massachusetts Spy*, November 14, 1771. Mayo, *Hutchinson's History*, 3, 229.

49. Ellen E. Brennan, *Plural Office-Holding in Massachusetts 1760 to 1780: Its Relation to the "Separation" of Departments of Government* (Chapel Hill: U of North Carolina P, 1945).

50. *Massachusetts Spy*, No. 37, November 1771.

51. *Boston Gazette*, October 7, 1771.

52. Ibid., October 14, 1771.

53. Thomas Hutchinson to ?, March 23, 1772, Hutchinson Papers, 27, 306.

54. Timothy M. Barnes, "The Loyalist Press in the American Revolution, 1756–1781" (unpublished Ph.D. dissertation, University of New Mexico, 1970).

55. *Censor*, November 30, 1771; Mercy Otis Warren, *The Adulateur, A Tragedy, As It Is Now Acted In Upper Servia* (Boston: Printed and Sold at the Printing Office, 1773); *Massachusetts Spy*, March 26 and April 23, 1773; Maud MacDonald Hutcheson, "Mercy Warren, 1728–1814," *William and Mary Quarterly* 3rd ser. 10 (July 1953): 378–402.

56. *Censor*, November 23, 1771.

57. Ibid., December 7, 1771.

58. Ibid., 9–10.

59. Ibid., 10.

60. Ibid., 11; *Censor*, May 2, 1772.

61. Thomas Hutchinson to Richard Jackson, October 1771, Hutchinson Papers, 27, 436.

62. Mayo, *Hutchinson's History*, 3, 235.

NOTES TO CHAPTER SEVEN

1. Thomas Hutchinson to John Hely Hutchinson, February 14, 1772, Hutchinson Papers, 27, 521.
2. Thomas Hutchinson to ?, January 24, 1772, Hutchinson Papers, 27, 498; Thomas Hutchinson to Lord Hillsborough, January 31, 1772, Hutchinson Papers, 27, 509.
3. Thomas Hutchinson to ?, April 28, 1772 and to Francis Bernard, January 29, 1772, Hutchinson Papers, 27, 567, 502–504.
4. Thomas Hutchinson to Lord Hillsborough, January 24, 1772, Hutchinson Papers, 27, 500.
5. Thomas Hutchinson to John Pownall, April 1772, Hutchinson Papers, 27, 557.
6. Thomas Hutchinson to Francis Bernard, January 13, 1772, Hutchinson Papers, 27, 486; Thomas Hutchinson to Lord Hillsborough, May 9, 1772, Hutchinson Papers, 27, 599; Thomas Hutchinson to William [Billy] Sanford Hutchinson, May 17, November 3, and December 22, 1772, Hutchinson Papers, 27, 602–603, 731–732, 792.
7. Bradford, *Speeches*, 313–325; Thomas Hutchinson to Thomas Pownall, June 22, 1772, Hutchinson Papers, 27, 627.
8. Bradford, *Speeches*, 325.
9. Ibid.; Mayo, *Hutchinson's History*, 3, 257, 404–410.
10. Bradford, *Speeches*, 325–326.
11. Thomas Hutchinson to ?, July 12, 1772, Hutchinson Papers, 27, 656.
12. Thomas Hutchinson to Francis Bernard, June 27, 1772, Hutchinson Papers, 27, 636.
13. Thomas Hutchinson to Lord Hillsborough, June 12, 1772, Hutchinson Papers, 27, 614; John R. Bartlett, *A History of the Destruction of His Brittanic Majesty's Schooner Gaspée* (Providence: A. C. Greene, 1861); David Lovejoy, *Rhode Island Politics and the American Revolution, 1760–1776* (Providence: Brown UP, 1958); William R. Leslie, "The Gaspée Affair: A Study of Its Constitutional Significance," Mississippi Valley Historical Review, 39 (September 1952): 233–256; B. D. Bargar, *Lord Dartmouth and the American Revolution* (Columbia: U of South Carolina P, 1965).
14. Thomas Hutchinson to ?, August 29, 1772, and to Samuel Hood, September 2, 1772, Hutchinson Papers, 27, 381–382 and 385; Thomas Hutchinson to James Gambier, no date, Hutchinson Papers, 27, no page.
15. Thomas Hutchinson to James Gambier, no date, Hutchinson Papers, no page. Here Hutchinson suggested that the authorities "carry a few of those who burned the Gaspée to the executioners dock in London."
16. Thomas Hutchinson to Lord Hillsborough, October 1, 1772, Hutchinson Papers, 27, 709–710; Thomas Hutchinson to William Palmer, September 11, 1772, Hutchinson Papers, 27, 704.
17. Richard D. Brown, *Revolutionary Politics in Massachusetts: The Boston Committee of Correspondence and the Towns, 1772–1774* (Cambridge: Harvard UP, 1970); *The Votes and Proceedings of the Freeholders and Other Inhabitants of the Town of Boston,*

in Town Meeting Assembled, According to Law (Boston: Edes and Gill and T. and J. Fleet, 1772); Thomas Hutchinson to Lord Dartmouth, October 23, 1772, Hutchinson Papers, 27, no page.

18. "Fervidus," *Boston Gazette*, March 16, 1772; Cushing, *Samuel Adams*, 2, 234.

19. Thomas Hutchinson to John Pownall, November 13, 1772, Hutchinson Papers, 27, 751.

20. Brown, *Revolutionary Politics*, 68–80.

21. Thomas Hutchinson, "Account and Defense of Conduct," July 1776, Hutchinson Papers, Massachusetts Historical Society, 6; Thomas Hutchinson to Thomas Gage, January 7, 1773 and to John Pownall, January 1773, Hutchinson Papers, 27, 438 and 439.

22. Thomas Hutchinson to Lord Dartmouth, December 13, 1772, Hutchinson Papers, 27, 786–787.

23. *Censor*, February 8, 1772; Adair and Schutz, *Peter Oliver's Origins*, 36–43; Mayo, *Hutchinson's History*, 3, 252–253; Thomas Hutchinson to John Pownall, July 21, 1772, and to Sir Francis Bernard, December 3, 1773, Hutchinson Papers, 27, 658–659, 1097; Warden, *Boston*, 246–250.

24. Thomas Hutchinson to Francis Bernard, March 10, 1773, Hutchinson Papers, 27, no page; Bradford, *Speeches*, 336–396; Mayo, *Hutchinson's History*, 3, 266.

25. Adams, *Works*, 2, 310–313.

26. Hutchinson, "Account and Defense of Conduct," 6–7.

27. Thomas Hutchinson to Thomas Gage, March 7, 1773, Hutchinson Papers, 27, 461–462.

28. Bradford, *Speeches*, 337–338.

29. Ibid., 338.

30. Ibid., 339; Thomas Hutchinson to the Reverend Doctor Williams, November 13, 1773, Hutchinson Papers, 27, 1069.

31. Bradford, *Speeches*, 339–340.

32. Thomas Hutchinson, "A Dialogue Between an American and a European Englishman," *Perspectives in American History* 9 (Cambridge: Charles Warren Center, 1975), 343–410.

33. Ibid., 341.

34. Ibid.

35. Thomas Hutchinson to John Pownall, January 7, 1773, Hutchinson Papers, 27, no page.

36. Ibid., no page. Hutchinson wrote "I must have brought upon myself the indignation of Parliament if I had sat still when its authority was treated with so much contempt."

37. Thomas Hutchinson to John Pownall and to Lord Dartmouth, February 1, 1773, Hutchinson Papers, 27, no pages.

38. Thomas Hutchinson to James Gambier, February 1773, Hutchinson Papers, 27, no page.

39. Thomas Hutchinson to General Mackay, February 23, 1773, Hutchinson Papers, 27, no page; Albert Henry Smyth, ed., *The Writings of Benjamin Franklin*, vol. 6, 1773–1774 (New York: Macmillan, 1907), 51.

40. Smyth, *Writings*, 48–49; Bailyn, *Ordeal*, 215–219.

41. Thomas Hutchinson to ?, March 20, 1773, Hutchinson Papers, 27, no page: Thomas Hutchinson to ?, March 23, 1773, Hutchinson Papers, 27, no page; Thomas Hutchinson to William Sanford Hutchinson, April 20, 1773, Hutchinson Papers, 27, no page.

42. Thomas Hutchinson to Lord Dartmouth, no date, Hutchinson Papers, 27, 903–906.

43. Thomas Hutchinson to ?, June 14, 1773, Hutchinson Papers, 27, no page.

44. Thomas Hutchinson to Francis Bernard, June 29, 1773, Hutchinson Papers, 502; Hutchinson, "Account and Defense of Conduct," 7; *A Copy of the Letters Sent to Great Britain etc.* (Boston: Edes and Gill, 1773); John Temple to Thomas Whately, November 4, 1768, *Collections*, 6 (Boston: Massachusetts Historical Society, 1897): 111–113; Adams, *Works*, 2, 318.

45. Benjamin Franklin to Thomas Cushing, June 4, 1773, in Smyth, *Writings*, 6, 57.

46. Samuel Cooper to Benjamin Franklin, June 14, 1773, ibid., 6, 58–59; Thomas Hutchinson to Israel Mauduit, September 28, 1773, Hutchinson Papers, 27, 1014; Benjamin Franklin, "Tract Relative to the Affair of Hutchinson's Letters," in Smyth, *Writings*, 6, 258–289; ibid., "The Scene in the Cockpit," 10, 240–272.

47. *Copy of Letters*, passim.

48. Adams, *Works*, 1, 133.

49. Thomas Hutchinson to Francis Bernard, June 29, 1773, Hutchinson Papers, 27, 922–923; Hutchinson, "Account and Defense of Conduct," 8.

50. Thomas Hutchinson to Francis Bernard, June 29, 1773, Hutchinson Papers, 27, 922–923; Thomas Hutchinson to Thomas Pownall, July 3, 1773, Hutchinson Papers, 27, 931; Thomas Hutchinson to William Tryon, July 6, 1773, Hutchinson Papers, 27, 935; Thomas Hutchinson to [Lord Dartmouth], June 14, 1773, Hutchinson Papers, 27, 912; Thomas Hutchinson to ? [Smith], June 28, 1773, Hutchinson Papers, 27, 927.

51. Thomas Hutchinson to the Reverend John Lyman, July 16, 1773, Hutchinson Papers, 27, 944–945.

52. Thomas Hutchinson to Lord Hillsborough, letter fragment, no date, Hutchinson Papers, 27, 929; Thomas Hutchinson to William Sanford Hutchinson, August 21, 1773, Hutchinson Papers, 27, 983; Thomas Hutchinson to William Sanford Hutchinson, December 7, 1773, Hutchinson Papers, 27, 1101; Thomas Hutchinson to Israel Mauduit, September 28, 1773, Hutchinson Papers, 27, 1015; Jonathan Sewall as "Philalethes" in *Massachusetts Gazette and the Boston Weekly News-Letter*, June to August, 1773.

53. "The freemen of the province understand from good authority that there is a consignment of a quantity of tea to your House from the East India Company which is destructive to the happiness of every well wisher to this country therefore it is expected that you will personally appear on Wednesday next at 12 o'clock at noon day to make a public resignation of your commission agreeable to a notification of this day for that purpose: fail not upon your peril." Egerton Collection, November 2, 1773, Massachusetts Historical Society.

54. Thomas Hutchinson to Thomas Whately, October 30, 1770, Hutchinson Papers, 27, 11–12; Thomas Hutchinson to William Palmer, September 11, 1772, Hutchinson Papers, 27, 704.

55. Mayo, *Hutchinson's History*, 3, 303.

56. For example, the articles by "A Consistent PATRIOT," and "JOSHUA, SON OF NUN," in the *Massachusetts Spy*, October 14, 1773; "PRAEDICUS," *Boston Gazette*, October 18, 1773, and November 1, 1773; "A MERCHANT," *Massachusetts Spy*, October 28, 1773.

57. Benjamin Woods Labaree, *The Boston Tea Party* (Boston: Northeastern UP, 1964); Peter D. G. Thomas, *From Tea Party to Independence: The Third Phase of the American Revolution, 1773 to 1776* (Oxford: Clarendon Press, 1991).

58. Thomas Hutchinson to the Directors of the East India Company, December 19, 1773, Hutchinson Papers, 27, 597–599.

59. Thomas Hutchinson to Israel Mauduit, December 1773, Hutchinson Papers, 27, 1150.

60. Thomas Hutchinson to the Directors of the East India Company, December 19, 1773, Hutchinson Papers, 27, 1138.

61. Ibid., 1138.

62. Adams, *Works*, 2, 323.

63. Thomas Hutchinson to Lord Dartmouth, December 24, 1773, Hutchinson Papers, 27, 1148.

64. Thomas Hutchinson to ?, December 30, 1773, Hutchinson Papers, 27, 1158; Thomas Pownall later criticized Hutchinson personally for not taking action without the Council's permission. Peter O. Hutchinson, *Diary and Letters*, 1, 194–195.

65. Thomas Hutchinson to Francis Bernard, January 1, 1774, Hutchinson Papers, 27, 1161; Hutchinson, "Account and Defense of Conduct," 17.

66. Thomas Hutchinson to Francis Maseres, January 3, 1774, Hutchinson Papers, 27, no page.

67. Thomas Hutchinson to Lord Dartmouth, January 28, 1774, Gage Papers, no page; Frank W. C. Hersey, "Tar and Feathers: The Adventures of Captain John Malcolm," Colonial Society of Massachusetts, *Publications*, 34 (1937–1942): 429–473.

68. Peter O. Hutchinson, *Diary and Letters*, 1, 112–117.

69. Ibid., 112–117; Shipton, *Sibley's* 8, 217.

70. Adams, *Works*, 2, 233. Adams wrote that Rogers was "not one of the originals but came in afterwards." In March 1774, Adams seemed to think that Hutchinson would continue to be governor but retire to England allowing Peter Oliver to take over as lieutenant governor "and rule the province."

71. Adams, *Works*, 2, 150–151; *Boston Evening-Post*, December 6, 1756; *Copy of Letters*, no page.

72. *A Fair Account of the Late Unhappy Disturbance at Boston in New England* (Boston: October 1770); *Copy of Letters*.

73. Lord Dartmouth to Thomas Gage, April 9, 1774, in *The Correspondence of General Gage*, 2, 159–162.

74. Mayo, *Hutchinson's History*, 3, 327–329; Cunningham, *Letters and Diary*, 265; Peter O. Hutchinson, *Diary and Letters*, 1, 147.

NOTES TO CHAPTER EIGHT

1. Thomas Hutchinson to ?, December 31, 1765, Hutchinson Papers, 26, 373; Peter O. Hutchinson, *Diary and Letters*, 2, 353–355.
2. Peter O. Hutchinson, *Diary and Letters*, 1, 157–175.
3. Ibid., 1, 179–180.
4. Ibid., 2, 40.
5. Ibid., 1, 238; Bailyn, *Ordeal*, 290–292.
6. Peter O. Hutchinson, *Diary and Letters*, 1, 158; Jensen, *Founding*, 456.
7. Peter O. Hutchinson, *Diary and Letters*, 1, 158.
8. Ibid., 1, 176–178; Jensen, *Founding*, 582.
9. Bailyn, *Ordeal*, 334–340; Hutchinson, "Account and Defense of Conduct."
10. Mark A. DeWolfe Howe, "The English Journal of Josiah Quincy, Jr., 1774 to 1775," Massachusetts Historical Society, *Proceedings*, 50 (1916 to 1917): 433–470.
11. Ibid., 440, 444.
12. Ibid., 440, 443.
13. Peter O. Hutchinson, *Diary and Letters*, 311; Hutchinson, "Account and Defense of Conduct."
14. Gregory Oalmer, *Biographical Sketches of the Loyalists of the American Revolution* (London: Oxford UP, 1961); Hugh Edward Egerton, ed., *The Royal Commission on the Losses and Services of the American Loyalists, 1783–1785* (New York: Burt Franklin, 1915; reprint, New York: Lenox Hill, 1971); E. Alfred Jones, *The Loyalists of Massachusetts: Their Memorials, Petitions and Claims* (London: St. Catherine's Press, 1930); Lewis Einstein, *Divided Loyalties: Americans in England during the War of Independence* (London: Cobden-Sanderson, 1933); Mary Beth Norton, *The British-Americans: The Loyalist Exiles in England, 1774–1789* (Boston: Little, Brown, 1972).
15. Peter O. Hutchinson, Egerton Collection, 2664, October 1777, Massachusetts Historical Society, microfilm, reel 3; Ibid., Peter O. Hutchinson, *Diary and Letters*, 1, 261, 281 n3, 283, and 2, 290.
16. Ibid., 1, 476–477.
17. Ibid., 1, 390.
18. Ibid., 1, 410, and 2, 291.
19. Ibid., 2, 156 and 356.
20. Egerton Manuscript, 2664, Massachusetts Historical Society, microfilm, reel 3; Peter O. Hutchinson, *Diary and Letters*, 2, 343–345.
21. *Independent Chronicle and Universal Advertizer*, January 4, 1781; Lyman H. Butterfield and Marc Friedlaender, eds., *The Adams Family Correspondence*, vol. 4 (Cambridge: Harvard UP, 1973), 22 and 58–59.
22. Adams, *Works*, 10, 261.
23. Ibid., 261.

24. Edward Pierce Hamilton, *A History of Milton* (Milton: Milton Historical Society, 1957); Peter O. Hutchinson, *Diary and Letters*, 1, 557; Malcolm Freiberg, *Thomas Hutchinson of Milton*, (Milton: Milton Historical Society, 1971); James K. Hosmer, *A Life of Thomas Hutchinson* (Cambridge: Riverside Press, 1896; reprint, New York: Da Capo Press, 1972), 442; Arthur Lee to James Warren, August 8, 1782, Massachusetts Historical Society, *Collections*, 73 (1925): 171.

25. Peter O. Hutchinson, *Diary and Letters*, 1, 12.

Selected Bibliography

UNPUBLISHED PRIMARY DOCUMENTS

Belcher, Jonathan. Jonathan Belcher Letter Books, 1743 to 1755. Massachusetts Historical Society.

Bernard, Sir Francis. Bernard Papers. 13 Volumes. Massachusetts Historical Society. This collection is a microfilm copy of the original Sparks Manuscript in the Houghton Library, Harvard University, Cambridge, Massachusetts.

Davis, Caleb. Caleb Davis Papers. Massachusetts Historical Society.

Gage, Sir Thomas. Gage Papers. Massachusetts Historical Society.

Hancock, John and Thomas. Hancock Family Letter Books, 1745 to 1782. Massachusetts Historical Society.

Hancock, John. John Hancock Papers, 1728 to 1775. Massachusetts Historical Society.

Hutchinson, Thomas. Account and Defense of Conduct, July 1776.

———. Hutchinson's Correspondence, 1774 to 1780. Massachusetts Historical Society.

———. The Hutchinson Papers, 1741 to 1774. Massachusetts Historical Society. Volumes 25, 26, 27. This collection is a typescript by Cathcrine Shaw Mayo of the originals held at the Massachusetts State Archive, Boston State House, Boston, Massachusetts. This collection is often referred to as "Hutchinson's Letter Books."

Loudoun, Lord. Loudoun Papers. Massachusetts Historical Society. This collection is a microfilm copy of the original manuscript holdings at the Huntington Library, San Marino, California.

Oliver, Andrew. Letter Book, October 20, 1767 to January 7, 1774. 2 Volumes. This collection is a typescript by Frederick L. Gay, Massachusetts Historical Society.
Paine, Robert Treat. Robert Treat Paine Papers. Massachusetts Historical Society.
Williams, Israel. Israel Williams Papers, 1728 to 1785. Massachusetts Historical Society.

NEWSPAPERS AND BROADSHEETS

The Boston Chronicle (1768 to 1769) .
The Boston Evening-Post (1760 to 1774)
The Boston Gazette (1760 to 1774)
The Boston News-Letter (1768 to 1769)
The Boston Post-Boy and Advertizer (1763 to 1774)
The Censor (1771–1772)
The Independent Advertizer (1749)
The Massachusetts Gazette (1768–1769)
The Massachusetts Spy (1770 to 1774)

The Massachusetts Historical Society holds thousands of broadsheets and pamphlets from the colonial era. I made use of many of these for the period 1711 to 1774.

PUBLISHED PRIMARY DOCUMENTS AND OTHER
SECONDARY SOURCES INCLUDING UNPUBLISHED
THESES AND DISSERTATIONS

Adair, Douglass, and John A. Schutz, eds. *Peter Oliver's Origins and Progress of the American Rebellion: A Tory View*. Stanford: Stanford UP, 1961.
Adams, Charles Francis, ed. *Familiar Letters of John Adams and His Wife Abigail Adams During the Revolution*. New York: Hurd, Houghton, 1876.
———. *The Works of John Adams*. 10 vols. Boston: Little, Brown, 1850–1856.
Akers, Charles K. *The Divine Politician: Samuel Cooper and the American Revolution in Boston*. Boston: Northeastern UP, 1982.
Anderson, Benedict. *Imagined Communities: Reflections on the Origin and Spread of Nationalism*. London: Verso, 1983.
Anderson, George P. "Ebenezer Mackintosh: Stamp Act Rioter and Patriot." *Publications* 26. Boston: Colonial Society of Massachusetts, 1924–1926.
Bailyn, Bernard. *Faces of Revolution: Personalities and Themes in the Struggle for American Independence*. New York: Knopf, 1990.
———. *The Ordeal of Thomas Hutchinson*. Cambridge: Belknap Press, 1974.
———, ed. "A Dialogue Between An American and a European Englishman, 1768," by Thomas Hutchinson in *Perspectives in American History* 9 (1975): 343–411.

Bancroft, George. *The History of the United States.* New York: D. Appleton, 1886–1888.

Bargar, B. D. *Lord Dartmouth and the American Revolution.* Columbia: U of South Carolina P, 1965.

Barnes, Timothy. "The Loyalist Press in the American Revolution, 1756–1781." Unpublished Ph.D. Dissertation. University of New Mexico, 1970.

Bartlett, John R. *A History of the Destruction of His Brittanic Majesty's Schooner the Gaspée.* Providence: A. C. Greene, 1861.

Batinski, Michael Clement. "Jonathan Belcher of Massachusetts, 1682 to 1741." Unpublished Ph.D. Dissertation. Northwestern University, 1970.

Battis, Emery. *Saints and Sectaries: Anne Hutchinson and the Antinomian Controversy in the Massachusetts Bay Colony.* Chapel Hill: U of North Carolina P, 1962.

Beeman, Richard R. "Deference, Republicanism, and the Emergence of Popular Politics in Eighteenth-Century America." *William and Mary Quarterly* 3rd ser. 49 (July 1992).

Bell, Hugh. "'A Personal Challenge': The Otis-Hutchinson Controversy, 1761–1762." *Essex Institute Historical Collections* 106 (January 1970).

Bernstein, Barton, ed. *Towards a New Past: Dissenting Essays in American History.* Cambridge: Harvard UP, 1968

Billias, George. "The Massachusetts Land Bankers of 1740." *University of Maine Studies* 2nd ser. 74 (April 1959).

Boston Town Records 1631–1822. Boston: Rockwell and Churchill, 1881–1906.

Bonomi, Patricia U. *A Factious People: Politics and Society in Colonial New York.* New York: Columbia UP, 1971.

Boyer, Paul. "Borrowed Rhetoric: The Massachusetts Excise Controversy of 1754." *William and Mary Quarterly* 3rd ser. 21 (July 1964).

Boyer, Paul, and Stephen Nissenbaum. *Salem Possessed: The Social Origins of Witchcraft.* Cambridge: Harvard UP, 1974.

Bradford, Alden, ed. *Speeches of the Governors of Massachusetts, 1765 to 1775.* Boston: Russell and Brown, 1818; repr. New York: Da Capo Press, 1971.

Brennan, Ellen E. *Plural Office-Holding in Massachusetts, 1760 to 1780: Its Relation to the "Separation" of Departments of Government.* Chapel Hill: U of North Carolina P, 1945.

Bridenbaugh, Carl. *Cities in Revolt.* New York: Knopf, 1955.

———. *Seat of Empire.* Williamsburg: Colonial Society of Williamsburg, 1950.

Brown, E. Francis. "The Law Career of Major Joseph Hawley." *New England Quarterly* 4 (July 1931).

Brown, Richard D. *Knowledge Is Power: The Diffusion of Information in Early America, 1700 to 1865.* New York: Oxford UP, 1989.

———. *Revolutionary Politics in Massachusetts: The Boston Committee of Correspondence and the Towns, 1772 to 1774.* Cambridge: Harvard UP, 1970.

Brown, Richard M. *Strain of Violence: Historical Studies in Early American Violence and Vigilantism.* New York: Oxford UP, 1975.

Brown, Robert E. *Middle-Class Democracy and the Revolution in Massachusetts, 1691–1780.* Ithaca: Cornell UP, 1955.

Brown, Wallace. *The King's Friends: The Composition and Motives of the American Loyalist Claimants.* Providence: Brown UP, 1965.

Bullion, John L. "British Ministers and American Resistance to the Stamp Act, October-December, 1765." *William and Mary Quarterly* 3rd ser. 49 (January 1992).

———. *A Great and Necessary Measure: George Grenville and the Genesis of the Stamp Act, 1763 to 1765.* Columbia: U of Missouri P, 1982.

———. "Honor, Trade, and Empire: Grenville's Treasury and 'the American Question,' 1763–1765." Unpublished Ph.D. Dissertation: University of Texas, 1977.

Bushman, Richard. *King and People in Provincial Massachusetts.* Chapel Hill: U of North Carolina P, 1985.

Butterfield, Lyman, ed. *John Adams's Diary and Autobiography.* Cambridge: Belknap Press, 1961.

Butterfield, Lyman H., and Marc Friedlaender, eds. *The Adams Family Correspondence.* 4 vols. Cambridge: Harvard UP, 1973.

Cain, P. J., and A. G. Hopkins. *British Imperialism: Innovation and Expansion, 1688–1914.* London: Longman, 1993.

Carr, Edward Hallett. *What Is History?* New York: Knopf, 1961.

Carter, Clarence E., ed. *The Correspondence of General Thomas Gage with the Secretaries of State, and with the War Office and Treasury, 1763–1775.* 2 vols. New Haven: Yale UP, 1931–1933.

Champagne, Roger J. *Alexander McDougall and the American Revolution in New York.* (Schenectady: Union College Press, 1975).

Channing, Edward, and Archibald C. Coolidge, eds., *The Barrington-Bernard Correspondence and Illustrative Matter, 1760–1770.* Cambridge: Harvard UP, 1912.

Colley, Linda. *Britons: Forging the Nation, 1707 to 1837.* New Haven: Yale UP, 1992.

Conroy, David W. *In Public Houses: Drink and the Revolution of Authority in Colonial Massachusetts.* Chapel Hill: U of North Carolina P, 1995.

Cook, Edward. "Social Behavior and Changing Values in Dedham." *William and Mary Quarterly* 3rd ser. 26 (1970).

Countryman, Edward. *The American Revolution.* New York: Hill and Wang, 1985.

———. "The Problem of the Early American Crowd." *Journal of American Studies* 7 (1973).

Cunningham, Anne Rowe, ed. *The Letters and Diary of John Rowe, Boston Merchant, 1759–1762, 1764–1779.* Boston: W. B. Clark, 1903.

Cushing, Harry A., ed. *The Writings of Samuel Adams.* 4 vols. New York: Octagon, 1968.

Davis, Andrew MacFarland. "A Calendar of the Land Bank Papers." *Publications 4.* Boston: Colonial Society of Massachusetts, 1910.

———. "Currency and Banking in the Province of the Massachusetts Bay." *Collections 2.* Boston: Colonial Society of Massachusetts, 1901.

———. "Papers Relating to the Land Bank of 1740." *Publications.* Boston: Massachusetts Historical Society, 1910.

Day, Alan, and Katherine Day. "Another Look at the Boston Caucus." *Journal of American Studies* 5 (1971).

Demos, John. *A Little Commonwealth: Family Life in Plymouth Colony.* New York: Oxford UP, 1970.

Dexter, Franklin Bowditch. *Biographical Sketches of the Graduates of Yale with the Annals of the College History.* New York: Holt, 1919.

Dickerson, Oliver M., ed. *Boston under Military Rule 1768 to 1769 as Revealed in a Journal of the Times.* Boston: Chapman and Grimes, 1936.

———. *The Navigation Acts and the American Revolution.* Philadelphia: U of Pennsylvania P, 1951.

Douglass, William. *A Discourse Concerning the Currencies of the British Plantations in America.* Boston: Kneeland and Green, 1740.

Draper, Theodore. *A Struggle for Power: The American Revolution.* New York: Random House, 1996.

Egerton, Hugh Edward, ed. *The Royal Commission on the Losses and Services of American Loyalists, 1783–1785.* New York: Burt Franklin, 1915; repr. New York: Lenox Hill, 1971.

Einstein, Lewis. *Divided Loyalties: Americans in England during the War of Independence.* London: Cobden-Sanderson, 1933.

Eliot, John. *A Biographical Dictionary.* Boston: Cushing and Appleton, 1869.

Erikson, Kai. *Wayward Puritans.* New York: Wiley, 1966.

Fischer, David Hackett. *Paul Revere's Ride.* New York: Oxford UP. 1994.

Fiske, John. *Essays Historical and Literary.* 2 vols. New York: Macmillan, 1902.

Fitzmaurice, Edmond. *The Life of William, Earl of Shelburne.* London: Macmillan, 1875.

Freiberg, Malcolm. *Prelude to Purgatory: Thomas Hutchinson in Provincial Massachusetts Politics, 1760 to 1770.* New York: Garland, 1990.

———. "Thomas Hutchinson and the Province Currency." *New England Quarterly* 30 (June 1957).

———. "Thomas Hutchinson: The First Fifty Years." *William and Mary Quarterly* 15 (January 1958).

———. *Thomas Hutchinson of Milton.* Boston: Massachusetts Historical Society, 1971.

Friedman, Bernard. "The Shaping of the Radical Consciousness in Provincial New York." *Journal of American History* 56 (1970).

Galvin, John. *Three Men of Boston.* New York: T. Y. Crowell, 1976.

Gilje, Paul. *The Road to Mobocracy.* Chapel Hill: U of North Carolina P, 1987).

Gipson, Lawrence Henry. "Thomas Hutchinson and the Framing of the Albany Plan of Union, 1754." *Pennsylvania Magazine of History and Biography* 74 (January 1950).

Gordon, William. *The History of the Rise, Progress, and Establishment of the Independence of the United States of America.* 4 vols. New York: Hodge, Allen & Campbell, 1789.

Greven, Philip. *The Protestant Temperament: Patterns of Child-Rearing, Religious Experience, and the Self in Early America.* Chicago: U of Chicago P, 1977.

Hall, David D., ed. *The Antinomian Controversy, 1636–1638: A Documentary History.* Middletown: U of Connecticut P, 1968.

Hamilton, Edward Pierce. *A History of Milton.* Milton: Milton Historical Society, 1957.

Henretta, James. "Economic Development and Social Structure in Colonial Boston." *William and Mary Quarterly* 22 (January 1965).

———. *The Origins of American Capitalism: Selected Essays.* Boston: Northeastern UP, 1994.

Hoerder, Dirk. "Boston Leaders and Boston Crowds, 1765–1776." In Alfred Young, *The American Revolution.*

———. *Crowd Action in Revolutionary Massachusetts 1765–1780.* New York: Academic Press, 1977.

Hosmer, James K. *The Life of Thomas Hutchinson.* New York: Da Capo Press, 1972.

Hulton, Ann. *Letters of a Loyalist Lady: Being the Letters of Ann Hulton, Sister of Henry Hulton, Commissioner of Customs at Boston, 1767–1776.* Cambridge: Riverside Press, 1896; repr. Cambridge: Harvard UP, 1927.

Hutcheson, Maud MacDonald. "Mercy Warren, 1728–1814." *William and Mary Quarterly* 3rd ser. 10 (July 1953).

Hutchinson, Peter Orlando, ed. *The Diary and Letters of His Excellency Thomas Hutchinson.* 2 vols. Boston: Houghton, Mifflin, 1884.

Hutson, James. "An Investigation of the Inarticulate: Philadelphia's White Oaks." *William and Mary Quarterly* 3rd ser. 28 (January 1971).

Jensen, Merrill. *The Founding of a Nation: A History of the American Revolution, 1763–1776.* New York: Oxford UP, 1968.

Jones, E. Alfred. *The Loyalists of Massachusetts: Their Memorials, Petitions, and Claims.* London: St. Catherine's Press, 1930.

Kammen, Michael. *Empire and Interest: The American Colonies and the Politics of Mercantilism.* New York: J. B. Lippincott, 1970.

———. *A Season of Youth: The American Revolution and the Historical Imagination.* Ithaca: Knopf, 1978.

Kaye, Harvey, ed. *The Face of the Crowd: Selected Essays of George Rudé.* London: Harvester, 1988.

Kimball, Everett. *The Public Life of Joseph Dudley: A Study of the Colonial Policy of the Stuarts in new England, 1660 to 1715.* New York: Longmans, Green, 1911.

Koehler, Lyle. "The Case of the American Jezebels: Anne Hutchinson and Female Agitation during the Years of Antinomian Turmoil." *William and Mary Quarterly* 3rd ser. 31 (January 1974).

Kulikoff, Alan. "The Progress of Inequality in Revolutionary Boston." *William and Mary Quarterly* 3rd ser. 27 (January 1971).

Labaree, Benjamin Woods. *The Boston Tea Party.* Boston: Northeastern UP, 1964.

Labaree, Leonard Woods. *Royal Government in America: A Study of the British Colonial System before 1783.* New Haven: Yale UP, 1933.

Langford, Paul. *A Polite and Commercial People: England 1727–1783.* Oxford: Oxford UP, 1992.

Lax, John, and William Pencak. "The Knowles Riot and the Crisis of the 1740s." *Perspectives in American History* 10 (1976).

Lemisch, Jesse. "History from the Bottom Up." In Bernstein, *Towards a New Past.*

———. "Jack Tar in the Streets: Merchant Seamen in the Politics of Revolutionary America." *William and Mary Quarterly* 3rd ser. 25 (July 1968).

———. "Listening to the Inarticulate." *Journal of Social History* (Fall 1969).

———. "Review of Hiller Zobel's Boston Massacre." *Harvard Law Review* 84 (1970–71).

Lincoln, C. H., ed. *The Correspondence of William Shirley*. New York: Macmillan, 1912.

Lockridge, Kenneth A. "Land, Population and the Evolution of New England Society, 1630 to 1790." *Past and Present* 39 (April 1968).

———. *A New England Town: The First Hundred Years. Dedham, Massachusetts, 1636–1736*. New York: Norton, 1970.

Lovejoy, David. *Rhode Island Politics and the American Revolution, 1760–1776*. Providence: Brown UP, 1958.

Lynd, Staughton. *Class Conflict, Slavery and the U. S. Constitution*. Indianapolis: Bobbs-Merrill, 1967.

Maier, Pauline. "Popular Uprisings and Civil Authority in Eighteenth-Century America." *William and Mary Quarterly* 3rd ser. 27 (January 1970).

———. *From Resistance to Revolution: Colonial Radicals and the Development of American Opposition to Britain, 1765–1776*. New York: Knopf, 1972.

Main, Gloria L. "Inequality in Early America: The Evidence from Probate Records of Massachusetts and Maryland." *Journal of Interdisciplinary History* 7, 4 (Spring 1977).

Main, Jackson Turner. *The Social Structure of Revolutionary America*. Princeton: Princeton UP, 1965.

Martin, James K. *Men in Rebellion: Higher Governmental Leaders and the Coming of the American Revolution*. New Brunswick: Rutgers UP, 1973.

Martin, James K., and Karen R. Stubaus, eds. *The American Revolution: Whose Revolution?* Huntington: Robert E. Krieger, 1981.

Mauduit, Jasper. Jasper Mauduit, Agent in London for the Province of Massachusetts-Bay, 1762–1765. *Collections* 74. Boston: Massachusetts Historical Society, 1918.

Mayo, Lawrence Shaw, ed. *Thomas Hutchinson's History of the Province of Massachusetts Bay*. 3 vols. Cambridge: Harvard UP, 1936.

McCusker, John J., and Russell R. Menard. *The Economy of British America, 1607–1789*. Chapel Hill: U of North Carolina P, 1991.

Miller, John C. "Religion, Finance, and Democracy in Massachusetts." *New England Quarterly* 6 (1933).

———. *Samuel Adams: Pioneer in Propaganda*. Stanford: Stanford UP, 1936.

Miller, Perry. *The New England Mind: From Colony to Province*. Cambridge: Harvard UP, 1953.

Morgan, Edmund S. *Inventing the People: The Rise of Popular Sovereignty in England and America*. New York: Norton, 1988.

———. "Thomas Hutchinson and the Stamp Act." *New England Quarterly* 21 (1948).

———, ed. *Prologue to Revolution*. Chapel Hill: U of North Carolina P, 1955.

Morgan, Edmund S., and Helen Morgan. *The Stamp Act Crisis: Prologue to Revolution.* Chapel Hill: U of North Carolina P, 1953.

Moscovici, Serge. *The Age of the Crowd.* Cambridge UP, 1981.

Namier, Sir Lewis, and John Brooke. *Charles Townshend.* London: Macmillan, 1964.

————. *The House of Commons, 1754–1790.* 2 vols. New York: Oxford UP, 1964.

Nash, Gary. *Race, Class and Politics: Essays on American Colonial and Revolutionary Society.* Urbana: U of Illinois P, 1986.

————. "Social Change and the Growth of Prerevolutionary Urban Radicalism." In Alfred Young, *The American Revolution.*

————. *The Urban Crucible: Social Change, Political Consciousness, and the Origins of the American Revolution.* Cambridge: Harvard UP, 1979.

————. "Urban Wealth and Poverty in Pre-Revolutionary America." *Journal of Interdisciplinary History* 4 (Spring 1976).

Nelson, William E. *Americanization of the Common Law: The Impact of Legal Change on Massachusetts Society, 1760–1830.* Cambridge: Harvard UP, 1975.

Nelson, William H. *The American Tory.* Boston: Beacon Press, 1961.

Norton, Mary Beth. *The British-Americans: The Loyalist Exiles in England, 1774–1789.* Boston: Little, Brown, 1972.

Olton, Charles S. *Artisans for Independence: Philadelphia Mechanics and the American Revolution.* Syracuse: Syracuse University Press, 1975.

Palmer, Gregory. *Biographical Sketches of Loyalists of the American Revolution.* London: Meckler, 1984.

Pargellis, Stanley M. *Lord Loudoun in North America.* New Haven: Yale UP, 1933.

Patterson, Stephen. *Political Parties in Revolutionary Massachusetts.* Madison: U of Wisconsin P, 1973.

Pencak, William. *America's Burke: The Mind of Thomas Hutchinson.* Washington D.C.: UP of America, 1982.

————. *War, Politics, and Revolution in Provincial Massachusetts.* Boston: Northeastern UP, 1981.

Pickering, Danby, ed. *The Statutes at Large.* 36 vols. Cambridge, England: J. Bentham, 1761–1806

Quincy, Josiah, Jr. "The Journal of Josiah Quincy, Jr. in London, 1774 to 1775," *Proceedings* 50. Boston: Massachusetts Historical Society, 1916–1917.

Raimo, John W. *Biographical Directory of American Colonial and Revolutionary Governors, 1607–1789.* Westport: Meckler, 1980.

Rediker, Marcus. *Between the Devil and the Deep Blue Sea: Merchant Seamen, Pirates, and the Anglo-American Maritime World, 1700–1750.* Cambridge: Cambridge UP, 1987.

Riley, Stephen T., and Edward W. Hanson, eds. *The Papers of Robert Treat Paine.* Boston: Massachusetts Historical Society, 1992.

Rudé, George. *The Crowd in History, 1730–1848.* New York: Wiley, 1964.

Sawtelle, William O. "Thomas Pownall, Colonial Governor and Some of His Activities in the American Colonies." *Proceedings* 63 Massachusetts Historical Society, 1930.

Schlesinger, Arthur M. *Colonial Merchants and the American Revolution, 1763–1776.* New York: Columbia UP, 1968.

Schutz, John A. *Thomas Pownall: British Defender of American Liberty: A Study of Anglo-American Relations in the Eighteenth Century.* Glendale: A. H. Clarke, 1951.

―――. *William Shirley: King's Governor of Massachusetts.* Chapel Hill: U of North Carolina P, 1961.

Shaw, Peter. *American Patriots and the Rituals of Revolution.* Cambridge: Harvard UP, 1981.

Shipton, Clifford K., ed. *Sibley's Harvard Graduates.* Vols. 4, 8, and 10. Boston: Massachusetts Historical Society (1933, 1951, 1953).

Shy, John. *Toward Lexington: The Role of the British Army in the Coming of the American Revolution.* Princeton: Princeton UP, 1965.

Smith, William James, ed. *The Grenville Papers.* 4 vols. London, 1852; repr. New York: A.M.S. Press, 1970.

Sparks, Jared, ed. *The Library of American Biography.* 25 vols. New York: Harpers, 1840–1860.

Stark, James H. *The Loyalists of Massachusetts and the Other Side of the American Revolution.* Boston: James H. Stark, 1907; repr. Clifton, New Jersey: Augustus M. Kelly, 1972.

Sulloway, Frank J. *Born to Rebel: Birth Order, Family Dynamics, and Creative Lives.* New York: Pantheon, 1996.

Taylor, Robert J., ed. *The Papers of John Adams.* Cambridge: Belknap Press, 1977.

Thayer, Theodore. "The Land Bank System in the American Colonies." *Journal of Economic History* 13 (1953).

Thomas, Halsey M., ed. *The Diary of Samuel Sewell, 1674–1729.* 2 vols. New York: Farrar, Straus, Giroux, 1973.

Thomas, Isaiah. *The History of Printing in America with a Biography of Printers and an Account of Newspapers.* Worcester: Isaiah Thomas, 1810; repr. Barré, Mass: Imprint Society, 1970.

Thomas, Leslie J. "Partisan Politics in Massachusetts during Governor Bernard's Administration, 1760–1770." Unpublished Ph.D. dissertation. University of Wisconsin, 1960.

Thomas, P. D. G. *British Politics and the Stamp Act Crisis.* Oxford: Clarendon Press, 1975.

Thompson, Edward P. "The Moral Economy of the English Crowd in the Eighteenth Century." *Past and Present* 50 (1971).

Thrasher, Peter Adam. *Pascal Paoli.* Hamden: Archon Books, 1970.

Tucker, Robert, and David Hendrickson. *The Fall of the First British Empire: Origins of the War of American Independence.* Baltimore: Johns Hopkins UP, 1982.

Tyler, John W. *Smugglers and Patriots: Boston Merchants and the Advent of the American Revolution.* Boston: Northeastern UP, 1986.

Van Doren, Carl. *Jane Mecom: The Favorite Sister of Benjamin Franklin.* New York: Viking Press, 1968.

―――, ed. *The Letters of Benjamin Franklin and Jane Mecom.* Princeton: American Philosophical Society, 1950.

―――, ed. *Letters and Papers of Benjamin Franklin and Richard Jackson, 1753–1785.* Philadelphia: American Philosophical Society, 1947.

Walett, Francis G. "Governor Bernard's Undoing: An Earlier Hutchinson Letters Affair." *New England Quarterly* 38 (June 1965).

———. "James Bowdoin: Patriot Propagandist." *New England Quarterly* 27 (September 1950).

———. "The Massachusetts Council, 1766–1774: The Transformation of a Conservative Institution." *William and Mary Quarterly* 3rd ser. 6 (Winter 1949).

Walsh, Richard. *Charleston's Sons of Liberty.* Columbia, S.C.: U of South Carolina P, 1959.

Ward, George A., ed. *Journal and Letters of the Late Samuel Curwen.* New York: Leavitt, Trow, 1845.

Warden, G. B. *Boston: 1689–1776.* Boston: Little, Brown, 1970.

———. "Inequality and Instability in Eighteenth-Century Boston: A Reappraisal." *Journal of Interdisciplinary History* 4 (Spring 1976).

Warren, James. "The Warren-Adams Letters." *Collections* 72 and 73 Boston: Massachusetts Historical Society, 1917 and 1925.

Warren, Mercy Otis. *The History of the Rise, Progress and Termination of the American Revolution.* New York: A.M.S. Press, 1970.

Waters, John J., Jr. *The Otis Family in Provincial and Revolutionary Massachusetts.* Chapel Hill: U of North Carolina P, 1968.

Waters, John J., and John A. Schutz. "Patterns of Massachusetts Colonial Politics: The Writs of Assistance and the Rivalry between the Otis and Hutchinson Families." *William and Mary Quarterly* 3rd ser. 24. (Winter 1967).

Whitmore, William H. *The Massachusetts Civil List for the Colonial and Provincial Periods, 1630–1770.* Albany: Munsell, 1870.

Wickwire, Franklin B. *British Subministers and Colonial America, 1763–1783.* Princeton: Princeton UP, 1966.

Wilkes, John, and William Palfrey. "John Wilkes and William Palfrey." Eight letters edited by George M. Elsey. *Publications* 34. Boston: Colonial Society of Massachusetts (1943).

Williams, William Appleman. "Samuel Adams: Calvinist, Mercantilist, Revolutionary." *Studies on the Left* 1 (1960).

Winsor, Justin, ed. *Memorial History of Boston.* 4 vols. Boston: J.R. Osgood, 1880–1881.

Wolkins, George G. "Writs of Assistance in England." *Proceedings* 66. Boston: Massachusetts Historical Society, 1941.

Wood, Gordon S. "Rhetoric and Reality: A Note on Mobs in the American Revolution." *William and Mary Quarterly* 3rd ser. 23 (January 1966).

———. *The Radicalism of the American Revolution.* New York: Knopf, 1992.

Wroth, Kinvin L., and Hiller B. Zobel, eds. *The Legal Papers of John Adams.* 3 vols. Cambridge: Belknap Press, 1965.

Young, Alfred, ed. *The American Revolution: Explorations in the History of American Radicalism.* DeKalb: Northern Illinois UP, 1976).

Young, Edward J. "Subjects for Masters' Degrees in Harvard College from 1655 to 1741." *Proceedings* 18. Boston: Massachusetts Historical Society, 1881.

Zemsky, Robert. *Merchants, Farmers, and River Gods: An Essay on Eighteenth-Century American Politics.* Boston: Gambit, 1971.

Zobel, Hiller B. *The Boston Massacre.* New York: Norton, 1970.

Zuckerman, Michael. *Peaceable Kingdoms: New England Towns in the Eighteenth Century.* New York: Knopf, 1970.

Index

Abercrombie, James, 33
Acadian refugees, 29
Adams, John, 10, 14, 107; author of Hutchinson's obituary, 158; and the Boston Tea Party, 149; on colonial patriotism, 113; criticism of Hutchinson as Chief Justice, 102; criticism of Hutchinson's legal qualifications, 41; on Hutchinson's ambition, 73, 77; on Hutchinson's letters, 145; on Hutchinson's speech from 1773, 139; on Hutchinson's understanding of currency, 25; James Otis's decline in health, 104; journalist for the *Boston Gazette*, 108; on mercantile wealth, 72; opinion of Andrew Oliver, 151; view of the Land Bank dispute, 20; whig political theorist, 138; on the writs of assistance dispute, 44
Adams, Samuel, Jr., 14; as caricatured by John Mein, 107; and the committee of correspondence, 136; as a critic of the Bernard administration, 38; as a critic of Hutchinson's speech of 1773, 138; and crowd action 64, 94; opposition to the court party, 101; opposition to the presence of British troops in Boston, 121; organizer of the Sneider funeral, 113; and

personal animus toward Hutchinson, 40; as a popular party activist, 148; and public opinion, 80; as a radical policy maker, 69, 101; Thomas Hutchinson's view of him as a minority dissident, 137; and the rift with John Hancock, 126, 131, 132
Adams, Samuel, Sr. (Deacon), 19
Albany Conference, 26, 28, 30
Alford, Lincolnshire, 5
Allen, James, 26
American Board of Customs Commissioners, 89, 126
Amory, John, 113
Amory, Jonathan, 113
Andros, Sir Edmund, 6, 7, 21, 56
Antinomian conflict, 5, 6
Apthorp, Charles, 43
Auchmuty, Robert, 43, 144
Avery, John, 69

Bailyn, Bernard, 127
Barnard, Thomas, 57
Barnstable, Massachusetts, 38
Barré, Sir Isaac, 61
Barrington, Lord (William Wildman), 37, 157
Bass, Henry, 69

About the Author

Andrew Stephen Walmsley was born in Wakefield, West Yorkshire, England. He attended Sussex University at Falmer, near Brighton from 1975 to 1979 where he completed a B.A. degree in American studies largely under the tutelage of the late Professor Marcus Cunliffe. In late 1979 he moved from Great Britain to Houston, Texas, to attend Rice University from which he received his M.A. degree in American history in 1982. This second degree was supervised by Professor Allen J. Matusow and focused on the anticrime legislation of the Johnson and Nixon administrations. In 1983 Professor Walmsley began a long affiliation with the Houston Community College System where he teaches American history today. Dr. Walmsley received his Ph.D. degree in 1996 from the University of Houston where his dissertation advisor was Professor James Kirby Martin. Dr. Walmsley is a specialist in the political and social history of colonial and revolutionary America. He resides in Houston with his wife and son.